GROUP DISCUSSION

GROUP DISCUSSION

A Practical Guide to
Participation and Leadership

SECOND EDITION

JULIA T. WOOD
The University of North Carolina, Chapel Hill

GERALD M. PHILLIPS
The Pennsylvania State University

DOUGLAS J. PEDERSEN
The Pennsylvania State University

1817

HARPER & ROW, PUBLISHERS, New York
Cambridge, Philadelphia, San Francisco,
London, Mexico City, São Paulo, Singapore, Sydney

Sponsoring Editor: Louise H. Waller
Project Editor: Holly D. Gordon
Cover Design: Mary Archondes
Photo Research: Mira Schachne
Production: Jeanie Berke
Compositor: ComCom Division of Haddon Craftsmen, Inc.
Printer and Binder: R. R. Donnelley & Sons Company

Previously published by Houghton Mifflin Company

Group Discussion: A Practical Guide to Participation and Leadership,
  Second Edition

Library of Congress Cataloging-in-Publication Data

Phillips, Gerald M.
  Group discussion, a practical guide to participation and leadership.

  Includes bibliographies and indexes.
  1. Problem solving, Group.   2. Decision-making,
Group.   3. Discussion.   I. Wood, Julia T.   II. Pedersen,
Douglas J.   III. Title.
HM291.P488   1986   302.3'4   85-8469
ISBN 0-06-045218-8

88   9 8 7 6 5 4 3

CONTENTS

PREFACE

The trend to localization in industry and government is one of the important features of the last decade. More and more, management and decision-making has passed from a single executive to groups. Committees, commissions, task forces, planning groups, boards, and ad hoc organizations have been formed to deal with local community problems, management decisions, and policies and practices of organizations and institutions, as well as to influence the outcome of social and political controversies. In industry particularly, the challenge of competition from overseas has led to the quest to involve workers on all levels in making companies more efficient and profitable.

The quality circle is an important example. Originally, the idea of the quality circle was ascribed to Japanese management. It turns out, however, that the idea of worker involvement in planning, decision-making, and problem-solving is basically American. Growing from the group dynamics movement of the early 1950s, citizen and worker involvement in dealing with the problems that beset them has now been recognized as the most effective way of making organizations more cohesive and effective by using the intelligence, experience, and dedication of every one of us.

That is the spirit of this book. It is about how democracy can be made to operate on all levels by according each human being respect for having lived and loved and solved problems.

The main theme of this book is that collective action for problem-solving must be systematic, for within a system is the greatest chance of displaying mutual respect and encouraging creativity. This book does not reflect a "paint by numbers" approach to problem-solving. The authors have had more than fifty years of collective experience working with a great many types of groups in communities, education, industry, and government. Ours is a practical approach that recognizes the creative potential of the individual human and acknowledges that synergy between individual and group is the best way to realize that potential.

We hope to help people become effective participants and leaders in whatever groups they serve. We have combined theory and practice in an effort to offer a great many options for individual behavior, backed by good theoretical explanations and advice regarding that action.

The first chapter explains how groups serve society and how individuals serve the group. It is an idealistic chapter about the practical realities of individuals in a democratic society working together for both individual and collective good. The second and third chapters explain the group as a task system by considering the relationship between the group and its setting. Group discussion is an interaction among individual, group, organization, and society. The complicating fabric of the system is sensitive to individual influence; individuals are responsive to broad changes in the world around them. The small group is the interface of all these forces, easily influenced by individuals and highly influential on the surrounding environment.

Within this complicated framework lie a virtually infinite number of personal choices to be made by members and leaders. These choices are the substance of Chapters 4, 5, and 6. Chapter 4 offers some options to participants. Chapter 5 defines alternative ways of leading. Chapter 6 deals with the issue of conflict, describing the many ways in which it can be managed.

Chapter 7 initiates an explanation of the group system. Tying together the most advanced information on system-based decision-making with traditional patterns of thinking, we describe the standard agenda, a procedure for dealing with problems while allowing the widest range of choice for the individual talent in every group. The standard agenda is a powerful heuristic system. It applies to all discussion groups, but it is not rigid. It consists of general questions, the answers to which differ in every case, and guides individuals to thorough consideration of the many sides of problems they confront.

The standard agenda is explained with a great many examples and brought to fruition with a description of the connections among decision-making, problem-solving, policy formation, and management/administration. The final chapter deals with presentation, the way the findings of a small group enter the larger community.

We regard speaking in groups as a special form of rhetoric, a way for the individual to exert his or her influence, to work for the common good, and to enhance self-esteem by contributing to the welfare of all. Such a powerful system demands skill, experience, and knowledge. We offer the background and the instruction by which knowledge can inform performance, informed performance can become skill, and constant skillful behavior can become experience. The classroom teacher and the students who use this book become the actors in the American drama of learning to work together.

Julia T. Wood
Gerald M. Phillips
Douglas J. Pedersen

Group Discussion

chapter 1

Introduction to Group Discussion

In a letter to a friend, Ben Franklin wrote in 1789: "In this world nothing is certain but death and taxes." If Franklin were to take a look at life in contemporary America, he would probably amend his statement to include group discussion.

Our democratic society is run by groups. Groups run industry, government, even the educational enterprise. Boards of directors, trustees, planning commissions, zoning boards, legislative committees, and on and on, deal with the complex demands for food, shelter, organization of communities, employment, government, defense, and even recreation. It is the group that protects our individual rights and allows all our voices to be heard.[1]

Particularly in government, the group historically has been employed for the common good. Any evening in your town or ours, the local paper will report on the work of dozens of groups that keep government moving, some by administering programs to meet new problems and some by discovering new problems that need programs. Deliberation by groups prevents the kind of arbitrary government that characterizes dictatorships.

Management, too, has shifted away from the old-fashioned autocrat who ran his shop his own way. Most industries are corporations, owned collectively by many people who are represented by boards. Boards of directors or trustees set policy; administrators use planning groups to discover the best ways to implement policy and coordinate its implementation. Group solutions even characterize labor disputes in which management and unions alike recognize their common interests and work together for the common good.

Your membership in an organization usually means you are willing to

1

engage in discussion. The popularity of quality circles, where workers discuss and agree upon production and work quality issues, means that even the assembly line worker can contribute to the solution of problems. As specialization and technological advancement have increased, so has the need to coordinate potentially disparate interests and activities. At all levels, administrators have been selected for their ability to solve problems, their technical knowledge, and their ability to inspire workers. Now there are additional criteria: the ability to reconcile factions and the ability to lead problem-solving groups, as well as the capacity to communicate effectively and to create a climate of cooperation and teamwork through discussion. Effective use of groups has become essential to the smooth operation of the modern corporation.

In education, more and more teachers use classroom discussion and small-group exercises to help students use the facts they have learned. Such educational techniques help to involve students in the learning process and prepare them for the kinds of group situations they will encounter on the job or in the community. And if you look around your campus, you will discover that committees abound. You will find a faculty rights committee, a curriculum committee, even a student affairs committee. Today, college teachers expect to have a share in governing their institutions and in making the decisions that affect them. In the public schools the increase in teacher power through professional associations has led to joint administration, with community and faculty committees both working to solve problems.

There is no escaping the committee. Much of what goes on at the typical company or institution is handled through groups. You have probably discovered already that people who are skilled at working in groups are in demand and influential. They feel good about themselves and what they can accomplish. It is possible to affect organizational decisions, provided that you are skilled in the techniques of small-group discussion—techniques that will help you become an effective planner and problem-solver.

"Yes, indeed," the skeptic responds. "Whatever happened to good old self-reliance? If groups are as inevitable as death and taxes, they are about as popular as well."

It does appear paradoxical that American culture emphasizes individuality and yet relies so heavily on groups for problem-solving and decision-making. How can individuals maintain the integrity of their personal values in a society that so often demands they reconcile these values with those of others? "Give a little, get a little" seems to characterize the way people do business. The individual doesn't seem to stand alone any more.

The authors of this book are not groupies; we do not say that groups will make you healthy or sane or even happy. What we do say is that the group is inevitable and that if you are to have any individuality at all, you will be most likely to discover it through your work with others in the small group. We haven't really lost our ideals about individuality; it is just that society is so big, so complex, and so anonymous that one voice alone cannot be heard or may not be given the opportunity to be heard because most problems and issues are too important to trust to a single person. On the other hand, because groups are small and because much of what they deal with is immediate and personal, individuals have a great many opportunities to represent themselves as individuals *in* groups.

Historically, Americans have relied on group deliberation. Think about how our nation came together in the first place; how individuals sat together to solve problems of taxation, government, manufacturing, and foreign relations, and how their efforts resulted in one of the few national constitutions that affords dignity to the individual.

The authors of this book propose that skill at group discussion can help preserve and protect our democracy. It may not be popular to take such a patriotic position, but we do not apologize for it. In fact, we find this position confirmed by the great number of students we have encountered who want to learn how to participate in groups. On campus, in continuing education, and in the community, people want to know how to size up a group, how to discover what a group might accomplish, how to talk in ways that might influence others, and how to avoid or resolve the conflict that sometimes impedes groups. Their questions come thick and fast, and mostly they want to know whether there is an orderly procedure, whether there is something they can learn about participation that will help them advance professionally and develop personally as they seek to influence the issues and matters they believe are important.

There is one additional point. Students who have graduated and gone on to their careers frequently report back how important their group discussion class has been to them. Whether you plan a career in accounting, medicine, teaching, management, engineering, agriculture, or social work (to name just a few), training in how to participate in group decision-making and how to lead a discussion can give your career a valuable boost. Learning how to be productive in group discussions is basic to succeeding in our society. It is as inevitable as death and taxes, but neither so final as death nor so painful as taxes. In fact, it may be one inevitability that people will enjoy and find productive.

OUR PERSPECTIVE ON GROUP DISCUSSION

Many kinds of experts have studied how people behave in groups. Social psychologists believe we can learn about groups best by discovering regularities in how people behave when they are in contact with other people and making generalizations from our observations. Using these generalizations, we can predict and even control some human behavior.

Psychiatrists and psychoanalysts believe that the study of groups should focus on individual experience. Sociologists seek to understand how groups influence society. They observe groups as collectivities and deemphasize the study of the individual participant. Speech communication focuses on the speech behavior associated with effective group performance.

In Chapter 2 we examine some generalizations made by researchers studying the group process and show how those discoveries may be useful to you as you participate in groups.

Yet, as useful as research generalizations may be, they are at best incomplete guidelines for your own discussion behavior. They are incomplete for two reasons: (1) Research conclusions most often describe the general case—that regularity in human behavior most likely to occur under the conditions in which the research was conducted. Your group, on the other hand, is a particular case that may or may not fit the generalization or the conditions from which the generalization was made. (2) Much of the research on groups has paid little attention to the content of the discussion—an analysis of what was said, by whom, with what effect—and has therefore left unexamined communication variables capable of exerting considerable influence on participants, processes, and outcomes.

We are teachers of speech communication. Our perspective on group discussion assumes that human beings are able to manage the words that come from their mouths and by so doing are able to alter the outcomes of situations in which they participate. We believe that regardless of the influence of other factors on the discussion process, it is most important for you to manage your own talk. As speech teachers, we are concerned with what is said in the group, by whom, and with what effect. Thus, we are concerned with helping you make choices about your own behavior: what to say, how to say it, to whom, when and where, with what anticipated effect. We believe you can plan your speech behavior and carry out your plan, and we believe that by learning to do so, you increase your value to the group as well as to yourself.

Our purpose in writing this book is to clarify the choices you have when you participate in discussions and to help you improve your own personal participation. We will suggest things you can do and say to help make group discussion work both pleasant and productive. Our advice is directed to members and leaders of all kinds of discussion groups: committees, planning groups, governing groups, and learning groups. Our main concern is with you as an individual and with what you can accomplish in a group of other individuals.

WHERE YOU WILL USE DISCUSSION IN YOUR LIFE

Discussion is an integral part of the democratic process. It is also an imperative to survival in contemporary social, professional, and political life. You can expect to find discussion groups operating no matter where you work and where you live. Today's problems are so complicated that no one person can be trusted to solve them. Today's society is made up of so many special interest groups that all their concerns must be considered in community action. Corporate executives and legislatures both depend on the discussion process for information about alternatives. Discussion groups rarely proclaim the solutions to problems: Their main role is to offer options to those who must make the decisions.

In industry, discussion groups will often prepare reports on the nature of a problem, including information about previous attempts to solve it. They may then work out several possible solutions, or they may work out a proposal. They transmit their report to the individual or board finally responsible for making the decision. In legislation, committees actually prepare the bills and resolutions presented for final action. They gather data, examine precedent, secure legal opinion, solicit testimony from interested groups, and sometimes work to resolve disagreements among legislators.

In the community, discussion groups plan fundraising, community service activities, and political action. Candidates use campaign committees not only to schedule events, but to develop the "tone" of the campaign, build the candidate's image, recruit volunteers, and pay the expenses. Lobbying organizations, political activist associations, minorities, special interest caucuses, and civic clubs all rely on groups to plan activities and solve problems. Whether you join Sierra Club, NOW, or the Rotary club, if you are active at all, you will very likely be acting with others.

Committees

Most organization-based groups are formed as committees. The committee holds a very special place in American government and civic activity. Committees are provided for in the basic rules of parliamentary procedure based on the classical idea that one form of talk is needed to examine issues and propose alternatives, while another form is required to mobilize opinion for and against. These activities, traditionally referred to as *dialectic* and *rhetoric,* are counterparts. In dialectic, several people will work together to discover or construct ideas. In rhetoric, people will exchange ideas and arguments designed to persuade people of the "truth" or acceptability of particular proposals. Rhetoric is employed in the courtroom to argue guilt or innocence. Dialectic is used in the courtroom to examine possible programs of punishment or rehabilitation.

Committees are used in industry for a great many purposes. Sometimes they are called *task forces* or *planning groups.* In this case they are usually set up ad hoc—that is, after the fact. Something happens, a new problem arises, the competition begins to make inroads into the market, there are unexpected financial emergencies. There is no plan in place to handle the problem, no group charged with regular responsibility for it. Committees are quickly set up to define the problem, examine its possible effects on the organization, and explore possible solutions.

Most organizations and companies also have regular committees dealing with recurring problems. There is usually a committee working on sales programs and merchandising plans, one to handle regular problems of receiving and disbursing funds. There may be committees planning community relations, research and development, or examining potential acquisitions. Civic and social organizations usually have a committee system built into their constitutions.

Regardless of the name given to it, a committee is a small discussion group. It usually has no more than seven members sitting at a table, talking face to face. Committees can be characterized as follows:

They have a particular task to do in a larger organization.

Members serve on them because of particular knowledge or interest.

They meet regularly.

Members are not necessarily linked by personal or social connections.

There are few enough people so that everyone can address everyone else by name at meetings.

When committees have more members than can conveniently talk face to face, they usually function through subcommittees. At some point, however, most planning, researching, examining, and proposing is done by a committee. Here are some examples of how committees are used:

> Most companies have new products groups to examine consumer needs and consider ideas about innovative ways to meet those needs. Groups may also deal with design innovations, merchandising, and public relations campaigns.

> Most hospitals have a variety of functioning committees. There are tissue committees to examine and evaluate pathological diagnoses. There are ethics committees charged with handling complaints about procedure or public treatment. Committees decide on new personnel and appointments and deal with public issues confronting the hospital or the profession. There are even educational committees set up to provide continuing education programs to the medical or nursing staff.

> Most professional organizations have committees to review complaints about ethical standards, evaluate the suitability of individuals for membership, and devise and initiate policies.

> Most organizations have standing committees to deal with matters of finance, membership, and ceremonies and awards, as well as the various ongoing activities of the organization.

Commissions, Authorities, Boards, Investigative Bodies

Local government employs citizens in a variety of small groups. Such bodies as zoning authorities, planning commissions, shade tree and parking boards, and other groups that hear citizen complaints, plan for the future, propose legislation, and generally supervise activities under statutes qualify as committees. Mostly people serve without pay; it is their way of providing service to the community and having an influence on its future.

Most public groups have little actual authority; they neither pass legislation nor enforce it. On the other hand, legislation could not be prepared without them, for they serve as clearinghouses for information about problems and alternatives for solutions. By combining the talents of informed and interested people, information can be synthesized and practical solutions can be proposed.

Furthermore, by separating the process of the preparation of legislation from the process of passing and administering it, bias is reduced. A public group knows that it does its best work by generating several alternatives. If one fails, another is ready to go.

The Quality Circle

Precisely what is going on in Japanese industry is hard to say. We can agree, however, that workers are being called on to participate in management, particularly in matters of cost reduction and quality control. The *quality circle* is a management innovation that forms worker groups to discuss improvements in the way products are made and distributed and to suggest ways to improve company operations.

Involving workers in management is very important. In the United States, labor unions and management take an adversary posture; each bargains to its greatest advantage. This has a great many benefits in prosperous times. Management improves morale, workers are better paid. On the other hand, in times of tight competition, maximum cooperation is necessary. Discontented workers are not productive. Management cannot afford to exploit personnel. By the same token, management cannot afford to give up its profits. When workers and management learn they have a common stake, they are able to work together for mutual benefits.

This is the principle on which quality circle groups are based. The usual procedure is to have regular meetings so workers can identify problems and consider solutions. Management has the option of presenting problems as it sees them as well. We have long known that people work harder to implement solutions they have had a hand in preparing. Constant collaboration thus increases involvement, which in turn enhances commitment.

We do not yet know the implications of quality circle type operations, but we can predict they will become more prevalent in the future. Virtually every employee can count on being called on to participate in solving common problems. This increases visibility—that is, makes both strengths and weaknesses more apparent. By cultivating skill in discussion, individuals can concentrate on putting their best foot forward.

Teleconferencing

A great many companies are conducting business through telephone and video connections. Travel time is very expensive. Recently, a major motel chain announced televideo linkups at various locations so companies can schedule conference time locally, make a national connection, and conduct business together without the expense in time and money associated with travel.

Teleconferencing is still very new, and it is difficult to pinpoint the elements of successful participation. Conferees see each other face to face, mostly one at a time. There is not the sense of human contact characteristic of other types of group activity. Yet the agendas of a teleconference are the same as if the conferees were face to face. It is equally important to present unbiased information, to avoid confrontation, and to collaborate on solutions. The teleconference offers an instance of machine-mediated discussion that may become more common in the future. Studies of the effects of teleconferencing on decision-making are now underway, and soon it may be possible to develop methods of training people to be effective at teleconferencing.

Learning and Personal Improvement Groups

A great deal of group activity has learning and therapy as its goal. These groups differ from task-oriented group discussions because they emphasize personal

Teleconferencing is an innovation in discussion methods. (Mancuso, Jeroboam)

goals. In a task group, all members should focus on common goals; personal gain is incidental. In a learning or therapy group, individual gain is imperative; group gain is merely a method by which individuals gain.

It is important not to confuse the processes and outcomes of the two types of groups. We mention learning and therapy groups here only to point out that sometimes task-oriented discussions are criticized because individual members do not benefit from either process or outcome. While it is important to be respectful of individual members' concerns and needs, they are not the goal of task-oriented discussion. They must, however, be the goal of learning or therapeutic discussions. In setting your own goals, be careful not to expect more than the *type* of group can deliver. In a task group, your best personal gain is the feeling of satisfaction you get from participating in the development of a good group solution. In a learning or therapy group, you have the option of setting your own personal goals and use the group to help you achieve them.

AND LO AND BEHOLD, THEY PRODUCED A CAMEL

We started this chapter by telling you about death and taxes and groups. One colleague put it this way: "Groups are like the weather; everyone complains about them, but no one does anything about them."

True, the complaints abound! Meetings are too long or too short. There is too much talk or too little; too much conflict or too much levity. Sometimes people try to respond to complaints. One chief executive officer we know recently ordered the chairs removed from the corporate conference rooms under the mistaken belief that if participants had to stand, the meetings would be more efficient and unnecessary talk would be eliminated. He seemed genuinely surprised when members of the organization began to complain even more about the group discussions.

Recent research (see Sorenson) has identified persons whose dislike for the discussion process is so intense that their attitude may be called "group hate." We asked some of these people to identify what they disliked about discussion groups. Because their responses may represent some of your own attitudes or experiences, let's take a moment to examine the four most frequent complaints.

Efficiency

First, many people told us they felt most discussions were a waste of time. They were cynical about the efficiency with which groups function. One person grumbled, "A camel is a horse designed by a committee." They complained that many people in groups like "to hear themselves talk," or that most people "had nothing to say, but took too long to say it."

Admittedly, like most other human endeavors, discussion can be nonproductive and a waste of time, but not because of some inherent weakness in the process. Nothing magical happens just because people gather together to discuss. Like everything else, group discussion works when we make it work. When members fail to prepare for a discussion, there is no reason to expect them to have anything useful to say. When leaders are not skillful in guiding members in productive directions, discussions are likely to degenerate into chaos or pleasant but nonproductive bull sessions. When members and leaders do not understand and implement the requirements for effective, purposive discussion, the process will probably be needlessly time-consuming and minimally productive. As you read subsequent chapters, you will understand more about the choices and options available to you that will help you make what you say in a discussion worthwhile.

Facility

A second complaint was that people often feel suppressed during a discussion. There are aggressive talkers everywhere, and most people are not really prepared to compete with them. After being squelched two or three times, a person usually keeps silent. Many people feel intimidated by conflict and seek to avoid it; others may respond by open combat.

However, these difficulties also are not inherent in the discussion process. People must be trained to work well in groups. Human beings are not innately able to work well in committees, even though there does seem to be a bit of the herd instinct in all of us. The idea of dealing with ideas in an analytical way is frightening to many people largely because these people have not learned how to do it. Discussion groups are neither debating societies nor arenas for interpersonal combat.

Leaders must therefore be trained to keep people from suppressing one another. Participants must learn to put the good of the group above their own personal gain. Everyone must learn to focus on data and reasoning rather than personalities. The qualities necessary for effective participation and leadership can be learned. In subsequent chapters, we will explore choices available to leaders and participants to help guard against these particular problems.

Personal Feelings

A third complaint, related to individual suppression and conflict, reflected confusion over the appropriate role of personal feelings in discussion. People sometimes get very involved in their ideas or in dedication to the cause or group they represent. These feelings are important in discussion. People are often put in groups simply because they reflect particular concerns and can represent them well. But it is difficult for such persons to keep from focusing attention on themselves and their ideas. It is easy to confuse representation and suppression.

During the past few decades, groups have been used increasingly for therapeutic purposes. People in these groups talk about potentially emotional issues. Support groups are used to help rehabilitate drug addicts or alcoholics, to help patients with terminal illness, for victims of rape or violent crimes, for persons seeking to share aspects of domestic or religious experience, to name but a few. When dealing with such issues, group training has often been—as it may need to be—focused on helping people learn how to manage feelings in groups. A great deal of attention has been devoted to ways of achieving harmony among group members. Some authorities claim that a group cannot be successful unless the members get along; others claim that goodwill is a result of successful completion of a group task. The main problem with this aspect of therapeutic groups is that focusing attention on the feelings of group members in nontherapeutic contexts often represents a cure that is worse than the disease. Some people claim that a little disharmony is necessary so various sides of the issue can be examined. Others complain that when too much attention is devoted to getting along with others, too little time is devoted to the topic of discussion.

We believe that the task aspects of the problem-solving group should receive primary emphasis. We also believe that such an emphasis can develop friendly and satisfying interpersonal relationships. By channeling emotions into the hard work of gathering and evaluating information, personal feelings can support problem-solving rather than interfere with it. Subsequent chapters will have more to say about the choices regarding the role of personal feelings and the effects of those choices.

Personal Integrity

The fourth and final complaint, and perhaps the most troublesome one of all, came from individuals who felt they had to sacrifice personal integrity in order to work with the group. Often, when five members of the group agree on an idea, the sixth person goes along with the majority to avoid being a holdout. He or she actually capitulates. It isn't a consensus at all; the dissenter feels embarrassed by holding out and doesn't want to endure the group's resentment for taking up valuable time.

The tendency of all group members to move into narrowly confining frames of thought has been called *groupthink.* There has recently been much concern about groupthink as it affects decision-making in government. Back in the 1950s, our concern was with conformity. We now know that techniques of participation and intervention can prevent conformity for the sake of harmony. In a well-trained group, people can avoid becoming puppets by setting norms of critical analysis and participation. The point is that no one has to capitulate. Everyone has the opportunity to alter the way the group is operating, to set new norms, and to influence the other members into productive postures if that person understands when and how to do so.

It is important for individuals to remain individuals in the group. Group process is designed to synthesize individual ideas to obtain "the greatest good for the greatest number." Individual points of view cannot be synthesized unless they are expressed. Effective expression requires effective documentation. Effective synthesis requires careful bargaining in the interests of all. In the chapters to come, we will offer some techniques for encouraging individual expression and using it in the construction of collective solutions.

We have examined four participant complaints about the discussion process:

1. Some people felt discussion was a waste of time and nonproductive.
2. Some complained that individuals could be suppressed and that conflict in groups was intimidating.
3. Some were confused about the role of personal feelings and the degree to which the group should be used to explore these.
4. Some were concerned about abandoning their own ideas and succumbing to the pressure for group agreement.

These problems are not inherent in the group discussion process. Unlike the weather, something can be done about them. Every one of these problems can be remedied through training. They do not come about because of the process; they come about because individual members are unable to handle the business before them effectively.

The purpose of this book is to help you discover your opportunities for making choices and to help you select from among the alternatives available. With this skill you will not only be able to help prevent problems from arising in your group, but you will be on the road to personal success whatever your vocational choice.

HOW TO LEARN ABOUT GROUP DISCUSSION

Whether you are a member of a discussion class or simply a person who wants to improve your discussion skills, there are two ways in which you can learn about discussion. First, you can find a source of information about discussion. This book is such a source. Your class instructor will also be able to provide information. Once you begin to get information, you might begin thinking about what this new information can mean in your life. Examine your past experience with groups.

How well did you do? Did you feel satisfied with your contribution? Were you prepared? Did you have the influence you wanted to have? Did people pay attention to you? Compare your behaviors to those outlined in this book. What do you think you need to learn? Think about the role of discussion in your future career. How will information about group discussion help you when you assume new responsibilities?

The second way to learn is to develop discussion skills through practice. Learning about the skills required of an effective discussion group member doesn't guarantee that you will be able to execute them. What you need is formal practice and criticism, preferably in a classroom, and a willingness to try your hand in real discussions outside the classroom. By reading and participating and by watching others, you will be able to develop your own style. By listening to criticism from your instructor and others, you will be able to correct your errors and learn more effective ways of behavior.

We do not believe you can learn to master discussion merely by learning about it. We urge you to observe and engage in discussion whenever and wherever you can. Only by applying our ideas in real situations will you know whether they are worthwhile. You must also develop your own unique style, and this means that you try what you learn a number of times and in a number of different ways. We begin by offering you a list of some of the basic ideas that underlie effective discussion participation.

BASIC GUIDELINES FOR GROUP DISCUSSION

There is an ancient Chinese proverb, "If you don't know where you are going, then any road will take you there." If you believe that things just happen and that you are destined to just go along, you might make an excellent subject for an experiment in norm formation, but you will have little success at discussion. Our point of view on group discussion is rhetorical; we believe individuals can make things happen by saying what needs to be said when it needs saying. It also means that we make some basic assumptions about what happens in discussion.

Effective Discussion Is Goal-Directed

When we talk about group discussion, we do not include all the things people can do together in groups. We are not concerned with casual socialization, bull sessions, or even group therapy. A small number of people gathering and sharing ideas does not make a group discussion.

For example, if you recall your high school days, you may remember the teacher who told you to get into groups and "discuss" the American Constitution. Most of the time you "discussed," but it was more likely Fred's or Emma's constitution. The teacher did not specify what was wanted, and the resulting talk would be better classified as group conversation.

By contrast, when we talk of *group discussion*, we are dealing with a relatively formal process. It is purposive talk by people who have formed groups to make decisions, to solve problems, to declare policy, to evaluate programs, to collect and examine facts, to administer operations, to select personnel, and so forth. The kind of group problem-solving discussion that we have in mind almost always requires some kind of formal outcome.

Customarily, when people come together for problem-solving discussion, each member of the group is selected because of some special knowledge, skill, or interest in the group's problem. In industry, for example, groups are often composed of various division or department heads. Advertising knows little about the work of accounts receivable and vice versa, but both have to be considered before production can gear up for the fall schedule. In the community, citizens come to groups because they have a stake in the outcome of some issue or question. The downtown businesspeople, the residents of center city, and the suburbanites all come because they want to be heard. Sometimes people are together because it is their task to be together. They may be members of a standing committee of an organization, or they may have formed an organization to work for some political, economic, or social purpose in which they are all interested.

Whether in industry, the community, or the classroom; whether members have volunteered or have been assigned; the kind of discussion we are writing about is purposive activity intended to accomplish some goal that the individual acting alone could not attain or that no single individual could handle because so many people have an interest in the outcome.

Effective Discussion Is Regulated by a Public Agenda

Group discussion requires that a number of people with different ideas and points of view come together and talk in order to solve a problem they have in common. Because it is difficult to reconcile the different ideas of a great many people, it is important to have some method or procedure that all participants can follow. People need rules of order to prevent conflict or to resolve it if it arises. In a discussion, participants commit themselves to a common goal. To the extent that they can agree on some rules to follow in order to achieve the goal, they can proceed efficiently to share information and work out solutions. It can be very confusing if participants simply shout out their ideas or compete for attention. Thus, it is customary for members of a discussion group to follow some kind of agenda that permits a leader to "direct" them from individual commitment to group solution. When discussion participants follow a natural agenda, they can process their ideas intelligently. They increase their chances of achieving a workable solution to their problem.

Because of the need for order, this book is based on a method called the *standard agenda.* Our experience (and that of other experts as well) has been that every effective problem-solving group appears to follow a similar sequence in order to get its major task done. Although it is often necessary and convenient to modify the agenda slightly, most effective groups can usually be "graphed" through the steps of standard agenda. A number of modifications have been suggested. The important thing is to understand how important orderly procedure is and to resolve to contribute to maintaining that order when you participate in a group.

At the beginning of a discussion, it may be useful to concentrate on simple issues and permit members to ventilate a bit. However, at some point, some basic questions must be asked. The people in the group must agree on what they are to do together and what the outcome should be. Requiring them to follow an agenda helps them come to agreement on the main issues. Once this has been accomplished, it is possible to loosen up and permit some digressions when they appear necessary. Our advocacy of the standard agenda is based on our experience with its efficiency in helping people with very diverse communication styles and conflicting ideas work respectfully and calmly from initial anarchy to sensible solution.

Effective Discussion Requires That Every Member Be Responsible for the Group's Effectiveness

We noted earlier that some of the people we interviewed saw discussion as a waste of time. When we asked some of these people what they had done to improve the discussion, they said they had done nothing. Many of them quickly added, "You can't criticize us for doing nothing, can you?"

All too often discussions are marked by individuals abdicating personal responsibility to contribute to the outcome. Some people want everyone else to take responsibility. Frequently, these nonparticipants pop up at the end and criticize everyone else. This is an impossible attitude. One of the main premises on which group discussion is built is that people who participate in forming a solution to a problem usually support it and help it work. People who do not participate thwart the process. Sometimes, simply by not participating, they permit people with totalitarian ideas to take over a democratic process.

Almost forty years ago, Erich Fromm in his book *Escape from Freedom*[2] described this kind of withdrawal from the tensions of decision-making. He declared that making a choice—the essence of freedom—almost always produces anxiety, and that many people seek to avoid the anxiety by choosing not to choose. Fromm argued that the rise of Nazi Germany was caused in large measure by the desire of individuals to escape the tensions of decision-making in a free society. That is why it is so important to support problem-solving groups. They are the best way for you to exert your influence as a thinking, caring citizen.

Whenever one group member decides to escape the responsibility of making choices by letting others judge the information, make procedural suggestions, or do the work, that person weakens the final product of the discussion. The quality of the decisions of a discussion group is only partly judged by their effect on the problem to be solved. The decisions are also judged against this question: Did the group process improve on what could have been done by an individual? If the answer to this question is "no," then the group process is a waste of time.

The answer to this question can virtually always be "yes" if every member assumes an obligation to participate. All members must be committed to listen, to think through, to reason, and to share the results of their reasoning with the group. All members must adopt a critical attitude toward the information they present and that presented by others. To do this, all members must know what is expected, what possibilities exist for behaviors, and most important, how to separate personality from their own comments.

This may sound highly moralistic. However, we can go far beyond admonition, for the following chapters will give you ways of developing the appropriate critical attitude. We will show you how to question information and how to draw conclusions from what you hear, and we will describe the roles you can select. It is more than empty moralizing to say that a group is composed of individual, participating members, not of one or two participants and several spectators.

Effective Discussion Presumes Cooperative Efforts and Attitudes

Group discussions are not forums in which individuals may orate on behalf of their favorite causes or charities. Discussions, as we have already noted, require participation. More than that, they require participation centered around a common agenda. This means that discussion is an inherently cooperative enterprise in which the success of the whole unit depends on the labors and attitudes of each individual. Every member is successful only when the group is successful, and the group cannot be successful unless most of the members succeed. There is no pleasure when the group simply ratifies the ideas of one aggressive member. Similarly, there is no joy when the group becomes polarized into warring camps, and one faction succeeds in beating the other into submission.

Saying that group activity is essentially cooperative implies that an effort should be made to resolve disagreements. Note: We did not say "avoid disagreements"; we said "resolve disagreements." Cooperation involves criticizing, dissenting, and arguing when you are legitimately motivated to do so, but it also involves trying as hard as possible objectively to entertain others' opinions and to resolve disagreements and make them into constructive capital for the entire group. The optimum in a group discussion is for people to speak their minds so the group can get an idea of the range of commitments, interests, and abilities represented in the group. From this point, the group must proceed carefully and meticulously through the steps required for people to "reason together."

We have not suggested that you should conform to a group's ideas. As a matter of fact, if you accept the statements above, simple conformity is impossible. What a group believes is a function of what the individual members believe. If every member has participated in shaping what the group believes, members cannot conform; they have to come to a consensus. *Consensus* is an agreement that may range from sincere unanimity to "Well, I can live with it." Consensus represents the ideal of group accomplishment. It happens when members have been so cooperative that they seek and support a collective decision which does not jeopardize their individual positions. Consensus cannot and does not happen all the time. Sometimes it is necessary for group members to negotiate and bargain about the solution; sometimes it may even be necessary to vote.

As a member of a discussion group, you are obligated to have ideas about the topic or question under discussion. You are obligated to present those ideas and to listen to the ideas of others. You are entitled, even urged, to be an advocate and to argue for those things you truly believe are right or meritorious. If you keep in mind that your goal is not for you to "defeat" the people who disagree with you, but for each of you to come closer to a common position, you will be doing your share to achieve the cooperative spirit of group discussion and help the group move toward its ideal of decision by consensus.

We cannot offer any prescriptions for bringing about consensus that you can use in all situations. We are not at all sure there are any. As professional teachers of discussion, the best we can do is to suggest ways to make consensus possible through educating group members as to their personal obligations and through teaching leaders how to play their roles skillfully.

Effective Discussion Requires Leadership

Discussion leadership is important, because group discussion is a complicated process and someone needs to be responsible for making it run.

A great number of tasks must be done by the typical problem-solving group. Someone needs to be responsible for liaison with agencies above and adjacent to the group, like the company executives or civic organizations in the community. Someone must coordinate the work that is assigned and see that it is done on time and in proper form. People need to be responsible for keeping proper records, for seeing that participation among members is in reasonable balance, and perhaps for refereeing conflict or judging when it is necessary to make a decision in equity. Someone has to maintain a file of information and ideas. Someone has to notify the group of the time and place of meetings and perhaps distribute the agenda in advance. Someone has to make reservations and provide for the amenities. Above all, someone has to lead.

In Chapter 5 we consider the popular idea that leadership can be identified by the performance of certain tasks that may be distributed among group members. Though effective discussion can take place without the guidance of a designated leader, we do not in general encourage this practice, since it often means that no one will perform the important tasks just mentioned. We believe one person should act as discussion leader. Even when regular members assume shared responsibility for leadership, it is a good idea to have one person to make sure that protocol details are handled and to represent the group to other agencies with which it is connected.

Leaders are made, not born. They may be appointed by a higher authority; they may have the privilege of rank; or they may be elected by or emerge from the group. Some groups even rotate leadership among the members. Whatever method is used to select a leader, we think that the group and its leader can be compared to an orchestra and its conductor. The members of the orchestra, like members of the group, provide the skill to produce the music, but the leader, like the conductor, must provide the downbeat and impose coordination on potential chaos. In this section, we have offered five basic guidelines for discussion:

1. Effective discussion is goal-directed.
2. Effective discussion is regulated by a public agenda.

3. Effective discussion requires that every member be responsible for the group's effectiveness.
4. Effective discussion presumes cooperative efforts and attitudes.
5. Effective discussion requires leadership.

These guidelines will serve as the foundation for learning about discussion as we examine the process in greater detail. Our final words to you in this chapter concern the choices you have when participating in discussion.

YOUR SECOND CHOICE

"Second choice? What happened to my first choice?"

You made your first choice by deciding to learn more about discussion and by reading to this point in the book. Forgive our devious way of bringing this to your attention, but we believe that your awareness of choice-making is a critical understanding.

Your capacity to make choices is one of your most valuable assets as an individual. You are not a creature of the fates and the furies. Although you may not be able to move mountains, each of you has the ability to influence the people around you. We want you to understand that your successful participation in group discussion is a matter of choice.

To be an effective choice-maker, you will need to understand both the opportunities that permit choice and the alternatives available to you. Some of your opportunities for choice are obvious. Others will be far more subtle and, given half a chance, may escape unnoticed. We want you to realize that you have countless opportunities for choice throughout the discussion process and that you will need to remain alert in order to exercise them.

Among your first choices, as we pointed out, was the decision to learn more about discussion and to improve your skill at participation. No one is born a good discussion group member. If you can learn what is expected of you as a member and then practice that skill until you are relatively proficient, you expand your capacity to choose.

Another of your choices concerns the groups with which you affiliate. If you are using this book in conjunction with a class, your instructor will probably present different ways of managing this choice. For example, to suggest only a few possibilities, you may form groups by instructor assignment, by random selection, or by grouping together persons with an interest in a particular problem. If you are a citizen participating in community groups, you also have choices about your affiliation. Though your concern with a particular problem may sometimes limit your choice of groups, you alone decide whether or not to get involved. Remember too that you can choose to form another group. If participation in a discussion group is part of your job, the nature of your work or the decision of a higher authority may have influenced the choice. Yet once again you still have choices, even if your choice is limited to finding another job.

You also can make almost unlimited choices about the nature and style of your participation. You need not regard yourself as locked permanently into one form of behavior or another. Even when you are with a group of people who have known you for a long time and expect a particular behavior from you, you have the ability to change. It may take longer to convince people who know you well to accept the fact that you have changed, but even so you have the right and the ability to make the effort.

If you are in a discussion course, what you do in the classroom can be regarded as a laboratory experiment. Take advantage of the opportunity to try things out and see how well you do with them. That's how learning takes place.

You even have a choice about how you use this book. In the next four chapters we will introduce some important theoretical ideas about group discussion. We hope that understanding the process will help you learn to participate well. The remaining seven chapters deal with the steps of the standard agenda. We will take you step by step through the process, in each case showing you what the group must accomplish and what each member and leader must do to bring about that goal.

If you like, you can move directly to Chapter 6 and begin working out discussion problems, saving the next four chapters till later. You may want to read chapters side by side—that is, read the next chapter and then start on your practical work with the standard agenda. You might even have a group discussion about the most effective way to use the book. Just keep in mind that learning about discussion doesn't necessarily make you effective, and participating in discussion can be improved only by learning new behaviors designed to fulfill the theoretical criteria for success. Theory and practice go hand in hand in learning group discussion, and through it all the choices you make are crucial to your own development.

However you go about learning discussion, remember that training and commitment to effective participation are the required ingredients for making group discussion work productively, efficiently, and perhaps enjoyably. This belief prompted us to write this book. We hope that some of our enthusiasm for group discussion and some of our confidence in its potential will rub off on you. We would like to see more group decisions like the response to the Cuban missile crisis and fewer like the Watergate coverup.

We think group discussion is most effective when people take the time to learn to be competent at it. The most important outcome of such training should be an awareness of the choices open to each person at each moment during a discussion. As we have noted, there are choices. In fact, each time you act or don't act, each time you speak or don't speak, each time you offer your comments in a dogmatic tone or with a conciliatory glance or with a high level of enthusiasm, you have made a choice. Consciously or unconsciously, you have decided to do one thing instead of another. No outside events and no other people forced you, although both could have influenced your decision. We have tried to make you more conscious of your choice-making capacity so that you will control it to your own advantage.

Each choice you make, of course, carries an obligation: the responsibility of accepting the consequences of your actions. For instance, if you fail to tell your leader what you want, then you had better be prepared for the consequence— accepting whatever is delivered by your leader. Likewise, if you choose not to take the time to help do research on your group's problem, then be ready for a superficial and spotty final report that probably will not be accepted. In each case you have made a choice, and every choice has consequences. It is for this reason that we urge you to consider carefully how you behave and what you say in discussions—you are going to have to live with the implications of your talk and actions.

Choices, of course, may be wise or unwise, effective or ineffective. For this reason we have devoted most of this book to giving you information and ideas for making sound choices about your own behavior in groups. In Chapter 1 we talked about our perspective on group discussion and presented five basic guidelines illustrating that perspective. Chapters 2 and 3 summarized a great many research findings so that you would be better able to size up discussion situations and decide what you had to do to represent yourself and your concerns well.

In Chapter 6 we will discuss behaviors associated with leadership in order to prepare you to be a leader should you choose to do so or if the position is forced on you. In Chapter 7 we will explain how both leaders and participants can cooperate to manage conflict and make it useful to the group. In Chapter 8 we will discuss specific steps you can take to prepare yourself for discussion, and in the remaining chapters we will explore each phase of the standard agenda, focusing on its goals and outcomes, describing the obligations of members and leader. Using this approach, we can show you what you have to do and say in order to help achieve group objectives during each stage in problem-solving.

We will conclude with a description of how to present the final report. In preparing the final report, the group is transformed from an objective investigative unit into a partisan and highly persuasive group. At this point the group has reached its decision, and the new goal becomes to convince someone else—the community, the president of the company, the board—to accept and act on that decision. We will show you how to analyze your audience so that you can present the report persuasively.

REFERENCES

1. Lou Harris, "The Emerging Shape of Politics for the Rest of the 1970s," speech given before the National Conference of State Legislators, Philadelphia, October 7, 1975.
2. Erich Fromm, *Escape from Freedom* (New York: Holt, Rinehart and Winston, 1941).

RECOMMENDED READINGS

Bormann, Ernest G. *Discussion and Group Methods,* 2d ed. New York: Harper & Row, 1975. In Chapter 3, Bormann presents an excellent discussion of the individual versus the group.

Haiman, Franklyn S. *Group Leadership and Democratic Action.* Boston: Houghton Mifflin, 1951. This is one of the early books on discussion that remains a worthwhile classic.

McBurney, James H., and Kenneth G. Hance. *Discussion in Human Affairs.* New York: Harper, 1950. This is another classic text in the discussion field that set the pace for several decades.

Olmstead, Michael. *The Small Group.* New York: Random House, 1959. Olmsted presents a good general discussion of the origins, structures, and varied functions of small groups in American society.

Sorensen, Susan. "Investigation of the Concept Group-Hate." Unpublished M.A. thesis, Pennsylvania State University, 1980.

Steiner, Ivan D. *Group Process and Productivity.* New York: Academic Press, 1973. Steiner's discussion in the first chapter deals with the potential for human choices in group settings. It makes an excellent supplement to the philosophy presented in the first chapter of this text.

chapter 2

Understanding the Group as a System

During your lifetime you've probably taken part in a number of group discussions. The meetings of the school spirit committee, planning sessions for the senior prom, organizing ticket sales for the school play, and the group assignments you worked out in class all qualify as formal problem-solving discussions. If you're like most people, you've been pleased with your participation in some cases and less satisfied in others, yet you might find it difficult to explain why some discussions seemed more productive and comfortable than others. It is easy to feel frustrated and confused in group situations and even to conclude that groups are so chaotic they defy understanding by sane people.

Groups are not really as chaotic as they sometimes appear. They are, however, very complex, since a variety of influences operates within them. Because groups are so complex, understanding them requires a theoretical perspective sufficiently powerful to explain the many forces that work simultaneously within them.

The purpose of this chapter and the one that follows is to enhance your understanding of group situations by providing a theoretical approach to group discussion and by summarizing significant research about how and why groups operate as they do. The theory and research we present form a foundation for informed participation in group deliberations. Once you recognize key aspects of group interaction and appreciate the ways they tend to influence individual and collective behavior, you'll have a basis for making sound choices regarding your own actions in group situations.

You may select your behaviors based on awareness of the dynamics of participation and on reasoned predictions of how alternative choices on your part are likely to affect what others do and what the group achieves. Toward this goal, this chapter explains the *systems* perspective that provides our theoretical basis. Then we examine the nature and functions of features comprising the initial group system. Chapter 3 continues this analysis by examining the process features and outcomes of discussion.

   Fair warning: These chapters necessarily contain a high volume of information. More than a single reading may be necessary.

THE SYSTEMS PERSPECTIVE

Of the many theories about human social behavior from which we could choose, *general systems theory* seems especially appropriate to the study of the small group. General systems theory originated with Ludwig Von Bertelanffy, a theoretical biologist, as a way to think about and study the constant, dynamic adjustments of living phenomena. His ideas have subsequently been adopted by many social scientists and humanists who seek to understand complicated interpersonal interaction. Many who study group discussion regard general systems theory as the most useful approach to teaching and research in small-group behavior.[1]

   According to the theory, an open system such as a group is defined as an *organized set of interrelated and interacting parts that attempts to maintain its own balance amid the influences from its surrounding environment.* Think, for example, about your college or university. It can be analyzed in a great many ways. We could consider students, faculty, maintenance personnel, administration, alumni, and so on as components made up of people. We could also consider teaching/learning, research/publishing, maintaining/caretaking, fundraising, and so on as activities carried on in the university. However we choose to divide it up, our metaphor would be to a living organism—a plant, for example. A plant is made up of roots, leaves, stem, flowers, all of which contribute to the nature of the organism. What happens to the roots affects leaves, stem, and flowers. Any outside force that affects the plant affects all components of the plant. Turning back to your school, an outside force affecting the institution as a whole (like the amount of money given by the legislature or the trustees) affects each component of the system. If faculty salaries go up, the faculty changes accordingly. A change in the faculty changes the influence on the students, which in turn might alter administration, and so on. From this model of an *open system,* we can derive four premises to guide how we think about group discussion.

Any Part of a System Can Be Understood only Within the Context of the Entire System   We cannot understand one part of a group in isolation. To take it out of the group context produces distortion. For instance, we cannot account for how one member acts without considering group norms, the power structure, leadership, and so on. Similarly, to explain a group's decisions we need to analyze member goals, leadership style, resources available to the group, and a host of other factors. (Consider, for example, how the faculty at your school makes decisions about teaching based on the nature of the students; how the nature of the students depends on the tuition, how the tuition depends on the funding, and conversely, how funding affects the morale of the faculty, which in turn affects how they deal with the students, who in turn respond to teaching, and so on.) As you participate in discussions, try to avoid analyzing parts of your group out of context. Remember that any components can be understood only in light of the whole system.

A System Is More Than the Sum of Its Parts   At first glance, this premise seems odd. However, it is central to a systems view of groups. The premise suggests that we cannot understand a group simply by adding up all its separate parts. If we add members, physical setting, communication patterns, and decision reached, we will not have an accurate picture. What is missing is the interactions; how physical setting affected members' communication patterns and how the result affects the outcome.

Within a group, the parts interact dynamically to create new features not present at the outset. For example, Smith may be naturally quiet outside the group, but the presence of Jones gets him excited. Smith and Jones develop a relationship unique to a particular group. The group is confronted with more than the behavior of Smith plus the behavior of Jones. They are confronted with a Smith/Jones dyad. Other members will relate both to the individuals and to their relationship. The total pattern of relationships forms the group norms against which the behavior of individuals is judged. The behavior of individuals, however, forms the norms. Norms are not present when the members first sit down; they result from interaction. Over time, the relationships take on new qualities in response to the pattern of responses. The process reflects the dynamic interactions characteristic of living (open) systems. Once formed, a system engages in an ongoing process of defining and redefining itself, constantly changing as it attempts to sustain itself against events inside and outside. (For example, we may be enjoying a party, nibbling away on the food, which gives us heartburn, which makes us irritable, which interferes with the conversation we are having, which has been interrupted several times by other people, which. . . . And if someone asks how was the party, would it be possible to single out just one feature?)

All Parts of a System Interact Dynamically and Constantly   This premise extends the previous ones. The parts of a group are intricately interconnected; each part affects all others. Many systems theorists point out that a change in any part of a system creates change in all other parts. This is because the parts are so interrelated that any change reverberates throughout the whole system. When one element alters, all others must adjust to accommodate it if the system is to survive in a healthy state.

Some changes have obvious and immediate effects. For example, when participation is stifled, member satisfaction declines. There is a direct relationship between participation and satisfaction. (What would be the effect on a group if the boss dropped in to hear a discussion on problems with his latest policy proposal?)

At other times, the influence is indirect. For instance, inhibiting participation reduces members' satisfaction (direct impact), which in turn reduces their commitment to the group, which in turn materially decreases the probability that the group will achieve a top quality outcome. In both cases, stifling participation is the action that influences other events in the group system, but some of the responses are easier to discern than others.

If we pursued this example even further, we'd need to ask why the participation was stifled. To answer this, we'd need to analyze the entire group system. Why did the boss come in to listen? Was she dissatisfied with what she heard was going on? Who might have directed information outside the system? Notice that events inside the system can have an effect outside the system, which in turn can influence the system itself. Each time we ask why something happened, we are pushed to further appreciation of the complex interrelationships among parts of a group system, along with the pressures and influences from outside the system that affect the system as a whole and individual elements as well. To think systemically is to think in very complex fashion. It is inappropriate to think in terms of specific causes of events in a system.

An Open System Interacts with Its Environment in Mutually Influential Ways
Just as we cannot consider parts of a group in isolation, neither can we consider the group apart from its context. Any group is embedded in many other systems, such as organizations, companies, communities, and cultures. Because they are parts of their larger environments, groups influence these environments and are influenced by them. There is, for example, a constant exchange of resources so that a committee produces policies for the institution it serves. The institution provides the meeting place and the salaries for the members. It also shapes member attitudes toward the institution, which are reflected in opinions expressed inside the group, which have an impact on the policies the group lays down, which affect the institution in ways that affect the members, and so on. Furthermore, members come and go. Each new member brings a new cargo of influence from outside. Each departing member changes the shape of the interactions inside the group.

Because groups interact with other parts of their environment, there is always the potential for conflicts arising from incompatible demands of multiple systems. Individuals may lack the time and energy to participate effectively in work groups, social action groups, and interpersonal systems. Tension arises, stress increases. Either individuals sacrifice membership in some of their systems, reduce investment in some, or suffer the consequences of burnout. In addition, people sometimes experience conflict of interest between the values of two or more systems. It may, for example, be to the interest of an employee's family to keep salaries high; it may be to the interest of the company to keep salaries low. High salaries may put the company out of business, but low salaries may make it difficult to live. How will any given employee respond? Consider how a person who worked for a nuclear power plant and belonged to the Sierra Club would feel. The two systems have clashing values. Furthermore, the values, expectations, and rules of the social milieu constrain and shape the ideas a problem-solving group may prudently recommend. To understand any group, we must recognize its place in the broader environment.

The four premises we've just discussed summarize the systems approach to small-group problem-solving. We can now build on this orientation by examining some of the components of group systems. We may have to focus on one part at a time in order to explain it clearly. Keep the system perspective in mind as we go on to remind yourself that each component interacts with *all* the others. We start with a discussion of the importance of a group's environment on its problem-solving activity. Then we consider four initial elements of groups: members, group size, group record, and group purpose. In Chapter 3 we will consider seven process elements that arise out of the initial elements. We will also discuss three possible outcomes from group systems. Throughout, the systems model below will guide our discussion.

Small-Group System and Surrounding Environment

	Surrounding environment	
Initial elements	**Process elements**	**Outcomes**
Members	Verbal communication	Satisfaction
Group size	Nonverbal behavior	Decision Effectiveness
Group record	Norms	Change in environment
Group charge	Power distribution Decision-making style Group autonomy Cohesion	

THE ENVIRONMENT SURROUNDING A GROUP

Our fourth premise about systems stated that groups interact with their environments in mutually influential ways. We want to explain how this idea applies to problem-solving groups. Any group is influenced and sometimes pressured by the institution to which it belongs, as well as by other groups within that institution. For example, a task force (committee) charged to plan a sales campaign is primarily responsible to the company that sets it up and pays its members. In addition, the task force must coordinate its efforts with the group that plans production, as well as the sales staff. In order to operate effectively, groups must work within the general guidelines and policies established by the company and administered by its executives. They must also stay within the limits of their setting. Thus, the task force must take into account the limitations of production and the capabilities of the sales force in its planning. It cannot, for example, cut prices despite the fact that doing so would bring more sales, if doing so would compel production to reduce quality, counter to company policy. Furthermore, the sales campaign planners cannot anticipate a campaign that would require sales personnel to cover more territory than is reasonable. They cannot add to the sales force if the size of the sales force is limited by policy. They can recommend changes in company policy, but if they do, both production and sales personnel will be affected by the changes. Thus, the external environment limits the behavior of the group. If, on the other hand, the group succeeds in changing the external environment, other groups will be affected, which in turn will affect the group that initiated the change.

A group also functions within a community. Each social layer exerts influence to the extent that the group is part of it. A public group attempting to establish group homes for retarded citizens will be constrained by the politics of the community regarding zoning and taxation, as well as the perceived interests of householders in the neighborhood where the group home is to be located. Church and civic groups will have attitudes on the question. So will real estate agents and merchants. Moral values of those who want to "do right" by the retarded citizens may clash with economic values of householders who believe the group home will reduce property values. Even students in college discussion classes must fit within the community, including the university, the town, the state, and society in general. Their conduct during discussion sessions, the topics they choose to discuss, and the manner in which they conduct the discussions will be affected by rules of conduct applying to classes, goals and objectives of the instructor, potential to interact with the community, obligations of members to other courses and activities in both university and community, and space available in which to conduct business.

Constituency is very important for problem-solving groups. A company's product must be desired by someone, otherwise there is no point in making it. The best designed "kadody" will not sell if no one knows what it is for and no one wants to pay money for it. Educational policy in universities may be controlled by faculty committees, but academic institutions will collapse if they alienate students, trustees, or contribution-giving alumni. The faculty committee may decide it is desirable that all students take Sanskrit, but if the students do not see the point, they may go elsewhere. If enrollment drops, contributions may dwindle. If both happen, faculty members may be terminated. Thus, any decision-making or problem-solving body must take into account the impact of decisions on *all* those who will be affected. Furthermore, they must consider how those constituents, once affected, may behave in ways that affect the decision-makers or problem-solvers. The faculty committee must be sensitive to the various constituencies as a matter of simple survival.

Prevailing public standards or norms affect the manner in which groups do business. Prior to widespread concern about fuel supplies, for example, car manufacturers produced powerful engines and sleek designs. Public demand for economical fuel consumption, a direct result of dwindling fuel supplies and growing environmental awareness, pressured companies into producing cars that consumed less fuel, which required changes in design, which affected costs, which affected the rate at which the public bought cars. If a pulp mill believes it can reduce costs by reducing the expense of waste disposal, it must take into account the effects of its action on both a national and local level.

Thus, to ensure survival, group members must be sensitive to the values of their communities. Some of those values are brought into the group by members who represent outside constituencies. A group member does not sacrifice other loyalties when she or he comes into the group. On the contrary, it is important that the member adequately represent those concerns. On the other hand, group members must consider the principle of equity in dealing with people who represent other interests so there is fairness in the exchange between the group and the community.

It is important for groups that lack official status to secure constituencies. Student task groups, for example, generally have no formal titles or recognized status. They may be regarded as upstarts not only by the faculty, but by other students. To win support from the external community may mean securing representation from the community, opening dialogue with it, or anticipating its needs and interests and taking them into account. A student group which advocated a textbook exchange on campus might find objection from bookstore owners, from faculty who believe books for low enrollment courses might be more difficult to obtain, and from others whose ability to move about might be affected by a change in traffic flow brought about by the book exchange. The students must find a way to enlist existing agencies in their campaign. Faculty might be invited to participate. Merchants could be solicited for information about their needs. Existing organizations could be canvassed to secure secretarial assistance, computer accounts, or funds for a survey. It is, after all, very easy to make decisions about other people so long as the other people don't know you are doing so and so long as the decisions will have no effect. If a group expects to be influential, members must be sensitive to their context.

Groups are materially influenced by adjacent groups. Recurrent problems arise from competition between groups.[2] Group morale and cohesiveness increase in a group that perceives itself in competition with another group, often to the point of antagonism toward both the other group and individuals in it. Members of both groups may unrealistically evaluate their work. They may overevaluate their own work and underestimate the work of their competitors. This may lead to a decline in self-criticism and to the care taken with decisions. Competition may lead to overconfidence and groupthink. The result is usually sloppy and ineffective recommendations. In the final analysis, it is not the competing group whose positive evaluation is necessary, it is the rest of the environment's. Groups contending for research funds, for example, need not solicit the approval of other competing groups. Their effort should be focused on their proposal and the demonstration of how it will serve the environment in general.

Finally, every group exists within the context of an overall culture that influences both individual members and the group as a whole. Most of us take for granted a broad array of values, expectations, and codes of conduct that we have learned over the years. Our table manners, the way we greet acquaintances, our small talk, the way we dress are all features of our culture. They are so familiar to us we do not even realize we're operating from internalized cultural assumptions. Yet to understand much of what happens in a group, we must raise our cultural assumptions to a conscious level.

The sense of how a group should operate is culturally influenced. For instance, most groups in America adopt a more or less democratic style of leadership (or at least claim to). Group members rarely discuss matters of style, yet most seem to find democratic process quite familiar. It is a culturally conditioned belief. Similarly, some groups typically expect a male to act as leader and a female as recorder. Regardless of qualifications for the position, most of us succumb to sex stereotypes that influence expectations of who should do what.

The influence of cultural assumptions is clearly reflected in the contrast between Japanese and American styles of decision-making. Typically the Japanese devote extensive time to defining and analyzing problems, but move with great speed in making final decisions. Americans follow an opposite path in which minimum time is devoted to analysis, while making the final decision consumes substantial time. No wonder international negotiations are often so frustrating for all parties.[3] We all reflect the culture in which we have been socialized through our participation in discussion. We are so tightly bound to our culture that sometimes Americans of different ethnic origin or from different parts of the country have to work at synthesizing differences in the way things are done.

Thus, it is a good idea to reflect on the influence exerted by the surrounding environment. By consciously identifying major influences, members find it easier to discover common ground in the way they talk to one another. Furthermore, they are sensitive to differing needs and values and take them into account in problem-solving.

INITIAL ELEMENTS IN GROUP SYSTEMS

At the outset, there are four main features in a work-oriented (problem-solving or decision-making) discussion group: individual members, size of the group, group record, and group purpose.

Individual Members

Groups are made up of individuals. Each member has a unique personality, personal needs, abilities, and self-esteem. In addition, the nature of membership is often affected by entrance requirements—that is, their specialties or the fact that they represent an outside reference group.

The work of Murray[4] and Edwards[5] is especially helpful in understanding how personality styles and needs influence group interaction. Between them, Murray and Edwards identified fifteen personality needs we each have:

Achievement	Deference	Order	Exhibition	Autonomy
Affiliation	Intraception	Succorance	Dominance	Abasement
Heterosexuality	Nurturance	Endurance	Aggression	Change

We don't offer this list for you to memorize but to illustrate the complexity of individual needs that come into play as people interact in discussion. Personality needs clearly influence individual styles of participation, as well as goals for membership in groups. Consider the personality profile of a student in one of the author's discussion classes:

> I think my highest need is for achievement, followed closely by needs for order and endurance (sticking with the task). I have pretty low needs for deference, affiliation, and nurturance. I like to concentrate on getting a job done as quickly and well as possible, and I don't need a lot of recognition for doing it.

As you may have inferred, this student was a workaholic, a perfectionistic, highly task-oriented person, and he seized leadership of his group and proceeded to run it as a one-man show. Would you consider this effective? Actually, it's impossible to judge his effectiveness solely on the basis of what we know about him as an individual. We must consider his personality in relation to others in his group. He would be effective with members who had high needs for deference, order, and abasement. On the other hand, he would clash with individuals who had high needs for dominance, change, and aggression, or with those who required a lot of nurturance and affiliation to motivate them. There is no ideal discussant personality; what matters is that the members' personalities fit together to form a workable system.

Gender was once considered an important personality influence on group interaction. Research dating back to the 1920s identified differences in the content and style of male and female participants. One major finding was that men tended to talk about task issues, while women dealt with interpersonal issues and matters of climate.[6] More recent studies, however, failed to confirm these early findings.[7] Rosenfeld and Christie summarized five years of research with the report that men and women do not differ appreciably in their participation styles.[8] In a later study, Rosenfeld and Fowler found men and women did not differ in the way they exercised leadership either.[9] Although sex stereotypes still exist in many people's minds, there is compelling evidence that there are no important differences between men and women as leaders or members of discussion groups. Despite this evidence, however, biases persist and seem to influence how men and women judge each other.[10] In a problem-solving model, these judgments often get in the way of consensus and sometimes deprive the group of important contributions from highly competent members.

In addition to personality, each member brings particular abilities to the problem-solving scene. Some are meticulous researchers, others may be skilled interviewers. Some may have the ability to write and edit; others may be able to ferret out important facts and subtle details. Some abilities are not so welcome. Some members may be more skillful at argument than others. They may be able to use sarcasm and ridicule, or display the ability to criticize others severely. Nobody is talented in all dimensions. The real problem for the group is to find and utilize member strengths, while discouraging the display of skills that might subvert the work of the group.

Each member has some image of self. Self-esteem has impact on participation. Those who have high regard for themselves are willing to take risks in offering ideas, can take criticism, assume their share of blame, and take credit graciously. By contrast, people with low self-esteem tend to be hypercritical of themselves and others, defensive about their worth and efforts, pessimistic about what the group can achieve, and in constant need of assurance of their merit (although often they are unable to accept compliments).[11] Members can affect the self-esteem of colleagues by rewarding constructive contributions and diverting counterproductive activity.

In addition to personality-related variables, groups can be affected by formal or informal membership requirements. Almost all groups limit membership at least to the extent that membership in the larger setting is restricted. The potential membership of any student group is affected by the entrance requirements of the college. Memberships in community action groups are limited by residence, interest in the issue, and economic and social factors that prevail in the community. In addition, there are informal requirements, such as visibility in context. People who are asked to serve on committees, for example, are those the person appointing the committee can remember.

Membership is sometimes limited by self-screening. People decide what groups they want to join. They may favor a cause supported by one group, or share a hobby with members of another. When individuals seek to join an established group, they do so on the basis of some "advertisement." They believe the group stands for something and membership might be profitable because it is compatible with what they think represents the group's norms. We can assume they are committed and motivated.

But a drawback of voluntary groups is there may be little sense of responsibility. If the group doesn't live up to what the new member imagined, he or she drops out. If there are no standards for membership, newcomers often make little commitment to the group. Others, however, may have a deep commitment. But the rule of voluntary organizations is that those who volunteer in can volunteer out. Hard workers can burn out, become discouraged, or be distracted by rewards promised by other groups. Those who are lukewarm can remain on the group rolls for a long time, but never contribute anything. Furthermore, volunteers often want to do things their way and resist leadership. They may be uncritical and argumentative in problem-solving, seeking mainly to persuade others to support their pet biases. And if everyone in the group has exactly the same beliefs and goals, there is little that can be done besides mutual reinforcement. Consensus may be too easy and consequently unproductive.

Membership qualifications may be set by the group itself. Some groups are open to all, others maintain a numerical quota, and still others use elaborate screening procedures. The way members are picked affects group morale. In one of the author's colleges, for example, there is a hierarchy of committees. Professors struggle to get on what they regard as major committees, appointment to which is a sign of the dean's favor. There is a group of committees newcomers start with, and if they behave properly, they may work up the ladder until they are appointed to the Promotion and Tenure Committee, which gives them considerable power over their colleagues. There is a striking similarity between this process and the process of rushing and pledging fraternities, securing new members in lodges and fraternal organizations, or admitting people to membership in learned societies and professional associations.

A now-classic experiment conducted in 1959 demonstrated the impact of entrance requirements on member attitudes toward groups.[12] In response to a membership appeal, a number of college women applied to join a club that would spend its time discussing sex (something not openly done in 1959). The applicants were told by the experimenters that they had to be screened, so those who were excessively embarrassed by talking about sexual topics could be excluded.

For one-third of the women, the screening procedure consisted of reading to the male experimenter twelve obscene words and two sexually explicit passages from novels. This was considered an extreme initiation. For another third, the procedure consisted of reading aloud five words related to sex, but not obscene. This was mild initiation. The final third, the control group, was simply asked whether sexual discussions would cause embarrassment. All the women were then informed they had been admitted to the club.

The women were then taken into another room, where they were told to listen to a discussion already in progress by members of the club they had just joined so they could get an idea of what the group was like and be ready to participate at the next meeting. What the women really heard was a tape recording the experimenters had designed to be as uninteresting and unprovocative as possible. After hearing the recording, the women were asked to evaluate the overall worth of the discussion and the quality of the club members.

When the responses were analyzed, the experimenters found that the women who had had the mild initiation and those in the control group had about the same evaluations of the discussion and the club members. Those who had undergone the severe initiation, however, rated the worth of the discussion as much higher than the other two groups. They also judged the quality of club members to be higher. From these results, the researchers concluded that when it is costly to enter a group, the investment leads the new member to place a higher value on the group.

This kind of experiment could not take place today because researchers are now bound by government guidelines for treatment of human subjects. (Researchers too are constrained by the rules of their contexts!) Throughout this chapter we will report experiments in which subjects' rights were not adequately taken into account. However, the findings are very useful. In this case, the investigator discovered that the personal value assigned to membership in a group shapes the value the person assigns to the group. Even in your classroom groups, members will become intensely involved depending on their commitment to the task, to learning in general, and to a grade. It is important to consider individual commitments, for the interaction of personal commitments will have a great deal to do with the norms of newly formed groups.

Group Size

The size of a group is a second initial feature that influences the process and outcomes of problem-solving. There seem to be limits to the size of a problem-oriented group beyond which efficiency drops. Based on the early work of Robert Bales, most authorities believe five or seven is the ideal size for a problem-solving group.[13] With less than five, a group lacks the diversity of opinion necessary for a broad perspective and consideration of various solutions. Furthermore, members are reluctant to disagree in groups of four or less. They fear alienating their colleagues. The sense of closeness that develops impedes critical, reflective analysis of issues.

Equally serious problems affect groups with more than seven members. As the group grows in size, there is a tendency for hierarchies to develop. Once status is assigned, higher-status members affect participation of lower-status members. The stronger members dominate and feel good about participation, while the weaker members suffer a drop in self-esteem and are dissatisfied with their participation.[14] Subgroups also tend to develop in larger discussion groups. When this happens, discussion becomes an exercise in politics, rather than a deliberation about issues. Power plays may disrupt group cohesion, which in turn leads to dissatisfied members, some of whom may decide to leave the group.[15]

Often you do not have control over how many members there are in the group. The information we have just presented should alert you to potential problems so you can do your best to minimize their effect. At other times you may be able to suggest breaking an oversized group into subcommittees to encourage more intense participation. If your group is too small or has lost membership over time, you can encourage increasing the size by appointing replacements or by recruiting new members. It is worthwhile to try to get groups to optimum size in order to facilitate effective participation and quality output.

Group Charge

Groups do not come into being by accident. They are formed for reasons that provide a collective goal which should unify members. In the early days of group discussion instruction, students were often put into groups and told to find a topic

Group size influences process and outcomes. (Bodin, Stock, Boston)

to discuss. This is unrealistic. It does not happen in commerce or government, where groups are created to respond to conditions in the larger organization. A group's charge or purpose may be as explicit as designing a new method of parceling out dormitory rooms on campus or very vague, like trying to improve student morale. The purpose may be imposed from the outside, as in the case of a committee created and charged to submit recommendations to meet some emergency condition, like adjust the college budget to accommodate to reduced appropriations. It may be generated from the inside, like a faculty committee to find ways to distribute limited funds.

If your classroom group is assigned to find a topic for discussion, it is important to agree on something that interests all the members—a real topic on which the group might exert real influence. Your group must seek a topic feasible to discuss, where information is readily available. A group interested in the general topic of campus safety, for example, might narrow its focus to consideration of the services provided by campus police. It may narrow down even further to find ways and means to inform other students about services provided by campus police. From any general topic different charges may be generated, but groups can pursue only one at a time. Effective groups narrow the scope of their topics to a manageable size.

Understanding the purpose is crucial to success. It is not possible for a group to be effective unless all members understand precisely what the task is and what the final outcome is to be. For this reason, groups that are charged from the outside often need to ask for clarification of purpose. Charging authorities are not always clear in explaining why the group was formed and what is wanted as a final output. A group without clear purpose or in which members disagree about the goal tends to falter. Members become disillusioned as the group becomes paralyzed with the apathy of confusion. Clarification of purpose is the first active step toward success.

Group Record

The final influence in the initial group system is the history of past work by the group. This feature is relevant only in groups that have a history. However, a newly formed group begins writing its history from the moment its members sit down at the first meeting. Each event affects those that follow.

Standing committees and other groups that have existed for a long time can be viewed as products of their own evolution. Studies of developing groups suggest strongly that members increase their commitment to groups that achieve their goals; the more successful the group, the more interested the members.[16] Initial success leads members to have confidence in the group's capacity to meet future challenges.

When a group fails, however, members tend to be disappointed and frustrated. They may seek a target for blame. Once blaming starts, the group can factionalize, or resentments can fester below the surface. Members will set low goals for future work because they have lost confidence in each other as well as the group. Some groups do not turn inward after suffering failure, however. They may blame someone or something outside the group. Members find it comforting to believe that "the system was rigged against us from the start," or "rejecting our proposal was a typical muddle-headed bureaucratic decision." Excuses are easy to find, and sometimes they are legitimate.

In either case, it is important to recognize the consequences of scapegoating. Finding the person who caused the failure is not as productive as seeking a way to be successful the next time. Furthermore, groups can become very cohesive on the issue of blaming. They may pull together under the stress of threat and engage in groupthink, setting excessively high goals for themselves and deluding themselves about the quality of their work. Supergroup, after all, can do anything, even jump mile-high administration buildings in a single bound.

You may not be able to guarantee that your group will succeed (although skillful participation surely increases the odds that it will), but you can use what you know about how groups operate to help guide you toward behavior that facilitates success.

We have examined the elements that form the initial system of problem-solving groups and considered the environment in which groups operate. At the outset, groups consist of individuals with diverse personalities, abilities, and degrees of self-esteem. They have different sizes, charges, and histories. These elements interact with one another and the environment to influence both the process and the outcome of group discussion. In the next chapter, we examine the features that evolve out of the initial group system.

REFERENCES

1. Ludwig Von Bertelanffy, *General Systems Theory* (New York: George Braziller, 1968); John K. Brilhart, *Effective Group Discussion,* 4th ed. (Dubuque, IA: William C. Brown, 1982), pp. 23–24; Stewart Tubbs, *A Systems Approach to Small Group Interaction* (Reading, MA: Addison-Wesley, 1981).
2. Muzafer and Carolyn W. Sherif, *Social Psychology* (New York: Harper & Row, 1969), pp. 221–266.
3. William Ouchi, *Theory Z: How American Business Can Meet the Japanese Challenge* (Reading, MA: Addison-Wesley, 1981).
4. Henry Murray, *Explorations in Personality* (New York: Oxford University Press, 1938).
5. Allen Edwards, *The Edwards Personal Preference Schedule* (New York: Psychological Corporation, 1953).
6. Steven M. Alderton and William E. Jurma, "Genderless/Gender Related Task Leader Communication and Group Satisfaction: A Test of Two Hypotheses," *Southern Journal of Speech Communication,* 46 (Fall 1980), pp. 48–60.
7. Steven M. Alderton, William E. Jurma, and John E. Baird, "Sex Differences in Group Communication: A Review of Relevant Research," *Quarterly Journal of Speech,* 62 (1976), pp. 179–192.
8. L. B. Rosenfeld and V. Christie, "Sex and Personality Revisited," *Western Journal of Speech Communication,* 38 (1974), pp. 244–253.
9. L. B. Rosenfeld and G. D. Fowler, "Personality, Sex, and Leadership Style," *Communication Monographs,* 43 (1976), pp. 320–324; G. D. Fowler and L. B. Rosenfeld, "Sex

Differences and Democratic Leader Behavior," *Southern Journal of Speech Communication,* 45 (Fall 1979), pp. 69–78.

10. E. G. Bormann, J. Pratt, and L. Putnam, "Power, Authority, and Sex: Male Response to Female Leadership," *Communication Monographs,* 45 (June 1978), pp. 119–155.

11. G. E. Meyers and M. T. Meyers, *The Dynamics of Human Communication* (New York: McGraw-Hill, 1973), pp. 109–110.

12. E. Aronson and J. Mills, "The Effect of Severity of Initiation on Liking for a Group," *Journal of Abnormal and Social Psychology,* 50 (1959), pp. 177–181.

13. R. F. Bales and E. F. Borgatta, "Size of a Group as a Factor in the Interaction Profile." In A. P. Hare, E. F. Borgatta, and R. F. Bales (eds.), *Small Groups: Studies in Social Interaction* (New York: Knopf, 1955), pp. 396–413.

14. P. E. Slater, "Contrasting Correlates of Group Size," *Sociometry,* 21 (1958), pp. 129–139.

15. B. Indik, "Organization Size and Member Participation: Some Empirical Tests of Alternative Explanations," *Human Relations,* 8 (1965), pp. 339–350.

16. H. P. Shelley, "Level of Aspiration Phenomena in Small Groups," *Journal of Abnormal and Social Psychology,* 40 (1954), pp. 149–164.

chapter 3

Developing the Group System

The preceding chapter introduced the systems perspective, which defines groups as systems of interacting, interrelated elements. We explained that a group is more than the sum of its parts, that any part of a group can be understood only in relation to all other elements of its system, and that parts of a system interact constantly with each other and the surrounding environment. In this chapter, we explain how a group evolves as a result of dynamic interaction among the initial elements. We identify process features and outcomes common to all small-group systems.

PROCESS ELEMENTS

Group members, size, purpose, and history interact dynamically to create new elements of groups that further affect the process and outcomes of problem-solving discussion. We will examine six such features of interaction: verbal communication, nonverbal behavior, norms, power, cohesion, decision-making style, and sense of group autonomy.

Verbal Communication

Communication is probably the single most important influence on how a group operates and what it achieves. Talking and listening are the substance of problem-solving. People are brought together in groups so they can talk, listen, and respond to one another. Talk is immediate and responsive. It is much more effective in sorting out ideas, picking up feelings, and identifying values and beliefs

36

than writing memos. By communicating face to face, people can negotiate and bargain in the interest of all.

However, you cannot estimate the quality of talk by counting. The person who talks most is not necessarily the person who talks best; one group is not better than another simply because people talk more. Sometimes productive group members are the ones who talk most, but conversational bullies and time wasters also talk a lot. Furthermore, a focus on talk alone does not take into account the importance of listening. Quantity of talk alone is a poor index of effectiveness. Both quantity and quality of participation must be considered, and listening must be recognized as an integral part of effective communication.

Relatively equal participation by group members is desirable for a number of reasons. First, if everyone has a fair chance to speak, there is a greater chance that important ideas will be expressed. Second, participation is closely related to satisfaction; if all members are active, there is a greater chance they will be pleased with their participation. Third, when people participate, they are likely to become committed to the group and its outcomes. People are more willing to work to implement solutions they had some role in shaping.

When people contribute freely, they are likely to offer useful ideas, listen thoughtfully, give appropriate criticism, ask insightful questions, and raise important arguments.[1] A problem-solving group needs all these if it is to be successful. Furthermore, members tend to feel satisfied with their participation if they believe they have had a fair opportunity to talk. Satisfaction encourages members to invest time, energy, and thought in the task. Communicative balance is a key to making each member feel he or she is a valuable part of the group.

The link between participation and commitment was found in pioneering research by Lewin. In one experiment, he tried to persuade people to eat "undesirable meats" during the national meat shortage. Lewin lectured to one group of housewives, and led a group discussion by others in which involvement was encouraged. He discovered that women who participated in the discussions were much more likely actually to try the meats than those who only heard the lecture.[2]

The contemporary management philosophy of teamwork is based on Lewin's work. Cooperative and balanced discussion seems to encourage people to contribute more and better ideas, as well as be loyal and diligent at implementing the decisions made by the group. Likert has conducted an impressive series of studies that confirms the positive relationship between participation in decision-making and efficient goal accomplishment in business and industry.[3] A recent study by Harper and Askling further supports the connection between active, balanced participation and successful group work.[4]

Various communication roles performed by members make up participation in the group system. Effective problem-solving discussion requires three basic communication roles that address the group's task, procedures, and climate.[5]

Task roles involve communication about the information that is the basis of problem-solving: asking for ideas and information, giving ideas and information, elaborating and evaluating information that has been introduced into deliberations. Each of these task roles assists a group in its effort to gain valid, reliable information on which to base a sound decision.

Procedural roles organize collective efforts: establishing and maintaining agenda, coordinating various ideas before the group, summarizing progress, and recording key ideas and agreements. Procedural roles are marked by comments that help members sustain a common course of thought.

Climate roles contribute to creating and maintaining a healthy, cooperative tone in group interaction. They include recognizing others' ideas, reconciling conflicts, releasing tension in the group through humor or other means, and emphasizing collective goals and values. A climate role can help sustain an atmosphere conducive to cooperative, productive discussion.

There is a fourth kind of communication role; one that is not constructive. *Egocentric roles* reflect individual concerns and interests, but often hinder collective communication. Examples of egocentric roles are personal socialization, refusing to permit the group to move on, seeking personal attention and recognition, making personal attacks on others, pleading for special interests, bringing up personal concerns, and withdrawing from participation. Any behavior that places personal concerns above those of the group should be discouraged. In effective groups, responsible members tend to reprimand and discipline members who waste time with individualistic behavior. It is important that each member have a fair chance to contribute. It is equally important to recognize that a task-oriented group is not suitable for personal therapy.

Each member of a group is personally responsible for contributing to balanced participation. It is important to make it possible for quiet members to participate, to discourage those who speak a lot, and to take care not to talk too much yourself. It is also important to recognize that listening is just as important a part of the communication process as talking. Each member can choose what role to play at particular points in the discussion; members are not confined to one role only. In the next chapter, we will discuss your choices in participation.

Nonverbal Behavior

When most people think of communication, they typically think of words. However, the actual words comprise a very small portion of our communication. The greater part consists of *nonverbal messages,* which are any behaviors of face and body without or in addition to words from which listeners can draw inferences about meaning.

Authorities estimate that nonverbal behavior accounts for between 65 and 93 percent of the emotional meaning of human behavior.[6] Research by Leathers, as well as by Gouran and Fisher, demonstrates that nonverbal behavior has considerable impact on group discussion. Similarly, our nonverbal behaviors are often interpreted by others as indicators of our intentions toward them and our evaluations of their ideas.[7]

Four types of nonverbal behavior are especially pertinent to group discussion: interaction cues, spatial networks, seating positions, and physical setting.

Interaction Cues   In group discussions, nonverbal behaviors provide many cues for interactions. One of the ways they do this is by reflecting attitudes toward others and their ideas. Facial gestures, physical position, eye contact, and tone of voice indicate feelings and levels of interest. For example, boredom is suggested when a member turns away or looks aside when someone else is speaking. Conversely, keen attention is indicated by a member who sits erect, faces the speaker, and maintains direct eye contact. Typically, listeners will regard nonverbal messages as more powerful than verbal in drawing inferences about the speaker's meaning, and speakers must base their conclusions about listener attitudes on what they see listeners doing.

Sometimes nonverbal cues are complete messages in themselves. Examples include a head nod to signal agreement, or a raised hand to indicate a desire to speak. In other cases, nonverbal behaviors supplement verbal messages. For instance, you might say "I disagree" while shaking your head; verbal and nonverbal behaviors work together to form the message.

Nonverbal behaviors also regulate interaction in groups. We use nonverbal cues to regulate or control the flow of discussion. In problem-solving, members take turns speaking, and nonverbal cues are the primary method of informally coordinating those turns. Someone who is speaking and intends to keep speaking tends not to hold sustained eye contact with another member. When that person is ready to yield the floor, however, she or he may indicate this by making eye contact with another person whose nonverbal behavior suggests he or she wants to speak.

It is sometimes possible to identify cliques or factions in a group by observing the turn-taking cues by which members of a clique keep the conversational ball in their court. It is also possible to use knowledge of turn-taking cues to invite quiet members into discussion and to discourage overly talkative ones from dominating. The interactional cues provided by nonverbal behaviors are a subtle yet very important part of the ongoing communication process in groups.

Spatial Networks   The spatial network of a group is the overall arrangement of seating. There are two basic types of networks: *centralized*, in which one person occupies a central position, like these:

and *decentralized*, in which all member have equally prominent spots, like these:

```
    X                      X                        X
  XX  XX             XXXXXXX                     X
  XX  XX                                        XXX


    X                      X                        X
 X      X            X           X           X           X
 X      X                                    X
    X                      X
```

The differences between the patterns should be obvious. In a centralized arrangement, communication flows through one person whose central position makes him or her powerful. In decentralized patterns, participants have an equal opportunity for face-to-face discussion with other members.

Studies comparing the two types of networks demonstrate that the decentralized pattern leads to more balanced participations and thus greater satisfaction among members. The decentralized style also seems to promote fuller analysis and more vigorous interaction. In addition, surprisingly enough, decentralized seating is actually more efficient than centralized. Complex problems require careful consideration and deliberation, processes encouraged by a decentralized network and impeded by a centralized one. We also know that fewer errors in reasoning are made in decentralized networks, probably because members are better able to talk over ideas and check and double-check inferences and conclusions.[8]

Seating Positions   Where a person sits is also important. It appears that whoever occupies a central position exerts more power than those whose positions are peripheral.[9] People on the physical edges of a group may feel they are also on its substantive edges, and their participation may wane. The effect of physical constraints in the meeting room that make a decentralized arrangement impossible (as in most board rooms) can be minimized by changing seating positions at each meeting to give everyone a fair chance to be central.

Physical Setting   The physical setting can influence both the tone of deliberation and patterns of interaction. Relaxed settings such as apartments or homes tend to promote a good degree of social talk and digression. In addition, casual settings often feature comfortable furniture that encourages people to unwind and take it easy. Classrooms, on the other hand, tend to emphasize one central person.

Which kind of setting is better? That all depends on your goals for the group at a particular time. A relaxed environment may be ideal for an initial meeting when members need to get acquainted and become comfortable with one another, but it might undermine the group later on when efficiency and tight, probing analysis are the key requirements. Conference rooms and even classrooms offer such useful items as tables for writing, blackboards, and chairs sufficiently spartan to discourage lingering conversation. Even meeting times can influence interaction. Consider the difference in enthusiasm (and perhaps attendance!) that you could reasonably expect at an 8 A.M. versus a 3 P.M. meeting.

The nonverbal dimension of problem-solving is important. Understanding the ways in which nonverbal features influence group discussion provides you with a basis for interpreting much of what happens in the group.

Norms and Conformity

Groups form habits just as individuals do. Once people have been together for a time, they develop standardized ways of managing task, procedures, and climate. Norms are standardized patterns of belief, attitude, communication, and behavior within groups. They grow out of member interaction. Then, in systematic fashion, they influence future interaction.

Adherence to norms is necessary for effective group interaction. Groups, in fact, could not exist without norms of procedure. Norms guide members in acceptable ways to disagree, resolve conflicts, release tension, welcome new mem-

The physical setup for a discussion influences the participation of each member. (© Kroll, Taurus)

bers, and do business. We all count on regularity in our dealings with others. Social norms help us get along with strangers, as well as provide a convenient shorthand for cooperation with people we know well. Yet norms are not always constructive. When people comform to norms without thinking, trouble can result. The challenge in groups is to get members to conform in the way business gets done, but to encourage them to the widest possible expression of facts, ideas, criticisms, and solutions.

Norms are standardized codes of conduct and thought; they may characterize any area of group life from task to procedural to social. Norms may even apply to personal behaviors, such as how members dress (have you ever noticed the similarity in dress style among people of the same rank in an office?). Members are often unaware of the norms in their group, probably because they have become so used to operating by them. To an outsider or a new member, however, the norms may be very clear.

Recognizing norms is important to effective participation in group discussions. Once you learn to identify norms, you can control how you respond to them. It is possible to make informed choices about when to conform, when not to, and when to comment on norms.

Basic to identifying norms is the awareness that they exist and influence what happens in groups. Members who are aware of this are likely to notice and think about norms. Look for patterns in how your group operates. Can you see regularized procedures in meetings? Do members consistently occupy the same seats? Can you predict who will try to speak next when one person speaks? Do some members consistently talk to a regular group of others? Do members seem to demand that the same amount of time be devoted to socialization before and after meetings? Do you spot quick agreement on some issues and consistent bickering on others? Questions such as these help you tune into norms in your group.

To be most effective, you should pay attention to norms from the very beginning of your membership in a group. Norms form at the beginning, and they are easiest to modify at the outset. Once norms have operated long enough to become entrenched parts of a group's identity, it is very difficult to change them. That is why it is important for members to be attentive to interaction patterns and the roles individual members select at the outset, when it is possible to modify any norms that seem inappropriate or counterproductive for the group.

Members of problem-solving groups often develop norms of belief about the collective task. They may have a common view of the situation, similar attitudes about the organization in which the group is nested, and a consensus about criteria for identifying the "good guys" and "bad guys." Often they share common goals. They will adopt some procedural conventions to organize the way they approach their work. Some groups, for example, invariably socialize for five to ten minutes before getting down to work; some begin by reading minutes from the previous meeting; and others expect the leader to launch each meeting with a preview of the agenda. Groups follow regular "rules" for communication. In some committees interaction is very formal, while in others it is loose and free-flowing. In some groups members are very attentive to whoever is speaking, while in other cases interruptions are frequent and accepted.

Conformity to norms is a topic that has long interested both researchers and ordinary people. Although conformity is often regarded as undesirable, this is not necessarily so. As we have suggested, norms serve a valuable purpose in providing members with some conventions for how to go about their business. Without norms, groups would be inefficient, perhaps even chaotic, because each interaction would have to be structured anew. However, excessive conformity is undesirable. It can stifle originality and lead to groupthink, thus thwarting accomplishment of group goals.

To study conformity, Kelly and Volkhart designed an experiment in which Boy Scouts were offered various incentives to deviate from the norms of their troop. The only Scouts who deviated were those who did not consider their membership to be very important. From this, the researchers concluded that conformity is most likely when members prize belonging to a group.[10] Subsequent investigations supplemented Kelly and Volkhart's findings by demonstrating that conformity is related to the importance of a norm. Minor norms may be violated by even the most committed members. In fact, many groups have norms to which members give lip service only—consider the norm of parliamentary procedure, for instance.[11]

People tend to honor norms they consider relevant to what a group stands for and does, but they resist norms that appear outside the group's purview. It seems that members believe there is a limit to the areas in which a group should influence them. A very important early experiment attempted to find out how much control people would accept from religious groups. The experimenters met with Catholic, Protestant, and Jewish students and reminded them of religious beliefs concerning birth control. Only the Catholic subjects conformed consistently to their church's stance, because only the Catholics felt their church had the right to prescribe personal attitudes in this area.[12]

The link between leadership and conformity to norms is very intriguing. Early work in this area produced seemingly contradictory findings. Some researchers reported that leaders conformed more than other members, while others argued leaders conformed far less. The apparent conflict was reconciled by the discovery that leadership is a two-sequence process. At the outset, a person attempting to earn leadership must conform closely to all norms to demonstrate loyalty and "membership character." Once leadership has been achieved, however, the leader is more free than others to deviate from group norms. Due to special status, the leader is awarded "idiosyncrasy credits," which allow him or her to innovate and violate norms binding on members.[13]

Members who do not conform to norms are usually punished. Usually this is not formal (although highly organized groups like the U.S. Senate have formal procedures for censuring the conduct of members). Most groups attempt first to resocialize the deviating member by explaining why the belief or behavior is inappropriate. Next, the group may ignore the deviating member by refusing to listen to his or her ideas. Finally, the group may withdraw the privilege of membership either formally by expelling the member, or informally by failing to send notifications of meeting time and place.[14]

Groups must maintain norms in order to get their work done. However, groups can become oppressive when they insist on excessive conformity, or when urgency for conformity squelches constructive dissent and debate. Individual members must be alert to pressures for conformity. It is appropriate to question both norms and group pressures to conform. Furthermore, each member must reconcile conflicts between group norms and personal values. If you find yourself in a group which demands that you sacrifice important personal beliefs in order to remain a member, you may have to consider resigning or trying to alter the norms. As long as you are in a group, you will be expected to conform to most of its norms most of the time, so weigh the value of membership carefully and evaluate the norms to which your adherence is sought. A truculent member whose personal values lead to consistent resistance to group norms has no value to the group. Furthermore, when it is clear you can no longer influence the group, it may be wise to go elsewhere to work for your ideas.

Power

Power is the ability to influence others. Sometimes occupying a position (chief executive officer, chairman of the board) makes a person powerful. Power may also be earned by a demonstration of competence. Position power comes with the office. It belongs to whoever holds a particular title, position, or post. In an ideal world, people gain their positions by demonstrating ability, and thus their position power is appropriate. Sometimes this is true in the real world, though people often gain their positions through political or social connections. In such cases, their position power may not be respected. Position power is particularly important in bureaucratic institutions with heavy turnover. In universities and colleges, for example, power is characteristically tied to position, since faculty and administrators change frequently.

Earned power results from effective performance that earns approval and respect from others. In long-standing groups, members with a great deal of earned power can be as powerful, sometimes even more powerful, than officials whose power comes only from position on the organization chart. In fact, when earned power clashes with position power, the former typically wins out.

Recently we saw an example of this. At a large college, Dr. Lou Quarm was hired to head an academic department. He was unable to handle the details of his job. He did not distribute agendas for department meetings, vacillated in his attitude on important issues, and most of all, paid little attention to Professor Teresa Torial, the senior member of the department. The faculty attempted to cooperate with Dr. Quarm for a time, assuming he would grow into the position if given time and support. Gradually, they became disillusioned with his leadership. Throughout this process, Dr. Torial bent over backward to help Dr. Quarm. She often prepared agendas and tried to keep Dr. Quarm informed on some of the subtleties of issues. She also tried to reduce her colleagues' tension about the situation. Gradually, the members of the department began to recognize Dr. Torial as the informal leader of the department. Dr. Quarm retained his title, but his office had been stripped of power. After three years, he resigned. Dr. Torial was offered the headship, which she refused, preferring to exert influence because of her competence. She played a major role in selecting the new head, however.

Even though Dr. Quarm had power conferred on him, he could not lead effectively. He never won the respect of his followers, so his position power was counteracted by his lack of earned power. The faculty turned to someone who had earned the right to influence them by demonstrating both competence and commitment to the group. The sociologist Floyd Hunter points out that in examining any group, care must be taken to discover who has the real power.[15]

The position or earned leader generally has most power, but virtually all members have some degree of power. To earn power, a member must render service to the group. This can be done by contributing information, ideas, and criticism, expediting the discussion, resolving conflict, and looking after the needs of the members. If a group needs a particular service or skill, the member who provides it will earn power. Power may be permanent or temporary, and narrow or broad in scope, depending on the group's needs.

Researchers have discovered that powerful members are the centers of communication in a group—they talk more, and others talk more to them than to members with less power.[16] In addition, members with power can influence decisions. One reason for this seems to be that members with low or medium status engage in "social climbing." They seek to increase their own standing in the group by securing approval from powerful members.[17] Recent research has confirmed this early finding.[18]

In most groups, there are some members who have little power. Generally members with low power become marginal participants. Once a member becomes marginal, it is very difficult to get him or her back in the hierarchy. There seems to be a reciprocal relationship between participation and power. Interaction of forces within a group system renders people with little power unable to participate, which makes them even more marginal until they break off from the group or become hostile to it. This hurts the group, because it eliminates a potential contributor.

By now you probably realize that power hierarchies can create serious problems in groups. It is to the interest of every member to see to it that power is distributed equitably among group members. To accomplish this, you must be alert to shifts in the power balance and try to compensate members who appear to be losing power by assigning them responsibilities that will enable them to regain their positions. You can also try to equalize your responses to individuals. By giving courtesy to all, you support equity in power distribution. If you discover that you seem to be losing power, try to avoid social climbing. Concentrate on the task, and try to improve your performance in the group. In the following chapter you will find a list of behaviors from which you can choose to improve your power position in the group.

Cohesion

Cohesion refers to the team orientation or the "feeling of we-ness" in a group. Cohesion can be very helpful to problem-solving groups, but it can also be carried to such an extreme that it undermines quality. Generally, in cohesive groups members pull together and agree on major issues such as the nature of the task and the goals they hope to achieve. In noncohesive groups, members seem to care less about group goals than personal ones, and there is little sense of team.

There can be too much or too little cohesion. Too much cohesion tends to subvert individuality to the group and often deprives the group of the independent, critical, and creative thought that characterizes members who preserve autonomy in order to facilitate group goals. Too little cohesion, on the other hand, tends to result in a group that has no common objectives, beliefs, and motivations. Effective problem-solving requires a healthy balance between cohesion and individuality.

We have already noted that cohesive groups tend to pull in the same direction. This is true even when the direction is wrong! Watzlawick, Weakland, and Fisch's analysis of problem resolution led them to conclude that overly cohesive units often exacerbate problems by doing more and more of whatever is not working. This happens because the group has become so cohesive members cannot exercise the self-criticism necessary to see what is not working and to consider alternatives.[19] In *Sanctions for Evil,* the authors point out that excessively cohesive groups are likely to perpetuate evil because they will not admit they could do anything wrong.[20] The desire to be cohesive imposes heavy pressures to conform and preserve the sense of unity in the group. The consensus on continuing the Vietnam war was achieved and maintained this way. Analysis of deliberations on that issue suggests that it was simply more important to the men involved to feel part of the advisory group by sustaining a united view than to bring the war to an end.[21] In Chapter 5 we will discuss groupthink, a phenomenon in which excessive cohesion leads a group to suspend critical thought.

Yet a degree of cohesion is constructive in problem-solving. Members need to feel they are on a team working toward a common goal. People in moderately cohesive groups work hard, are satisfied with what they do, find the group comfortable, and respect one another. In groups lacking cohesiveness, members tend to be less willing to invest effort toward any group goals; there is less satisfaction with the group; respect may be minimal; and there may be a chilly, even antagonistic and competitive climate.

Cohesion is not necessarily characteristic of an entire group. Sometimes only part of a group is cohesive, or there may be two cohesive factions within a single group. Usually this happens when groups become too large to allow the informal, interactive communication conducive to building a sense of team. As the inner group becomes increasingly cohesive, it also becomes a clique that prevents others from contributing to the progress of the overall unit.

Now that we have discussed some effects of cohesion, we need to review three basic reasons for its development. First, cohesion is fostered when members value belonging to a group so much that they are willing to sacrifice personal opinions to uphold group norms. In extreme form, this motive impels people to agree with and support what is said, to withhold criticism, and to ally themselves with the members who have the most power.

A second basis of cohesion is shared needs, interests, and goals. The idea is to get agreement on the goals and methods of procedure, and to encourage disagreement on facts and solutions. Groups with broad goal structures, like student government, attract a wide variety of people. Some groups have members with divergent ideas, but the group is cohesive because all members are committed to some broad goal. Student government, for instance, often attracts people with drastically different ideas of how to deal with faculty and administration, but who nonetheless share a common interest in the university. Many volunteer organizations develop cohesion from the shared goals of members. Parents of handicapped children, for example, have common experiences and concerns that meld them into a highly cohesive group, capable of raising substantial funds and exerting political power.

A third source of cohesiveness is interpersonal rewards. Many people seek a group that confirms them personally by providing acceptance and a sense of belonging. Individuals may be willing to work hard and effectively on a task in exchange for the privilege of being accepted in a group. Most people, in fact, seek some personal confirmation. In really effective groups, members encourage each other by taking note of exceptional contributions. They also share socialization. For a great many people, task groups are the avenue to social contact. If this gets out of hand, however, the group becomes so familylike that the sharp and honest disagreement needed to forge workable solutions is absent.

Cohesion is a mixed blessing. You should recognize its advantages and disadvantages, as well as the symptoms of its extensiveness. Understanding these issues enables you to make informed choices about how much cohesion you want to encourage in your group and how you might go about doing that. Smart executives often manipulate membership in task groups to ensure constructive disagreement.

Decision-Making Style

When members get used to each other, they begin to develop unique ways to reach decisions. Groups do not normally discuss these methods. They develop as norms, yet they tend to be as consistent and binding as any formal policies. There are three basic ways of group decision-making, each of which may be appropriate in particular circumstances. Each method has distinct constraints and fairly predictable impacts on a group.[22]

Consensus is unanimous agreement of all members. It is a useful goal, for seeking it preserves group unity and member commitment by encouraging thorough consideration of complex issues. After all, much analysis and discussion must usually take place before everyone will agree to one decision.[23] The major drawback of seeking consensus is that it tends to consume a lot of time. For important policy issues central to the group's work, time spent seeking consensus may be a sound investment. On minor issues, consensus may consume more time than appropriate, and when there are emergencies the group may have to act so quickly that seeking consensus is not possible. A second potential weakness of consensus is that it can result in uninspired decisions because they have been so watered down by the compromises necessary to secure unanimous agreement.

A second method, *negotiation,* involves bargaining among members to build a solution that honors each person's position on particular issues. One member may be willing to bend on cost in exchange for others agreeing to a particular plan for implementing recommendations. Negotiating a solution usually takes less time than consensus, and it can result in bolder decisions, since not all members have to agree with all aspects of the solution. Its outstanding advantage as a method, however, is that it accommodates parties with divergent and even conflicting goals and allows them to come up with some reasonable agreement that may be nobody's idea, but that everyone can accept. Negotiation also has several drawbacks, including its tendency to result in piecemeal solutions that are sometimes less coherent than consensual decisions.

A third method is *voting* in which members vote formally or informally on ideas before a group. The obvious advantage of voting is efficiency; it is a quick, decisive means of settling issues. Against this the potential disadvantage of control by high-powered members who may pressure others into voting their way must be weighed. Voting may create divisions in a group, polarizing winners and losers, and generating resentment, frustration, and disillusionment.

None of these methods is *correct.* Each has its own strengths and limitations, and each can be useful in particular circumstances. What is important is that members understand there are alternative styles of making decisions and that they appreciate the probable impacts of each. Acquainting yourself with decision-making options assists you in making informed choices about when to employ each method in your group. Be wary of settling into a single method for making all decisions. Not all issues merit the time required for consensus, yet some matters are too important to risk factionalizing a group by voting. Let your selection of method be guided by the requirements of the decision you are making and the potential for your membership.

Group Autonomy

Over the course of problem-solving, members come to see their group in particular ways. Just as individuals develop self-images, so a group develops some sense of its identity or image. Central to identity is the degree to which members perceive their group as autonomous. *Autonomy* refers to the degree to which a group can operate independent of external controls, constraints, and directives for outcomes. If group members believe their group has little real power and exists merely to ratify what some superior has already decided, then motivation drops, creativity diminishes, and the quality of solutions is impaired. By contrast, when members think they do have power and responsibility as relatively independent agents, the result is likely to be a motivated, enthusiastic, and effective group.

One of the authors studied two university committees that had different perceptions of their autonomy. In one committee, the members believed they had been appointed simply to approve decisions made by higher-ups. Within this group, members came minimally prepared and information was often lacking; members did not become involved in vigorous discussion and analysis; there was very little cohesion or sense of group pride; and communication among members was punctuated by frequent references to administrative stances and opinions.

The second committee felt it had considerable leeway to deliberate and recommend policy; members felt their decisions would be accepted if they were sound. Members came prepared with ideas and information; they debated ideas intensely; they considered a range of solutions, including some that the administration was known not to favor; and there was decidedly high group cohesion and morale. The dramatic differences between these two committees demonstrate how the feeling of potency can affect group problem-solving. It is important for members to know that they have some freedom to act and some potential to make a difference.[24]

The importance of perceived autonomy has been underscored by the work of Tannenbaum and Kahn. In a study of union groups, they found that members who thought they had control over outcomes were more willing to invest effort in group work and were more committed to implementing group decisions than members who perceived their groups as lacking autonomy.[25]

Most groups have some autonomy; neither total autonomy nor total lack of it occur frequently. The perception of a fair degree of independence is critical to committed, effective problem-solving. Most important is attention to the tone and content of communication during discussion. Members may create a sense of autonomy or an image of the group as a rubber stamp through their communicative choices. Members who refer constantly to outside attitudes or to the effect of the group on its organization, or who seem to look over their shoulders for approval from reference groups not present, do not have an autonomous image.

As the initial elements of a group system—individuals, size, purpose, and record—interact dynamically, new features evolve. We have discussed seven of these process features: verbal communication, nonverbal behavior, norms, power, cohesion, decision-making style, and group autonomy. Consistent with the systems perspective, we remind you that each of these process features interacts with all others to interrelate them in complex and dynamic ways. In addition, all the features we have examined so far influence the *outcomes* of problem-solving deliberations. That is the focus of the final section of this chapter.

OUTCOME FEATURES

What are the outcomes of group problem-solving discussion? What results from the interactions we have described thus far? Three end results of discussion merit our attention: effectiveness of group decision, individuals' satisfaction, and change in the environment surrounding a group. We remind you that these outcomes are interrelated, each affecting all others.

Effectiveness of Group Decisions

The discussion outcome that first comes to mind is group decision. The effectiveness of a group's final product is, after all, the bottom line in evaluating the group's success. Quality of decisions is not as simple a concept as it might first appear. Maier's research illuminated two distinct dimensions of decisions: quality and acceptance. According to Maier, the formula for an effective decision is:

$$ED = Q \times A$$

An effective decision *(ED)* requires attention to both the quality *(Q)*, which is measured by objective information such as the problem situation, costs of implementation, and so forth, and acceptance *(A)*, which refers to the degree to which the decision garners commitment from those who must implement and work with it. Quality is tied to objective, empirical data; acceptance is based on subjective feelings.[26]

Most decisions entail both components, but the balance between them varies widely. Quality is the overriding concern in technical decisions, such as those calling for estimates on costs or safety provisions for new products. Acceptance is the most important criterion for decisions in which success will depend upon people's willingness to abide by new policies and for decisions in which issues of fairness are perceived. For example, acceptance is critical in deciding how to schedule unpleasant tasks or overtime work, or in determing disciplinary procedures that must be internally enforced. In still other cases, quality and acceptance are equally important. For instance, policies to ensure safety in a plant must be based on sound analysis of safety hazards and preventive measures and must be acceptable to the people who must follow the policies.

Decision effectiveness clearly affects other outcomes, such as individual satisfaction. Moreover, it is related to process features, notably to decision-making style. When acceptance is the primary concern, participatory methods like consensus are most appropriate; when quality is the dominant criterion, group methods may be abandoned in favor of expert opinion. Effective decisions tend to be based on sound information and reasoning (quality) and tend to have a substantial base of support from members and from people outside the group who will affect implementation. What you must keep in mind is that the final test of a group decision is whether it works. Usually it takes a great deal of time before a solution devised by a group can be thoroughly tested. During that time, new problems arise, and the solution is modified to respond to changing conditions.

Attempting to measure the quality of group decisions with precision is virtually impossible.

Individual Satisfaction

Throughout this chapter we have dealt with member satisfaction. It is one important measure of a group's effectiveness. How positively members feel about their group may be affected by a variety of factors, most of which we have already examined. Topping the list of influences on satisfaction is participation. Satisfaction tends to be positively related to the amount of talk a member engages in. Further, power is associated with participation, so it is indirectly related to satisfaction. Cohesion is another influence on satisfaction, since members tend to take pleasure in belonging to a tightly knit team. Similarly, participatory decision-making methods generally enhance satisfaction, while more autocratic or divisive methods hamper individuals' contentment with the group process.

Other factors that promote satisfaction are recognition, responsibility, interest in the task, and group achievement. If a group is successful and members feel they actively contributed to that success, satisfaction is likely to be high. Individual satisfaction is very complex. Success of the group motivates commitment to it. Commitment makes a member work harder. Hard work, in turn, improves the solution. There is so much involved in the issue of member satisfaction that it is central to the issue of group effectiveness.

Changes in Surrounding Environment

Problem-solving discussion normally occurs in an open system in which there is exchange between a group and its environment. Earlier we examined some of the ways in which a group's context constrains its activities in terms of resources provided and values that must be accommodated. Now we turn our attention to the other side of the coin to consider two significant ways in which groups influence their contexts.

A group that engages in careful, informed problem-solving is likely to generate solutions that alter the environment by eliminating or reducing the problem that originally brought members together. Student groups in discussion classes successfully enlarged the orientation program for junior transfer students, modified the procedure that financial aid students must follow to buy textbooks, participated in revising the public relations program for the campus counseling center, and secured student representation on a state-level task force working on the problem of driving while under the influence. Student groups have also gotten the university to provide additional bike racks near class buildings, gained adoption of a policy prohibiting smoking in classrooms, and persuaded administrators to earmark funds to renovate buildings so that they would be accessible to handicapped students. Any serious problem-solving effort can alter policies and even values by the decisions it reaches and implements.

A second way in which problem-solving affects the surrounding environment is through the group's impact on individual members. Through participation members become informed on issues; they learn of alternative solutions and the promises and pitfalls of each. As a result of intense deliberation, members often become advocates of particular solutions and the values entailed in them. Thus, they are changed personally by their involvement in discussion. In addition, members may act as agents of change to influence the attitudes of others with whom they interact. During and after problem-solving, members deal with people outside the group, and they influence what those people will know, believe, and endorse. This happens not only through formal advocacy of the group's recommendations, but also through informal conversations with colleagues, friends, and family. Grassroots organizations consider this sort of interpersonal persuasion between people to be a primary source of changes in broad social values. Thus, the environment surrounding a group is affected by actual decisions reached and by the presence in that environment of informed individuals who influence the attitudes, opinions, and actions of others.

The major outcomes of problem-solving discussion are decision effectiveness, individuals' satisfaction, and changes in the context in which a group is embedded. These are not discrete outcomes; rather, they influence each other and are themselves shaped by a complex matrix of influences present throughout problem-solving.

SUMMARY

Chapters 2 and 3 offered a great deal of information that should help you understand, analyze, and act effectively in the groups to which you belong. You may find it helpful to read these chapters more than once, since all the material is pertinent to your effectiveness in group situations.

By now you should realize just how complex group discussion is. The systems perspective provides a sound way of thinking about the dynamics of small problem-solving groups. It emphasizes the interrelatedness of all elements in a group system and demonstrates how they influence the discussion process. To be an effective participant, you need to understand these factors and how they interact over time. Most important, your awareness of the multiple elements of group systems allows you to exert some control over what happens. You can make informed choices about what goals you seek in group situations and what means are most likely to assist you in achieving them.

The following chapters deal with some of the major issues involved in leading and participating in group discussion. You will also find a chapter devoted to the use and misuse of conflict in problem-solving.

REFERENCES

1. G. Philipsen, A. Mulac, and D. Dietrich, "The Effects of Social Interaction on Group Generation of Ideas," *Communication Monographs,* 46 (June 1979), pp. 119–125.
2. K. Lewin, "Forces Behind Food Habits and Methods of Change," *Bulletin of the National Research Council,* 108 (1943), pp. 35–65.
3. R. Likert, *New Patterns of Management* (New York: McGraw-Hill, 1961); *The Human Organization* (New York: McGraw-Hill, 1967).
4. N. Harper and L. Askling, "Group Communication and Quality of Task Solution in

a Media Production Organization," *Communication Monographs,* 47 (June 1980), pp. 77–100.

5. K. D. Benne and P. Sheats, "Functional Roles of Group Members," *Journal of Social Issues,* 4 (1948), pp. 41–49.

6. R. L. Birdwhistell, *Kinesics and Context* (New York: Ballantine, 1970), p. 66; A. Mehrabian, "Communication Without Words," *Psychology Today,* September 1968, p. 53

7. D. G. Leathers, *Nonverbal Communication Systems* (Boston: Allyn & Bacon, 1976).

8. M. E. Shaw, "Communication Networks." In L. Berkowitz (ed.), *Advances in Experimental Social Psychology,* vol. 1 (New York: Academic Press, 1964), pp. 111–147.

9. L. W. Howells and S. W. Becker, "Seating Arrangements and Leadership Emergence," *Journal of Abnormal and Social Psychology,* 64 (1962), pp. 148–150.

10. H. H. Kelly and E. H. Volkhart, "The Resistance to Change of Group-Anchored Attitudes," *American Sociological Review,* 17 (1952), pp. 453–465.

11. C. A. and S. B. Kiesler, *Conformity* (Reading, MA: Addison-Wesley, 1970).

12. W. W. Charters, Jr., and T. M. Newcomb, "Some Attitudinal Effects of Experimentally Increased Salience of a Membership Group." In G. E. Swanson, T. M. Newcomb, and E. L. Hartley (eds.), *Readings in Social Psychology* (New York: Holt, 1952), pp. 415–420.

13. E. I. Hollander, *Leadership Dynamics* (New York: Free Press, 1978), pp. 40–43.

14. S. Schachter, "Deviation, Rejection and Communication," *Journal of Abnormal and Social Psychology,* 46 (1951), pp. 190–207.

15. Floyd Hunter, *Community Power Structures* (Garden City, NY: Doubleday, 1963).

16. K. Bach, "Influence Through Social Communication," *Journal of Abnormal and Social Psychology,* 46 (1951), pp. 9–23.

17. J. T. Hurwitz, A. Zander, and B. Hymovitch, "Some Effects of Power on the Relations Among Group Members." In D. Cartwright and A. Zander (eds.), *Group Dynamics,* 3rd ed. (New York: Harper & Row, 1968), pp 291–297.

18. P. H. Bradley, "Power, Status and Upward Communication in Small Decision-Making Groups," *Communication Monographs,* 45 (March 1978), pp. 33–43.

19. P. Watzlawick, J. Weakland, and R. Fisch, *Change* (New York: Norton, 1974).

20. N. Sanford, C. Comstock, and associates (eds.), *Sanctions for Evil* (San Francisco: Jossey Bass, 1971).

21. Ibid.

22. J. T. Wood, "Consensus and Its Alternatives: A Comparative Analysis of Voting, Negotiation and Consensus as Methods of Group Decision-Making." In G. M. Phillips and J. T. Wood (eds.), *Emergent Issues in Human Decision-Making* (Carbondale, IL: Southern Illinois University Press, 1984).

23. R. Y. Hirokawa, "Consensus, Group Decision-Making Quality of Decision and Group Satisfaction: An Attempt to Sort Fact from Fiction," *Central States Speech Journal,* 33 (Summer 1982), pp. 407–415.

24. J. T. Wood, "Leading as Rhetorical Action: A Reconceptualization of Leading in Purposive Discussions," unpublished dissertation, Pennsylvania State University, 1975.

25. A. S. Tannenbaum and R. L. Kahn, *Participation in Local Unions* (Evanston, IL: Row-Peterson, 1958).

26. N. Maier, *Problem-Solving Discussions and Conferences* (New York: McGraw-Hill, 1963).

chapter *4*

Understanding the Group Process

At this point you should understand some of the major influences on how a group system develops. With that foundation, we can focus on the discussion process that takes place within a group system. Like any other process, discussion may be conducted well or poorly, depending on the skills of the people involved. Our purpose in this chapter is to explain a method that promotes productive and thorough problem-solving discussion. We will also explain why we recommend one particular method for problem-solving discussion.

THE VALUE OF AN AGENDA

Sometimes people get together simply to talk. They come without clear goals, other than being courteous and friendly. That's fine for social interaction and casual conversation. It is, however, not useful for productive problem-solving discussion. Genuine problem-solving discussion should not be spontaneous and unstructured. For one thing, most people do not have the time to wander aimlessly through a problem. For another, productive discussion requires logical development, mastery of fact, and skill at presentation. To emphasize the task dimensions of discussion requires systematic development of ideas based on some sort of agenda or method for going about business.

There must be an agenda or method for handling business. Without a basic structure for discussion, it is unlikely that a group will conduct the kind of systematic, thorough investigation necessary for wise decision-making. For this reason, virtually every book on group discussion includes one or more recommended agendas groups can use as a basic plan for their work.

Dewey's Basic Thought Process

Without a formal agenda, discussion is most often rambling and pointless. Attention to process is important, for process provides a check for you on whether you are dealing with important issues. During the early days of group discussion, various authorities attempted to formalize discussion process around the "five phases of reflective thought" identified by the philosopher John Dewey.[1] The steps were originally intended as a description of *individual* problem-solving based on reports by Dewey's students of how they resolved personal problems. There appeared to be five steps involved in every case.

1. A person feels generally uneasy.
2. The person locates and specifies a problem.
3. The person sets standards by which to test a solution.
4. Several solutions are identified and tested (usually mentally).
5. A solution is selected and put into operation.

McBurney and Hance modified this process to apply it to group discussion.[2] They specified the following phases of the group process:

1. Definition and delimitation of the problem. (This step included phrasing the question and setting goals for solutions.)
2. Analysis of the problem. (This step included fact-finding and discovery of causes.)
3. Suggestion of hypotheses. (This step included proposals of various solutions, testing solutions, and predicting how they would work.)
4. Reasoned development of hypotheses. (This includes setting criteria for judgment and eventual selection of a solution.)
5. Verification. (This includes considering how to put the solution into operation.)

A later work by Scheidel and Crowell modified the steps as follows:[3]

1. Describing the problem. (This includes defining terms in the discussion problem, specifying symptoms of the problem, and appraising the gravity of the problem. This latter would also involve examination of present and past methods for solving the problem and setting priorities for the solution.)
2. Analyzing the problem. (This would include finding causes of the problem, deciding whether to deal with symptoms or causes, and setting criteria for judging solutions.)
3. Proposing solutions.
4. Selecting the best plan for solving the problem. The plan is to be tested against criteria for judging solutions. Residual problems are also considered to determine the worth of the solution.

Most other proposed patterns seem to include similar components in a similar sequence. It appears that in order to have an effective discussion, the group must specify its problem, find and analyze information, set some goals and standards against which to judge solutions, and examine a number of possible choices.

In this book we will offer you a pattern called *standard agenda,* which is also an extension of Dewey's basic process. Standard agenda was originally generated to fit contemporary management decision-making systems like PERT (program evaluation and review technique) and CPM (critical path method). These systems guided complicated scheduling of manufacturing processes and government administration.

In problem-solving discussion there must be a method to organize talk and focus it on accomplishment of shared goals. The group goal must have priority over personal goals. But you cannot ask people to give up their ideas and sacrifice their beliefs to accommodate some abstract goal. Thus, the group leader must have a system to direct each person's ideas toward the common good. That is the purpose of standard agenda. It serves as a guide to leaders and members alike to ensure that their talk will relate to matters important to the group as a whole. It also facilitates systematic study, corrective dialogue, helpful criticism, and constructive conflict. Finally, it provides standards by which leaders and members can judge progress and decide what has been done and what remains to do. Above all, standard agenda makes it possible for a group to fit its work within time limits so it can be responsive to pressure from the company, legislative body, or institution that needs effective solutions to problems delivered on time.

Standard agenda consists of the following steps:

1. *Understanding the charge.* Why is the group in existence? What is it to do? What form does its output take? Who gets it? What is to be done with it?
2. *Understanding and phrasing the question.* What, precisely, is the group to examine or inquire about? What do the words in the question mean? Are all technical words and issues clear to the members?
3. *Fact-finding.* What are the symptoms of the problem? What is the cause of the symptoms? What is happening that should not be happening? What is not happening that should be happening? Who is suffering from the situation? How badly? What will happen if the situation is not remedied? How must the question be modified in light of fact-finding?
4. *Setting criteria and limitations.* What is possible (as opposed to what is desirable)? What are the legal, moral, financial, practical, and logistical limits on decision-making? What would a solution look like? What would be happening that is not now happening? What will stop happening?
5. *Discovering and selecting solutions.* What are the alternatives? How does each meet the goals? How do they measure up against the limitations? Which provides more of what is wanted with the least new harm? Which one should be selected? Who is to do what about what, when and where, with what projected effect, and how will it be paid for? What evaluation plan can be used to measure the effectiveness of the solution?
6. *Preparing and presenting the final report.* What must be written down? What must be said? When, where, and to whom? How can the final report be most persuasively presented?

WHY THE STANDARD AGENDA?

Perhaps you're wondering why we choose to focus on a single method of conducting discussion. After all, group discussions occur for many reasons. Doesn't it seem reasonable to learn about a variety of formats? Besides, you may think that knowing only one method might limit your effectiveness in different situations. These are reasonable questions to ask. If they occurred to you, you are a thoughtful, careful reader. These questions deserve responses, so we will first explain why we concentrate on the standard agenda. Then we will describe, explain, and illustrate the method itself.

Three reasons underly our exclusive focus on standard agenda. It is *the most complete, the most flexible, and the best time-tested* method for problem-solving discussion.

Completeness   An important advantage of standard agenda is its completeness. It is the most comprehensive problem-solving method of which we are aware. Other methods typically adhere to the basic pattern of standard agenda but leave out some of its steps. For instance, the Scheidel and Crowell model, mentioned earlier in this chapter, includes four of the stages in standard agenda, but omits those dealing with criteria and limits and preparing the final report. We think leaving out these phases is unwise. Recent research has demonstrated that establishing criteria prior to discussing solutions enhances the probability that a group will avoid divisiveness and agree upon a final solution that all members find acceptable.[4]

Like the Scheidel and Crowell model, a number of proposed methods follow standard agenda's basic form, but delete some steps. In each case we find not a conceptual alternative to standard agenda, but a shortened form of it. Thus, these alternatives are less complete methods of problem-solving than is the one we recommend. Standard agenda provides a maximally comprehensive understanding of how to go about solving problems through group discussion.

Flexibility   The completeness just discussed leads to a second advantage of standard agenda. It is highly flexible, allowing leaders and participants to modify its use to suit particular circumstances. Standard agenda alerts you to the full range of steps that may be entailed in problem-solving and demonstrates how each one figures into the overall process. Thus, you have an informed basis for deciding how thoroughly to apply each step and when to skim or entirely skip parts of the process.

Sometimes it's appropriate to omit certain steps or parts of them. For instance, if you're appointed to a fact-finding commission, your goal is restricted to preparing a report on the facts of some situation. You need not develop criteria and limits nor identify and evaluate alternative solutions. The committee that follows yours, however, might be charged to make recommendations based on your factual report. It could legitimately omit the opening stages of standard agenda (covered by your commission) and deal with only the latter phases.

Once you learn the standard agenda, you have the understanding necessary to decide how much time and attention to devote to each stage. The agenda itself is a reminder of what you might have to consider. By using it as a basis for discussion, you are confronted with important choices about what you plan to do. Your work can be organized so you can meet both your obligations and your deadlines. This kind of decision-making is not possible with truncated agendas. If a group does not realize the full range of potentially pertinent steps, it may well omit an important component of the discussion. Learning the most complete and most flexible method permits the group to have the widest range of choices.

Time-Tested A third and especially persuasive reason for concentrating on the standard agenda is its demonstrated quality as an effective agenda. Since 1939, when McBurney and Hance introduced a preliminary form of the standard agenda, the method has been widely used in both training and practice. For at least forty years it has held a prominent position in teaching, research, and consulting.

Standard agenda is used in business schools and public planning; it is used in administrative and organizational settings. It is also used as the basic form of discussion in the social sciences. It is reasonable to assume that no method could enjoy such wide and sustained popularity unless it leads to good results. This assumption was born out, in fact, by a recent study that compared different problem-solving formats. The authors concluded that the model derived from Dewey (standard agenda) provides an ideal baseline that may be modified to fit particular groups and tasks. Because other methods lack the completeness and flexibility of standard agenda, their effectiveness is more limited.[5] The connection between standard agenda and computer-based methods of planning and controlling production as well as administering complex organizations was made in 1963 (see Phillips, *Communication and the Small Group*). It has been used in conjunction with such complex problem-solving ever since.

It appears that standard agenda is also the wave of the future. The quality circles now so prominent in participatory management are designed to provide worker and member input into organizational problem-solving. The quality circle operates by connecting past with present to anticipate the future and thus is suited to a Dewey model of problem-solving. You will find the standard agenda suited to virtually every discussion task you may confront.

In the following pages we will present an outline of the standard agenda and explain to you what it contains and how it works. We will specify the goals, outcomes, member tasks, and leader responsibilities for each phase. This discussion will provide the basis for the detailed presentation in Chapters 8 through 13 of how to use the standard agenda.

OUTLINE OF OBLIGATIONS IN STANDARD AGENDA

Phase One: Understanding the Charge

In this phase, the group considers its task, its logistics, its schedule and deadlines, and agrees on procedures and meeting times.

Goal   Each group member must understand what the group is to do, why it is important to do it, what its business is, what its output is to look like, who is to get it, and to what purpose it will be put. The group examines the time frame in which it is to work and schedules itself accordingly.

Outcomes   1. A written set of specifications for the final report.
           2. A set of main heads describing the final report.
           3. A routing schedule for the final report.
           4. A schedule of activities, including a statement of how the group is to know it is finished.
           5. A statement of what happens to the group once its work is done.

Member Tasks   1. Raise questions about what each member is to do.
               2. Raise questions about their own function in the group.
               3. Raise questions about what the group is to do collectively.

Leader Obligations   The leader must make sure all members' questions are answered to the members' satisfaction. The leader must also be sure each member understands his or her individual obligations and the collective obligation of the group. Limitations on group activities must be considered, as well as resources available to assist the group in its problem-solving. The leader must see to it that the five outcomes are accomplished.

Phase Two: Understanding and Phrasing the Question

Goal   The group must agree on what the problem is and phrase a question that indicates *who is to do what about what.* The group must agree on the level or levels of discussion—whether the group is to fact-find, evaluate conditions, set policy, or propose a solution to a problem. A group may do any or all of these.

Outcomes   1. A formally phrased question.
           2. Definition of all the technical or ambiguous terms in the question.
           3. Definition and specification of whether or not the group is to do fact-finding, evaluation, policy formation, or problem-solving.

Member Tasks   1. Raise questions about the level of the problem (fact, value, problem, policy).
               2. Register preliminary attitudes about the problem and its severity.
               3. Raise questions about possible misunderstanding or misinterpretation of the question or particular words in the question.
               4. Provide whatever information they have that is useful in phrasing and specifying the question.

Leader Obligations   The leader must be sure the question is properly worded and understood by the members.

Phase Three: Fact-Finding

Goal   The group should gather and store a body of facts understood by all members and confirmed for accuracy. The group should gather informed opinions from experts. The result should be a statement about the nature of the problem, its relevant history, who is affected and how, what might happen if the problem is not solved, and an estimate of possible causes. At the conclusion of fact-gathering, the problem should be summarized and the problem question rephrased if it appears necessary.

Outcomes   1. Summary of factual information.
2. Summary of opinions from authorities.
3. Estimate of causes of the problem.
4. Reworded question, if necessary.

Member Tasks   1. Do necessary research, fact-gathering, interviewing, assessing, confirming, criticizing, and questioning.
2. Obtain opinions of proper authorities.
3. Make an estimate of the causes of the problem.
4. State preliminary attitudes on the problem.
5. Participate in decisions about whether the problem needs symptomatic or causal approach.
6. Participate in decision about whether problem question requires rephrasing.

Understanding and knowledge are needed in order to prepare well for group participation.
(© Siteman, 1983, EKM-Nepenthe)

Leader Obligations   The leader must direct and expedite fact-gathering and solicitation of opinions, see to it that an estimate of causes is prepared, be sure each unit of information is properly checked and evaluated, and guide the group to decisions about an approach to the solution and rephrasing the question.

Phase Four: Setting Criteria and Limitations

Goal   The group should describe what the world would look like if the problem were solved. The group should state its most optimistic goal, its most pessimistic goal, and the most likely goal. The group should examine possible limitations on its solution power. The group should attempt to anticipate undesirable concomitants of a solution.

Outcomes   1. A description of the most desirable goal.
2. Counterestimates of the least possible to accomplish and most likely outcomes.
3. A specification of legal, moral, practical, financial, institutional, and persuasive limitations on a solution.
4. A set of standards for judging proposed solutions.
5. A projection of possibilities once the problem is solved.

Member Tasks   1. Participate in goal-setting and specification of limitations.
2. Participate in setting criteria for evaluation of solutions.
3. Anticipate hazards in problem-solving.

Leader Obligations   The leader must be sure that goals are properly set, limitations specified, and standards set for evaluation of proposals.

Phase Five: Discovering and Selecting Solutions

Goal   The group must propose and examine as many solutions as possible and select an optimum solution or construct one from among possibilities.

Outcome   1. A detailed statement of the solution, including a statement about who is to do what about what, when and where, for what reason, under whose supervision.
2. A statement of funding and budget where relevant.
3. A statement of how the effectiveness of the solution will be judged.
4. A statement directing the preparation of the final report.

Member Tasks   1. Participate in finding and proposing solutions.
2. Participate in evaluating solutions against criteria and testing to see if they exceed limitations.
3. Assist with preparation of rationale, evaluation procedures, and preparation for the final report.

Leader Obligation   See to it that all four outcomes are achieved.

Phase Six: Preparing and Delivering the Final Report

See Chapter 13 for detailed information on preparing both oral and written reports; see Chapter 14 for information on presentational speaking as it applies to final reports. Final reports commonly include:

1. A review of the problem.
2. A review of the problem-solving undertaken by the group.
3. A detailed statement of the solution.
4. An argued defense of the solution. (This commonly includes a list of other alternatives considered and reasons they were rejected.)

Since the final report is often prepared by one person or by a smaller task group, many members will have no particular tasks to perform in this phase. If all went well, however, they will have contributed their share in phase five.

REFERENCES

1. John Dewey, *How We Think,* rev. ed. (Boston: D. C. Heath, 1933).
2. James McBurney and Kenneth Hance, *Discussion in Human Affairs* (New York: Harper and Brothers, 1939, 1950).
3. Thomas W. Scheidel and Laura Crowell, *Discussing and Deciding* (New York: Macmillan, 1979).
4. Rensis L. Likert and Jane G. Likert, "A Method for Coping with Conflict in Problem-Solving Groups," *Group and Organizational Studies* (December 1978), pp. 427–434.
5. Marshall Scott Poole, "Decision Development in Small Groups I: A Comparison of Two Models," *Communication Monographs,* 48 (March 1981), pp. 1–24.

RECOMMENDED READINGS

Bitzer, Lloyd F. "The Rhetorical Situation." *Philosophy and Rhetoric,* 1 (Winter 1968), pp. 1–14. This is the standard presentation of talk requirements in any situation where persuasion is warranted.

Dewey, John. *How We Think.* Boston: D. C. Heath, 1902. This is the original discussion of the phases of reflective thought.

Didsbury, Howard (ed.). *Communications and the Future.* Bethesda, MD: World Future Society, 1982. This book surveys contemporary applications of communication, including teleconferencing and various uses of group methods in industry.

Gibney, Frank. *Miracle by Design: The Real Reasons Behind Japan's Economic Success.* New York: Times Books, 1982. This is a good introduction to quality circle and other Japanese management techniques involving worker participation.

McBurney, James, and Kenneth Hance. *Discussion in Human Affairs.* New York: Harper and Brothers, 1939, 1950. These two editions will show you how the Dewey system of reflective thought was applied to the discussion process. Chapter 12 is an excellent discussion of personal techniques of preparation for discussion.

Phillips, Gerald M. *Help for Shy People.* Englewood Cliffs, NJ: Prentice-Hall, 1982. This book is a systematic presentation of goal-setting with an explanation of how it functions in public settings.

Phillips, Gerald M. *Communication and the Small Group.* New York: Bobbs-Merrill, 1973. Chapter 4 offers a complete discussion of PERT systems applied to the discussion process.

Scheidel, Thomas M., and Laura Crowell. *Discussing and Deciding.* New York: Macmillan, 1979. This contemporary text offers a number of process formats to be applied to group discussion.

chapter *5*

Making Effective Choices When Participating

Choices are the foundation on which this whole book is based. Choices are also the foundation of the rhetorical mode of communication. Rhetoric operates in situations where the outcome is uncertain. Because of this uncertainty, there are no universal rules. Instead, people make choices based on insight and knowledge about the particular situation and the other people involved. When people try to persuade one another, they use rhetoric. They seek to gain agreement from listeners by appealing to their listeners' individual concerns. When you engage in rhetoric, you use speech in order to accomplish your goals. The process operates something like this:

1. Through analysis of a situation, you set a goal that you hope to accomplish through communication. (Example, Rita Book, the city planner at Forest Slough, wants to convince the city council that new parking regulations are necessary.)
2. You analyze the people to whom you will be speaking so you can prepare remarks that are appropriate, clear, and persuasive. (The planner not only wants to convince the council, she wants the merchants and consumers of the town to agree with her. She notes that council is cost-conscious, merchants are customer-conscious, and customers are convenience-conscious.)
3. You then put ideas in order and phrase them in words. (Ms. Book decides to divide her presentation into three main points: new parking regulations will save money, bring customers into the downtown areas, and provide convenient traffic flow for customers.
4. You observe your listener responses, which may be verbal or nonverbal.

(While she speaks, Ms. Book has identified some key people representative of each group. She observes their responses and adapts her remarks to them until she receives their approval.)

5. Based on the responses, you assess how closely you have approximated your goal and what your next goal is to be. You can speak again, if you need to. (She decides she had better give another speech to the Chamber of Commerce because her businesspeople did not seem convinced.)

This persuasive pattern is perfectly all right when the goal is to convince. But in group discussion, the purpose is to share information and reason together until the group goal is reached. How does rhetoric apply?

Consider Ms. Book's options when she met with the Planning Advisory Commission. She had a great deal of information to present. She had to convince her colleagues of the accuracy and validity of the information. Members of the commission had criticisms and objections to raise. She had to listen carefully and accept those suggestions that made sense. There were times when the rest of the groups seemed lined up against her. When that happened, she had to negotiate. Throughout, she sought to convince her colleagues that she was interested in the group outcome, that she had worthwhile information to contribute, and that she could analyze data intelligently. She also had to pay attention to the needs of the group, move the discussion ahead, avoid digressions, help quiet members get into the flow of talk, and help suppress (gently) those who talked too much. In short, she employed rhetoric to convince her colleagues she was interested in them and in the group outcome, as well as in the ideas she represented. Moreover, she used rhetoric to persuade the others of her personal credibility.

There are a great many goals you can seek to achieve in group discussion. Throughout, it is necessary to pay attention to your colleagues. In true rhetorical fashion, you take them and their ideas into account as you plan your communication. This requires attention to what they do when you talk and what they say when they talk. The major adjustment you must make in group discussion is that everything you do and say must be directed toward accomplishment of the group goals so long as it remains consistent with your personal integrity and value system. This chapter is about the choices available to you as a discussion participant. By following the suggestions given here, you will be able to manage your talk so that you can make real contributions to the groups to which you belong.

GUIDELINES FOR PRODUCTIVE PARTICIPATION

We could generate a list of do's and don'ts about participation that would rival the Scout Oath. Be courteous and kind; be trustworthy and loyal. Such advice can be inspiring but relatively useless to people who are trying to learn. For one thing, there is no ideal behavior pattern for discussion participants. Problem-solving groups are like snowflakes. No matter how similar they may appear, there are always some differences. A "do" in one situation can become a "don't" in another. The situation, the other members, and the leader are all issues the individual participant must deal with, and different groups will demand different kinds of behaviors from you. What might work in one group will not work in another.

That is why we advocate a rhetorical mode of participation. You are constantly on your rhetorical guard in a group discussion. Your basic tasks are to monitor conditions, to find the group needs, to consider alternate ways of meeting them, to discover what you can supply, and to provide it effectively. In addition, you have to fulfill your personal role—to contribute the information only you can provide; to represent the group that sent you to the committee; to uphold your own personal ideals. It is not an easy task to balance personal and group interests. It cannot be done if you pay attention only to yourself. A rhetorical point of view keeps your mind on your colleagues and the group goal, so you can synthesize your needs with theirs to accomplish the best for all.

THE PROCESS OF HUMAN COMMUNICATION

Effective participation is based on understanding that human communication is a complicated process. The late Wendell Johnson once defined communication as "a process with four legs."[1] This simple statement sums up the basic proposition that communication is something more than one person talking. In addition to being a process, communication is also a relationship. It involves at least two people who must do more than be present in the same place at the same time making words. They must attend to each other. The speaker must want to speak for some good reason, and the listener must want to hear for equally good reasons. Each participant may have different reasons; we would expect that to be the case, because the reason they speak to one another in problem-solving discussion is to revise reasons and come to some kind of agreement.

Communication can be seen as a system involving humans in the *transfer* of meaning, or the *exchange* of meaning, or the *stirring up* of meaning. We did not say that communication is the *expression* of meaning. Communication is much more complicated than simply reporting what is on your mind. The process of communication requires you to think in terms of a listener and to adjust what you say to what you know about the listener. The relationship involved in communication consists of your record with your listener. Who are you to the listener? What do you have to say that might be useful to the listener? Do you have a past history together? The same systemic elements found in groups exist whenever two people communicate.

To be effective as a communicator, you must have an idea in mind that you think can change something in the system. Then you must phrase it so your listeners can understand it. You must offer some reason your listeners should pay attention by telling them how they, as a group, will benefit by agreeing with what you say. You may only want them to take note of a fact. You may want them to change their attitude about something. You may want them to take some action. Your responsibility is to make sure your listeners understand what you want and why they should cooperate with you. When you communicate in this way, you are behaving rhetorically. Each time you speak in your group, you are speaking rhetorically. Can you see why it is not so simple to say *effective discussion depends on effective communication*?

Most experts agree that it is impossible not to communicate. What you fail to say, as well as what you fail to do, will plant ideas in the heads of those who happen to be with you. When you remain silent in a group discussion, you are often communicating as much as when you talk. Effective participation in group discussion requires careful management of what you say and do not say, because everything about you communicates to all the people around you.

None of us can control completely the ways other people will see us. They may get upset by what we say or do, or they may like us in spite of what we say or do. Since we can control only our own minds and mouths, the best we can do is to try to make some intelligent guesses about the possible effects of our actions and to direct ourselves toward other people as purposefully and as skillfully as we can.

Effective listeners engage in the active process of trying to understand what speakers intend to communicate. During interaction, listeners may become speakers, and speakers may switch to listening. In group discussion, this process goes on rapidly and continuously. Conversation in discussion is even more than a four-legged process, for each person talks to an anonymous entity, "the group" or "the audience," as well as directly to some individuals we know as "the other members." We must generalize about our listeners while we speak directly to particular individuals in order to catch the minds of the greatest number. The whole group listens and participates as we talk, even when we respond directly to only one individual. This situation requires careful control. To help you achieve that control, here are some guidelines appropriate to both particular listeners and whole groups.

Thinking the way listeners think will help to clarify communication. (McKoy, Taurus)

1. Try to be clear and simple. Make sure your listeners understand by testing them with questions and looks. Encourage them to question you.
2. Try to be audible, clear, and "interesting." Although you needn't be as concerned about performance in a group as you are in front of an audience, the group members represent your audience, and it helps to keep in mind that you must gain and hold their attention by skillful speech if you are to have maximum impact.
3. Try to offer reasons for what you say. Make sure these reasons refer to what other people feel and want. Aristotle once said, "The fool tells me his reasons, the wise man persuades me with my own." Give examples and evidence, and be careful with definitions. Expect to be questioned, and take care with your answers.

Consider the following examples.

DON'T: I think the problem is worded all wrong.

DO: The statement "How can we prevent young people from doing vandalism in the schools?" seems to beg the question. I think we rule out the chance of discovering other vandals with that wording. I suggest we look at "How can we detect who school vandals are, and what steps are necessary for prevention?"

or

DO: That wording seems to be awfully complicated, and maybe the first part of the question is contained in the second. Why not "How can we prevent vandalism in the schools?" That wording will make us find out who the vandals are, and we won't indict all young people right at the start.

Note that the two satisfactory statements raise objections, but also offer reasons for those objections. The reasons are not phrased in personal terms; they refer to reasons other members of the group might respect. Consider a second set of examples.

DON'T: You people are silly if you think it isn't the kids!

DO: No one is saying it isn't the kids. No one is ruling anything out. But it doesn't make sense to rule anything in automatically. We need a wording that will allow for whatever we find.

or

DO: Can we change the wording when we have more facts? Good. Then let's say somebody is vandalizing and let's go after the facts. If the facts say one group or another is guilty, we can name them in our question later on.

In discussion, each participant must talk enough to explain reasons for every statement. Nothing can be taken for granted. We are not advising filibusters or unnecessary wordiness. Be prepared, however, for questions. Assume your group members are intelligent and honorable. Like you, they have beliefs and feelings. You cannot expect them to agree simply because *you* say so. A proper rhetorical mode will take into account the integrity of others. It will also recognize that no one can know your thoughts if you don't express them well.

In addition to clarity, you need to be careful that your remarks reflect a respectful and cooperative tone. In the recommended statements above, the speakers use tact and diplomacy. Personal attacks or bald condemnations seldom contribute much to output and serve to destroy the underlying base of cooperation that discussion requires. Talk should be about the ideas, not about the people who offer them. For example:

> DON'T: You've got to be kidding. Only a person who doesn't know the facts would say that kids weren't vandals.
>
> DO: I never thought that there might be anyone other than kids that vandalize schools. Do we have any evidence about this?
>
> or
>
> DO: If that's so, then we need to word our question to allow for that possibility. My evidence tells me that kids do most of it, but it can't hurt to allow for the possibility that others are involved.

Irving Lee proffered the "shy, Socratic approach"[2] as a guide to performance in discussion groups. He meant talking softly, making concessions where possible, yet asking questions based on information and arguing based on evidence. Being quiet about a disagreement does not mean that you do not have opinions.

You will also be involved as a listener in discussion. Active listening is helpful to other speakers. Since nonverbal behavior communicates as much as talk, it is useful to demonstrate attention and interest. If you have questions, indicate that with your facial expression. If you disagree, indicate that. Encourage the speaker to provide as much information as possible. Woolgathering or dozing off is usually not that refreshing anyway; it gets you little more than a stiff neck.

As a listener, sort out ideas as they come to you and figure out whether you understand them. Decide whether you need to reply and if so, what your message will be. Make sure you understand what the speaker is saying. Do you have the same meaning for words as the speaker? For example, to one person "freedom" may mean the right to work out the way one does one's job; to another person, it may mean one's choice of job. Because meaning is in people rather than in the words they use, it is important as a listener to check the speaker's intended meaning by giving your interpretation of what was said or by raising questions that may clarify what was meant. Don't be content with "we'll work it out"; make sure all the kinks in understanding are removed by raising good questions.

Don't make the mistake of assuming that anyone who disagrees with you has no justification. Ask why the speaker believes what he or she says. Ask for evidence and justification. Encourage the speaker to offer justification from his or her point of view. After all, discussion is supposed to reconcile conflicting positions, and you can't reconcile differences until you understand them. Active listening includes careful attention to reasons, seeking and clarifying them if need be, and deciding whether or not they make sense.

Communication is a complicated process. By understanding your obligations as a speaker and by engaging in active listening, you can help prevent misunderstanding and harmful conflict from arising in your group.

RHETORICAL SENSITIVITY

Effective participation is characterized by rhetorical sensitivity. A few years ago, Rod Hart and Don Burks introduced a concept called *rhetorical sensitivity.* [3] Although rhetoric has traditionally been associated with talk on the public platform, recently the term has been associated with all forms of planned and conscious speech. Phillips and Metzger made the point that intimate relationships of high quality between human beings are the result of conscious control of verbal output.[4] Elwood Murray offered the concept of *negative spontaneity,* or the suppression of off-the-top-of-the-head comments, as an appropriate way of dealing with others.[5] We choose rhetorical sensitivity as our basic term for identifying the outlook of effective discussion group members. We prefer this term because the sensitivities to which the term refers sum up what governs superior, conscious management of verbal output. With apologies to the originators of the concept, we will take a few liberties with their ideas as we apply them to discussions.

Rhetorical sensitivity is a judgment other people make of you. It is based on your communication style toward them. When you appear rhetorically sensitive, you encourage others to cooperate with you. The message you declare to others is:[6]

1. I am aware of your existence and declare your importance and uniqueness. (Associated behaviors: Careful listening, patience, allowing the other person to talk it out, making room for the other person to talk, asking intelligent questions as if the other person was intelligent enough to give useful answers.)
2. I believe in what I am saying. (Associated behaviors: Speaking vigorously, associating nonverbal behavior with your remarks, demonstrating care in preparation.)
3. We are all going to get something out of this. (Associated behaviors: Giving your listener reasons for your point of view, showing what interests you have in common, suggesting ways that not reconciling your differences could hurt both of you.)
4. I am going to take care with what I say so you will understand it, and my reasons for saying it, in your own terms. (Associated behaviors: Sound documentation, adaptation of your ideas to the listener, willingness to answer questions, define terms, give examples, cooperating with the listener to reach common meaning.)
5. There is more to come. There may be more benefit in the future. (Associated actions: Demonstrating a willingness to cooperate, offering to exchange concerns, agreement to consider issues the other person raises.)

Let us now consider what these statements mean in terms of attitudes and actions you can develop in discussions.

To a group member, the first statement ("I am aware of your existence and declare your importance and uniqueness") means that you are neither indulgent nor hostile in the remarks that you offer to the group. A good member is courteous at all times—when speaking directly to an individual or to the whole group. This awareness of others must also be conveyed by eye and body movements. There is as much need for skill in delivery in a discussion group as there is on the platform. You want the best communicative style you can muster to convince others you think they are worth talking to (even if they oppose what you say).

It is important to remember the basic difference between platform speaking and group discussion. When you speak on the public platform, your goals are to convince the people who are neutral, to reinforce those who agree with you, and to soften the resistance of those who are hostile to your ideas. In a group, however, you must reach agreement with others, including those with whom you disagree. While it is appropriate to present your ideas persuasively, it is equally important to listen with an open mind to arguments offered by others. Your attitude and behavior, therefore, must match the group goal.

It is possible to respect people with whom you disagree vigorously. In fact, respect is the only basis on which differences can be resolved. Conciliation works best among equals. Furthermore, regarding the people with whom you disagree as honorable representatives of their point of view is contagious. Respectful disagreement begets respectful disagreement, which expedites productive, open-minded discussion.

The meaning of the second statement ("I believe in what I am saying") is more obvious. There is no point in talking in the group just to hear yourself talk. If you have no commitment to an idea or a bit of evidence, then perhaps it is not worth speaking. James McBurney once commented that a good group member thinks before he speaks, but he does not think too long.[7]

Any person in the discussion group can have just the right idea or remark at the given moment. Therefore, you must be willing to talk—thoughtfully. If you are a member of a discussion group, it means that whatever thoughtful remark occurs to you is worth saying, and since it makes sense to you, you must say it as if you believe it is worth saying—and give reasons. When the attitude of all members is mutually respectful, quiet members can often be stimulated to function as mediators between contending factions. Thus, commitment to difference can result in commitment to agreement.

The third statement of attitude ("We are all going to get something out of this") is an assurance that your motive for speaking is harmonious with the group goals. People who stand to gain from participation will not engage in time-wasting digressions. When group members believe discussion is a waste of time, they will behave in ways that subvert the group. But if everyone believes participation means progress, individual members can quickly synthesize their commitments into a group feeling. Once members are committed to the group goal, group standards can be used as a basis for resolution of conflict. Furthermore, committed individuals are willing to risk criticism and even argument because they believe both can be useful in moving the group toward its objectives. Involvement in the group cause is the best antidote for groupthink.

The fourth statement ("I am going to take care with what I say so you will understand it, and my reasons for saying it, in your own terms") is a profound rhetorical proposition. It means that as a member of a discussion group, you have the obligation to direct your remarks to your listeners. Participation in group discussion is not an egocentric act. Listeners must be able to understand what you say. They must see reasons why you believe what you are saying, and they must see how they can benefit from it. This obligation involves preparing ideas outside the group so that you can say them clearly when they are relevant. When you comment on or criticize someone else's remarks, you must consciously do so in a way that will help the group to understand why you are questioning and criticizing.

This attitude also implies that group members must be on their toes and alert to every nuance and subtlety in the discussion. There can be no letup in attention. The responsibility for respect is mutual, but committed talkers motivate committed listeners. (Actually, group participation can be very exciting, more exciting than possible distractions if, and only if, everyone involved is sufficiently respectful to solicit collaboration.)

To be effective in adapting your ideas to others, you must analyze the other members carefully. What do they represent? What ideas do you expect them to uphold? What are they experts at? What useful information and opinions can you get from them? As you begin to understand the value of what others say, you can become more vigorous in communicating your own value. This leads to animation, responsiveness, and effective analysis, all requirements of sound group decisions.

The final statement ("There is more to come; there may be more benefit in the future") means you are willing and prepared to continue to talk. It is particularly important in discussion to maintain a constant relationship with the other members. Questions like "Was I clear?" "What do you think about what I just said?" "Do you have any questions?" indicate that you are willing to keep talking until your thoughts are clear. Such questions also suggest your willingness to remain in close relationship with the other members of the group. Sometimes group members drop in and out of communicative relations for no clear reason; the effect is usually disruptive. Your obligation is to suggest constantly that you are a permanent, participating member of the group; you can do this by keeping your remarks open-ended.

Willingness to continue talking is the keynote of sensitive negotiations. Even when the situation looks bleak, it is imperative to sustain an attitude that "continued effort will be beneficial." In labor negotiations or the bargaining preceding complicated international treaties, contending parties often resort to power plays characterized by refusing to talk or listening. Such power plays are counterproductive in group problem-solving. Uncooperative members are normally easy to replace. Furthermore, refusal to participate is sufficiently disruptive to cause polarization and hostility. On the other hand, patience, tolerance, and stamina characterized by continuing to talk and listen encourages everyone to adopt placating and conciliating attitudes.

The five principles of rhetorical sensitivity we have just discussed are good standards against which to examine your participation. A person regarded as rhetorically sensitive expresses affiliation with the group and its goal, as well as demonstrating personal integrity. A rhetorically sensitive participant demonstrates concern for the group by trying hard to reconcile personal commitments and concerns with the group goal, and trying very hard to get everyone else to do the same. When opinions clash head-on, it may be impossible to reconcile them. When the group goal is placed between them, however, it may be possible to reconcile them through commitment to the common good. This is the way labor negotiations are carried out. Obviously, management wants the most work for the least pay, and labor wants the least work for the most pay. Neither profits if the company goes under. Thus, the good both sides can derive from the continued success of the company motivates them to make concessions leading to mutual benefit.

Individual Preparation

Effective participation is based upon careful individual preparation. We will discuss techniques of individual preparation in Chapter 7. To do your best in a discussion, you must be prepared not only with knowledge of the topic, but with knowledge of procedure, understanding of the other members, a feeling of compatibility with the leader, and awareness and understanding of the group goal. All this involves considerable thought.

Unfortunately, people often come to discussion groups directly from breakfast, lunch, or dinner. They have not reviewed their notes. They do not know what they believe in or what reactions would be reasonable. They may not even remember what happened at the last meeting. When they respond, they may respond off the top of the head by asking questions already answered or raising issues already disposed of. The prepared participant, on the other hand, comes ready to present both information and opinions and thus becomes a valuable group member.

Preparation is largely a matter of raising and then answering questions with yourself for the purpose of general understanding. By asking yourself questions and then thinking about responses, you are better able to cope with the give-and-take of the discussion process. In the following chapters we discuss various phases of the discussion process as we acquaint you with the standard agenda. For each phase, we will list the member behaviors associated with the best possible outcomes, and you will be able to make your choices to participate accordingly.

Reviewing Your Options

Another way to prepare in advance for discussion is to review your options for participation and to understand the obligations inherent in each choice. In general:

> *You may make categorical statements.* "The facts are. . . ." "The way I see it is. . . ." "I believe that. . . ."
>
> *You may make process statements.* "I think we agree that. . . ."

"Aren't we ready to move to the next point?" "The definition appears complete to me."

You may criticize. "I don't think that description of the facts is quite complete. May I add. . . ." "Are we all sure the authority that was just quoted is unbiased?" "Seems to me there were some flaws in the research on which that study was based."

You may question. "Do you believe that for the same reasons he does?" "What evidence does he offer for his position?" "If we added this idea, would you still support the solution?"

You may argue. "I believe that . . . for the following reasons . . . and I do not think that . . . is correct because. . . ."

You may reason. "If this is so, then we are obligated to take either this or that, but if that is flawed, then this is our only alternative despite its limitations."

You may use any of these behaviors in each phase of the standard agenda. We provide a chart at the beginning of each chapter showing the agenda steps. Check them carefully for a list of your participation options. You may also use leader behaviors to the extent you are encouraged to do so by your leader if you feel they are needed.

Obligations in Participation

Each comment you make has obligations associated with it. You should be prepared to back up your statements. If you offer an informative statement, you should be able to explain it by providing definitions or examples. If you offer an opinion, you should be prepared to give reasons for it that make sense to other members. If you offer a proposal, you must assume the burden of proof for it by showing that it is reasonable and has a chance to solve the problem for which it is offered as a solution. You are also obligated to offer reasons for disagreement. You cannot rely simply on your reputation to support your objections. It is as important to support critical statements as constructive ones. When you criticize, it is important to make clear the standards you use as a basis of your criticism. If others question them, you must be able to explain why they are relevant. In Chapter 10 we will discuss in detail methods of supporting your ideas.

Asking questions is particularly important. They are a way to express doubt or objection that does not threaten the speaker. Questions may be addressed to individuals or to the group, and they may be raised about any matter of content or procedure. But there should be a point to the question, and you should be prepared to clarify that point if necessary. Careful listening is important, because it is embarrassing to ask for information that has already been given. Questions should be asked mildly: "How could anyone believe that?" is not a reasonable question. Nor is "I bet you can't give me a good reason for believing that!" Questioning should be temperate, and where necessary your question should be explained. For example, "I heard Marilyn offer three reasons for believing what you oppose. Can you say anything to cast doubt on her arguments?" If you give the speaker a focus for response, you will help the group judge what to believe.

STICKING TO THE POINT

Effective participation requires attention to where the group is in the problem-solving process. There is nothing so disruptive as an out-of-phase comment in a discussion. It confuses the group, it makes the members who were on track wonder where you were, and for that matter why they were where they were and you weren't with them. Was that last sentence confusing? If so, it is confusion similar to what results from a poorly timed comment in discussion. Questions need to be asked when they are germane; dissent expressed when it is relevant. It is important to try to stay on track, to know what is being discussed, to remain aware of the main issue. (If we were to stop now and go on for three pages about the uses of discussion in the Japanese industrial complex without making a connection to material preceding or following, your confusion would be justified. Fortunately, we are not going to do this. We will return immediately to our main idea—how important it is to stick to the point.)

The classical philosophers referred to the central issue under discussion as the *stasis*. This is an important concept. Stasis represents the main point, the issue to be decided, the topic of the agenda. Was the argument about cost? Was practicality the deciding issue? In examining two conflicting statements of fact, could the issue be decided on the quality of the person giving the report? These kinds of questions are stasis-oriented. Comments should be relevant to the stasis.

Here are questions you can use to help you understand what is going on and what your options are in response (see Chapter 10 for a complete explanation of these topics).

1. Are we talking about something that happened? If so, are we talking about who said it happened and how reliable that person was? Are we talking about the reliability of another member? Are we talking about how relevant a fact is to our question? Are we talking about how typical the event is?
2. Are we talking about expression of opinion from an authority? Are we talking about how the authority got the information? Are we talking about possible biases of the authority? Are we trying to find out whether the authority was paid to say it?
3. Are we talking about issues of relationship? Are we talking about a logical relationship (cause, association, function)? If so, what rules guide our reasoning? Are we talking about a scientific experiment? If so, what rules guide our reasoning? Are we talking about inductive and deductive reasoning? If so, what rules of logic apply? Are we talking about a definition? Is it a dictionary definition or an operational definition? What rules apply? Are we talking about critical standards? What standards, and why are they relevant and useful?
4. Are we trying to make a decision about whether to deal with causes or symptoms? How can we find out what is desirable and what is doable?
5. Are we talking about whether we know enough? What do we need to

know? Why do we know we need to know it? Where can we find it out? How do we find it out? How do we know when we know enough?

6. Are we talking about altering our topic or our charge? Why must we make the change? How can we justify it?

7. Are we talking about ways to judge solutions? What standards should we use? What limitations are imposed on us? Fiscal? Member competency? Moral? Legal? Jurisdictional? Institutional? Logistical?

8. Are we talking about solutions? Do we have several to examine? Why not? Are we trying to pick one, or are we trying to put one together? Are we testing against limitations? Are we testing against criteria? How can we anticipate the best, worst, and most likely outcomes? How can we tell if we are realistic? Are we keeping in mind what our final report should look like?

9. Are we talking about selecting a final solution? Do we know who is going to do what? Do we know when we start? Do we know how much it will cost? Do we know where the money will come from? Do we need an organization chart? If so, what will it look like? Who must we convince of the worth of our solution? How?

10. Are we discussing the final report? Do we know who we have to persuade? Do we have information about what that person might find persuasive? Do we have a general public to appeal to? Do we know what will appeal to them?

These questions are based on the standard agenda (see Chapter 7). They will help guide you to intelligent participation. By being familiar with these questions and with the stages of the standard agenda, you will be more able to attend to where you are in the problem-solving process. Knowing where you are, and reflecting that knowledge in your choice of how to participate, are essential for effective discussion.

We have presented four general guidelines for productive participation:

1. Effective participation in discussion reflects the understanding that human communication is a complicated process.
2. Effective participation in discussion is characterized by rhetorical sensitivity.
3. Effective participation in discussion is based on careful individual preparation.
4. Effective participation in discussion reflects attention to where the group is in the problem-solving process.

By developing a style of discussion participation that follows these guidelines, you will increase the likelihood of your own personal effectiveness.

PRODUCTIVE PARTICIPATION IN PROBLEM-SOLVING DISCUSSION

We began this book by noting that group discussion is an inevitable aspect of twentieth-century America. Task groups have become integral parts of government, community life, industry, and education. To many people, the inevitability of group discussion has not made it any more desirable or tolerable. Countless individuals complain that group discussion is a waste of time, a means of suppressing individuality, or too social a medium for productive work. These complaints come from honest and sincere people who have not succeeded in discussion, so we do not disregard the legitimacy of the claims; they are potentially serious indictments of the discussion method. However, we earnestly believe that these problems are not intrinsic to the method. Rather, they result from improper management of the process; and management, as we have reminded you many times, is directly controllable by the members of a group.

Some people know or have learned how to participate effectively in group discussion, and the reward for their skill is access to decisions and policies that are better—more thorough and more effective—than any single individual could make. A secondary reward for such people is the increased prestige and respect accorded them by others who recognize their talents in managing group discussion productively.

We are not claiming that group discussion is the way, the truth, and the light. It is not a cure for all ills. It is not perfect. Group discussion can produce "camels" or poor decisions: the Pearl Harbor disaster, the continued United States escalation in Vietnam, the Bay of Pigs incident, the Watergate coverup, and the Environmental Protection Agency scandals are familiar examples of seriously inadequate group decision-making. In addition, we are sure you have seen countless other committee flops that are less famous (or infamous).

However, group discussion has also been the means to some of the best decisions we know of. The ingenious handling of the Cuban missile crisis resulted from discussion among President John F. Kennedy's advisers. Recently, the National Academy of Science discussed the dangers inherent in experimentation with genetic engineering and produced guidelines to ensure that ethical issues would be of primary importance in any future work of this kind. In the rural community of one of your authors, a group of citizens banded together to stop construction of an unsightly development. They succeeded. The Constitution of our nation and, in fact, the whole concept of a democratic form of government were born out of group discussion. And, most important of all, every day boards of directors, trustees, task groups, urban commissions, welfare agency groups, and interested citizens work together to solve the mundane problems that affect corporations and communities; problems that could not have been solved without effective group discussion.

Students in discussion classes have also had considerable impact. At one of the universities where your authors teach, campus health administrators have accepted one student group's recommendation that all dogs on campus be leashed or with their owners at all times, thus preventing the cruel practice of chaining a dog to a tree for hours without food or water while the owner attends classes. Another student group has received a positive preliminary reaction to its recommendation for changing the honor code system that has governed cheating since the university opened in the 1700s. Still another group received administrative approval for a book cooperative that should significantly reduce the cost of textbooks. And a group recommended an orientation program for junior transfer students that has just received substantial funding. At another campus, a group of students convinced administrators to install more bicycle racks in dormitory areas. The point is that group problem-solving can make real differences.

Students can use group discussion to solve problems that affect them. So can businesspeople. So can citizens. So can anyone who will take the time to understand and carefully apply the method.

REFERENCES

1. Wendell Johnson, "Speech Disorders of the Fluent." In Lee Thayer (ed.), *Communication: General Semantics Perspectives* (New York; Spartan Books, 1970), pp. 261–265.
2. Irving J. Lee, *How to Talk with People* (New York: Harper & Bros., 1952), p. 103 and chap. 9.
3. Roderick P. Hart and Don Burks, "Rhetorical Sensitivity and Social Interaction," *Speech Monographs,* 24 (June 1972), pp. 75–91.
4. Gerald M. Phillips and Nancy J. Metzger, *Intimate Communication* (Boston: Allyn & Bacon, 1976).
5. Elwood Murray, Gerald M. Phillips, and J. David Truby, *Speech Science-Art* (New York: Bobbs-Merrill, 1969), p. 236.
6. Roderick P. Hart, "Signposts on the Road to Effective Communication." Unpublished classroom handout, Department of Speech Communication, Purdue University, Lafayette, Indiana.
7. James H. McBurney and Kenneth G. Hance, *The Principles and Methods of Discussion* (New York: Harper & Bros., 1939), p. 95.

RECOMMENDED READINGS

Berne, Eric, M.D. *Games People Play.* New York: Grove Press, 1964. This is a very cogent and highly entertaining consideration of the kinds of ploys individuals execute in interactions with others. It is well worth the reading time for people who are serious about understanding the interpersonal dimension of group problem-solving.

Gibb, Jack R. "Defensive Communication." *Journal of Communication,* 11 (September 1961), pp. 141–148. In this article Gibb points out the specific kinds of communication that tend to produce defensiveness in others.

Lee, Irving. *How to Talk with People.* New York: Harper, 1952. This small book deals simply but effectively with many of the everyday problems that plague our attempts to communicate with others.

chapter 6

Making Effective Choices When Leading

This chapter should be read by everyone who participates in group discussions, because leadership is every member's concern and responsibility. Why? Most obviously because leadership affects every member, as well as the group's ability to achieve its goals. In addition, there is the practical fact that any member may be called upon to lead at any time. The original leader of a group may be weak or unable to keep up with the group's changing needs, in which case someone else must move in to keep the group on course. There may also be times when a leader is temporarily absent due to other commitments, illness, or a deliberate choice to avoid influencing a group. (Remember that President Kennedy felt it necessary to remove himself from the Cuban missile crisis discussions because members were too easily swayed by what he said.) All members should be prepared to move into the leadership position if the group needs them.

Most people can learn how to lead competently by gaining a perspective on what is involved in leadership. In this chapter we are going to talk about the choices that help individuals gain and hold on to leadership, as well as the choices they make about how to exercise leadership. Before we deal with these concerns, however, there are some preliminary issues to consider. First we want to explain why leadership is essential in problem-solving groups. Next we review five major theories of leadership to acquaint you with different views of the process. Then we introduce an adaptive view of leading which we think offers the most instructive and realistic approach to the topic. We also discuss important distinctions between gaining leadership and maintaining it. Finally, we identify some of the more important situations and choices that face leaders, and offer advice on how to deal effectively with them.

This chapter should increase your understanding of how to lead. Equally important, it should give you a sound basis for judging how well others are leading and for assisting them when appropriate.

THE ADVISABILITY OF SINGLE LEADERS

Research as well as experience and observation consistently demonstrate that groups with designated leaders perform better than those in which no single leader exists. During the 1950s and 1960s, misunderstanding of democratic principles led a great many authorities to argue that "leaderless groups" best served the interests of the members. They believed individual members could perform the functions of leadership without establishing a hierarchy. New information about leadership of groups nested in larger social units (companies, agencies, institutions) demonstrates that there are tasks associated with leadership for which responsibility must be firmly fixed. Furthermore, groups with single leaders work more efficiently, have fewer interpersonal problems, and produce better outcomes.[1] Single leaders provide guidance, coordination, and centralized authority, all of which are essential to smooth progress and goal achievement.[2]

Given the necessity to have a leader, there are three practical options when setting up a group: (1) Designate one person as leader, (2) take a chance that a leader will emerge, or (3) hope that among the various members all leadership functions will be handled and no power conflicts will occur. Making sure there is a person designated as leader is the safest bet. Most groups choose this course of action. When groups are connected with larger organizations, the act of appointing the group is usually accompanied by designation of a person responsible for leadership.

The second option, hoping a leader will emerge, is a serious gamble. If one doesn't, the group may falter. Even worse, two members seeking leadership may make their political rivalry the dominant issue, thus distracting everyone from the task at hand. Assuming that leadership can be distributed effectively among members is truly risky. Remember the power struggles in the Kremlin under the *troika* government. Eventually, Leonid Brezhnev defeated Kosygin and Bulganin and became sole dictator. The leftover hostility from a power struggle tends to divide a group for a long time after the issue of leadership has been decided.

Furthermore, members often lack sufficient experience to do what needs to be done. They simply do not know how to lead. In other cases, members may have the ability to lead, but none do because no one feels responsible. Sometimes members disagree on what act of leadership is relevant at the moment, and the group gets involved in an argument about whether members should do more research or move on to the next step of discussion. There is no way to resolve these kinds of conflicts without a leader, so the group is caught in a trap. You would have to look long and hard to find a leaderless administrative committee, board of directors, corporate committee, or other serious problem-solving unit. Specifying a leader and fixing responsibility in one person is the wisest general rule.

Not everyone believes that single leaders are advisable. Advocates of leaderless discussion (in which all members are expected to perform leadership tasks) argue that discussion should be a cooperative enterprise in which all participate equally. They also suggest that shared leadership facilitates democracy and that a single leader can lead to authoritarian control. Finally, advocates of leaderless discussion sometimes claim that a leaderless group can be as effective as one operating under a single leader. The operative word is "can." A leaderless group *can* be effective—if all members participate with a spirit of goodwill and are very considerate of one another. This kind of utopian situation is rare. Furthermore, if there is any conflict in the group, it is virtually impossible for a leaderless group to resolve it. A group with a designated leader can also be ineffective if the leader is incompetent or conflicts are irreconcilable, but it is easier to replace a leader than it is to train people to get along so well they do not need one. The odds are definitely with groups that have designated leaders.

Designated leaders perform a variety of important functions. They provide liaison with groups or other individuals in the surrounding environment; they furnish a central point of responsibility, which is especially significant in organizational settings that demand clear lines of accountability; they represent a central point of coordination and direction for all members of a group—a reference point when there are problems, changes in plans, complications, and so on. Without one person who assumes responsibility for these functions, a group may factionalize, become chaotic, or operate inadequately.

We are particularly troubled by the alleged association between single leadership and authoritarianism. There is no necessary connection between the two. Any person, including a leader, can be only as powerful as others permit. This point is well explained by Hollander, a prominent theorist of leadership, when he defines leadership as a "two way influence relationship [that] . . . is not the job of the leader but also requires the cooperative efforts of all others."[3] The mere presence of a person called leader does not imply dictatorship, manipulation, or even solo decisions. The degree of power and authority a leader possesses results from choices made by everyone in a group. It is certainly a fundamental premise of our democratic society that leaders govern with the consent of the governed. An alert membership prevents authoritarian leadership.

Like most people, we have seen dictatorial leaders. We don't deny they exist. However, when a leader is authoritarian, it is because members have encouraged him or her to assume primary control of the group. Members tend to reinforce the leadership style they want. In essence, they train a person how to lead them.[4] Often this is unintentional, as are many of the choices humans make. Erich Fromm theorizes that most people do not really want freedom and responsibility, although they claim they do; what they really want is to surrender control to someone else and to have someone else be responsible for what happens.[5] Group members who seek to escape the burden of freedom will reinforce controlling behaviors and respond negatively to democratic or nondirective behaviors from a leader. Over a period of time, the leader will adapt to group demands and become increasingly directive. Thus, members have a great deal of control over what kind of leader they will have. If members fail to exercise their control, they also sacrifice their right to complain. All members are responsible for contributing to the leadership of a group; all are responsible for making thoughtful choices in designing and responding to leadership.

Leadership is best thought of as a contract between a leader and members, and both parties have control over the details of the contract. One way to exercise this control is role negotiation, in which a leader and members tell each other what is expected and why. Members may specify they want a leader to enforce a schedule, design a schedule, or work with the members to develop a schedule; they may ask a leader to assign tasks to members or specify that members cannot be pressed into service without their consent; they may request that a leader run meetings formally, informally, or delegate running meetings to another member; and so on. Any issue of leadership is open to negotiation, so spend some time thinking about what you want in a leader and then explain your desires to the person selected to lead your group. If you are that person, spend some time thinking about what you want to invest in leadership, what you are and are not willing to do in terms of your style and responsibilities. Then alert members to your conditions. Reasonable people can usually work out a set of agreements acceptable to all and constructive for the group objectives. By negotiating the nature of leadership and the limits on it, members can be assured that a single leader need not result in authoritarian control. And they can reap the substantial benefits of having a central person charged with defined functions that will assist the group in doing its work with maximum efficiency and quality.

One of the important elements of the standard agenda is that it compels both group and leader to engage in reflective consideration of what they have done and what they need to do. Emphasis on personal responsibility facilitates assumption of responsibility. When members believe what they do makes a difference, they are less likely to concede power to an authoritarian leader.

THEORIES OF LEADERSHIP

There has been a great deal of recent scholarship on the topic of leadership. There is, however, no consistent view on what constitutes leadership or how a person can become a leader. In fact, there is considerable disagreement about what leadership is and should be, and how it works. Of the many existing theories of leadership, five stand out as particularly noteworthy. Each has held the limelight for a time. As we review these five theories for you, try to decide which one or which parts of each make sense to you.

Traits (1927)

The trait approach, or the "great man theory" as it was nicknamed, was the first serious effort to explain leadership. It was based on the assumption that leaders are people who possess certain innate qualities that most people either do not possess or possess in very limited degree. Researchers developed lists of physical, psychological, and social characteristics that supposedly distinguished leaders from nonleaders. Thrasher's classic study of boys' gangs in Chicago reported that the key attributes of leaders were bravery, physical ability, speed, and firm decision-making.[6] Other researchers claimed the traits of leaders were height (tall, but not too tall—between 5 feet 10 inches and 6 feet 1 inch), extraversion, a sense of humor, a tendency to dominate, and so forth. As you can see, quite a variety of answers were given to the question, "What are leadership qualities?"

In 1940 Charles Bird reviewed the work done on leadership traits and reported that of the 79 traits claimed to be associated with leadership, only about 4 had been mentioned by several different studies.[7] Stogdill then dealt the death blow to trait theory with an article in which he called the search for traits of leadership hopeless and ill-conceived.[8]

Styles (1939)

Kurt Lewin, among the most insightful social scientists of our century, decided to examine leadership as a social force rather than a simple set of traits. Lewin believed there were different kinds of leadership and that each would have specific effects on group productivity and climate.

To test this idea, Lewin conducted a series of experiments with ten-year-old boys in YMCA camps. He trained assistants to act as democratic, authoritarian, and laissez-faire leaders. Then he observed how the boys acted under the different styles of leadership. Lewin concluded that both democratic and authoritarian leadership result in a good quantity of work, but democratic leadership produces better quality work. The laissez-faire groups were not productive in any sense. Lewin also found that the different leadership styles had pronounced effects on group climate. The democratically led groups were participative; members were satisfied with interaction; and the boys were supportive of one another. Boys in the authoritarian groups tended to become apathetic and would work only when directed by the leader. Further, they became hostile toward one another and the leader. Democratic leadership seemed to produce friendly interaction and personal initiative, while authoritarian leadership fostered dependence and resentment.[9]

Lewin and his associates concluded that democratic leadership was the most effective style, a finding compatible with the political mood in wartime America. As a result of this work, leadership training programs sprang up around the country, and companies sent their executives to learn how to become democratic leaders. The training was not very successful for a variety of reasons, not the least of which was the fact that democratic leadership is not appropriate in all circumstances. (We'll say more about this later.) Furthermore, at the time the behavior characteristics of democratic leaders had not been identified, so most instruction consisted of telling people what they *ought* to do rather than explaining *how* to do it.

Lewin's work represented a substantial advance over the trait approach. The styles theory of leadership included primitive systems principles, although systems theory was not established when Lewin was working. This approach also contributes to our understanding of the impact of leadership on group productivity and climate.

These strengths notwithstanding, there are significant problems with the styles view. The most obvious flaw is the claim that the democratic style is always the best. As we explain later, no single style is invariably effective. Another shortcoming of the styles approach is the suggestion that style of leadership is objectively verifiable. Contrary to what style theorists imply, leadership style is not a matter of fact. Instead, it is a matter of perception and evaluation. What one person perceives as democratic, another may regard as laissez faire; what one person perceives as highly authoritarian may be judged by someone else as democratic guidance. In fact, an intriguing study by Rosenfeld and Fowler found that how a leader's behaviors are perceived depends on the leader's gender. Male leaders who try to guide without directing and who offer support to members are perceived as democratic and effective, but women who behave the same way are judged as nurturing.[10] Lewin's views did not account for the critical role of perception in labeling and evaluating leadership style.

Situations (1945)

By the mid 1940s the trait approach had been discredited and the styles approach seemed incomplete. After nailing the coffin shut on the trait approach, Ralph Stogdill launched a new wave of investigation that became known as the situational approach. This theory presupposed that there are no universal leadership traits, but that the qualities important in a leader will vary with task and situation. For example, physical ability and speed might well be leadership qualifications in a boys' gang, but they will not be valued in a complex corporation or in a volunteer church group. According to the situational approach, the situation determines what qualities are relevant to leadership.[11]

As Stogdill attracted followers, research from the situational perspective began to flow. One finding was that physical position makes a difference in who becomes leader. People in central positions are more likely to emerge as leaders than people on the sidelines.[12] Also, people who control the flow of information and who engage in heavy communication are likely to emerge as leaders. A number of findings of this type were forthcoming. They are useful generalizations about leadership and how it is influenced by situational factors. However, the situational approach left many important questions unanswered, especially those having to do with what a leader actually does and how a leader's acts shape perceptions of a situation.

Functions (1955)

During the 1950s and 1960s, our society became intensely interested in human relations and interpersonal development. This preoccupation pervaded the social fabric, including institutional life. Thus, industrialists were advised to consider the "human factor" in their organizations, particularly in training people for managerial roles. Teachers were told to deal with students as equals rather than to exert authority over them. Employers were encouraged to let employees participate in decision-making so that employees would feel they were a part of the organization.

This societal trend paved the way for a fourth approach to leadership, the functional theory. The basic idea was that leadership was not a person, but a set of functions that should be performed by all members of a group. Work by Bales,[13] Benne and Sheats,[14] and Barnlund and Haiman[15] resulted in two major categories of leadership functions: those that have to do with the group's task (asking for or giving information, providing evidence, maintaining procedures, recording ideas), and those that have to do with interpersonal climate in groups (balancing participation, relieving tension with jokes, seeking compromises). Once these two categories were established, researchers focused on specifying the appropriate balance between them. There was a quest for general rules or formulas for successful discussion.

You've probably already inferred one of the two major problems with the functional approach. Its preoccupation with developing general rules for effective group work is inconsistent with the varying requirements and constraints that characterize different groups. What works in one situation may be entirely inappropriate in another. The second problem with this approach lies in its fundamental assumption: that leadership can be distributed throughout a group. In order for leaderless groups to be effective, members must be sufficiently skilled to fulfill all necessary functions and they must assume responsibility, two conditions difficult to guarantee in the majority of groups. The functional approach to leadership is best regarded as a product of a particular era and mood in our country. It has not survived the test of time, and it is seldom practiced in real situations, where people cannot afford the gamble entailed in leaving important decisions to a group with no central organization.

Contingencies (1964)

Shortly after the functional approach appeared, Fred Fiedler proposed the contingency model as a comprehensive explanation of how leadership works.[16] Fiedler united ideas from the styles approach and the situation view to build a theory which claims that leadership involves a match between a person's given style and the requirements of a situation. After collecting data on over 1600 groups, Fiedler concluded that leaders who have a relationship-oriented style are most effective in situations where they have moderate amounts of power, but leaders who are task-oriented are most effective in situations that accord either very little or very much power to the leader.

The great strength of Fiedler's theory is its predictive power. Using instruments he has developed, Fiedler can predict what people will be effective in which situations, and he is right much of the time. What Fiedler cannot do is offer guidance to individuals regarding how they might improve their effectiveness. He assumes that individual personalities are set and not subject to substantial change. They can be effective if and only if they are placed in the appropriate situations. The primary use of Fiedler's theory is in placement, an inference you may have already drawn.

It should be apparent that each of these five theories is based on a static conception of leadership as an unchanging set of circumstances. Further, each neglects the individual's potential to influence factors relevant to gaining and implementing leadership. The theories have a decidedly deterministic flavor, suggesting that humans are programmed by forces external to their efforts (innate traits, situational requirements, fixed styles). A third criticism of all five theories is that they neglect communication, which is the crux of leadership. None of the theories we have examined explains how people use communication to earn and exercise leadership. These three deficiencies motivated the development of the adaptive approach, to which we turn now.

The Adaptive Approach

Unlike previous views of leadership, the adaptive approach regards leading as a highly dynamic, changing process.[17] Scholars who endorse this view believe there is no single correct style of leadership, nor is there a universal balance of behaviors comprising effective leadership. Instead, a variety of leading styles can be appropriate in varying situations and in response to the needs of different members. This approach assumes that every leadership situation is unique and calls for behaviors specifically tailored to the circumstances and people involved. There are no recipes that can be applied, but individuals can learn how to analyze particular situations to discover what is needed. The name *adaptive approach* stems from the basic assumption that effective leadership is essentially adaptive to particular circumstances, members, and tasks and to changes in all these aspects of problem-solving. In the pages that follow, we will explain how leaders analyze situations and how they adapt appropriately to the specific requirements confronting them.

SUSTAINING LEADER ACCEPTABILITY

Leaders do not exist in isolation. The very concept of leader presumes the existence of members. Consequently, those who lead are engaged in an ongoing effort to satisfy their members and to retain their confidence. In democratic societies, citizens judge the qualifications of their leaders through elections. In small groups, however, leaders sometimes volunteer or are appointed; they may get their position by virtue of their job description, or they may be placed in the position by consensus of the group. Seldom are there formal votes. Leaders who are designated by the members can be dismissed by the members when they cease to perform satisfactorily. Leaders who hold their jobs by virtue of their job description cannot be removed unless they are also dismissed from the larger system. A person cannot lead a group, regardless of how powerful his or her position, unless he or she is acceptable to the members.

In order to remain acceptable, a leader must stay in tune with the needs of the group and provide what members want and expect. To do this, the leader analyzes the members and situation, staying alert to changing requirements. In addition, the leader helps the members achieve their personal aspirations by finding ways to help each person be as effective as possible. For this reason, a leader should understand the special skills and deficiencies of each member.

Analyzing Member Needs

To analyze members, leaders must first realize that there is great diversity in what people want in a leader. Although many people like to be guided by a democratic leader who works with them, others prefer a directive leader who takes charge and even cracks the whip occasionally. The democratic style will not work well with followers who crave direction, and the authoritarian style will fail with followers who have initiative and the experience to back it up. In a recent study, Jurma found that people who are not highly organized prefer a leader who provides structure for them, while well-organized individuals do not appreciate so much direction.[18] So leaders need to adapt their actions not just to the group as a whole, but also to the needs and preferences of individual members—a challenging task.

Analyzing Situations

To be effective, leaders also need to analyze and adapt to their particular situations. The leader must recognize competition confronting the group and be sensitive to time pressures. Additionally, the leader should be aware of the record of successes and failures of the group and of individuals in it and should monitor role and status development among members. For example, if a group has suffered a recent defeat, the leader may need to give a pep talk, along with a lot of support as members get behind a new task. On the other hand, if a group has been together for a long time and has a star-studded list of accomplishments, the leader should be wary of the dangers of overconfidence and of excessive cohesion, which could interfere with constructive conflict in deliberations. In short, a leader needs to have a sense of the potential of the group. Careful, informed thought about the group and its members is a leader's basic tool.

Inspiring Commitment

Persuading each member to be as committed and effective as possible represents the real challenge of leadership. The leader of a small group can develop a personal relationship with each member, being inspirational to one person, collaborative with another, and directive with a third. Research on effective group discussions confirms the fact that successful leaders do indeed persuade members to do their best, all the while assisting the group toward its common goal.[19]

Behavioral Flexibility

Analysis of members and situations informs a leader of what is needed to make a group work smoothly. The next step is to provide what she or he has diagnosed as needed. It is clear that effective leaders have mastered a wide repertoire of behaviors, and they know how and when to employ each.

There appear to be a few expectations of leaders common to most group situations. Generally, leaders are expected:

1. To provide some basic organization for the problem-solving process by managing an agenda acceptable to the members
2. To boil down and summarize deliberations, particularly at points of transition from one agenda item to another
3. To indicate connections among issues discussed at different times by suggesting causes and consequences of decisions
4. To ensure that conflict does not impede the work of the group by discovering and using ways and means of resolving conflicts between members
5. To test for consensus before moving the group along, by whatever means are necessary, and to record agreements once made
6. To delegate responsibilities for recordkeeping, logistics, research, and so on, to members, and to supervise members to be sure assigned tasks are done

In addition to these task and procedural behaviors, leaders are generally expected to promote development of the group itself. They must encourage balance in participation, demonstrate rhetorical sensitivity, and promote group pride and member development. These basic responsibilities are associated with leadership in most contexts. Because they are widespread expectations, they may be regarded as the core or nucleus of effective leadership. Yet beyond these few common responsibilities, generalizations about the requirements of leadership are risky. Each group situation is unique and has unique needs and opportunities.

Leading is a dynamic process of analyzing and adapting to the complexities of problem-solving groups. A few examples should illustrate the kind of flexibility we are describing. First, there is the actual case of Professor Barbara Seville of the department of music, who was appointed chair of the curriculum committee at a large university. At an early meeting of her committee, she assumed a very casual demeanor. She encouraged members to talk, allowed minor tangents to punctuate discussion, and often solicited members' advice on directions the committee should pursue. She appeared to be a classic democratic leader. As the going got rougher and the deadlines for a report got nearer, however, Seville tightened the reins. She gradually increased the amount of direction she imposed, diplomatically but forcefully curbed digressions, and assigned specific subcommittee tasks to members. The group moved along efficiently and effectively, turning out a report that earned high marks for all from the university administration.

We interviewed Professor Seville and discovered that she knew exactly what she was doing each step of the way. In initial meetings, her goals were to build a sense of team spirit and to gain insight into how each member operated without any direction from her. As soon as she had a handle on the group's tendencies and the inclinations of individual members, she could define her own role appropriately. By the time the group had to buckle down, she had earned members' confidence, so they accepted the pressure she put on them and followed the directions she proposed. She analyzed her situation and did what was necessary to lead the group to success.

A second example is the case of Felix Eptable, who moved into a junior management position in a manufacturing company. He had studied human relations in college and had been taught that participatory decision-making was desirable. Felix's first assignment was to chair a committee charged to review the executive training program and recommend methods of improving it. Felix applied what he had learned by working on an equal-to-equal basis with the members who held positions similar to his in the company. The report was a smashing success.

A little later Felix was asked to head a committee of factory workers charged to recommend ways to increase production. Felix tried to run this group just as he had run the previous one. He treated the factory workers just as he had treated his executive colleagues. He encouraged everyone to participate. But the workers did not respond to his efforts. He might have failed completely had the union representative not offered some advice. The representative told Felix that the men were naturally distrustful of management, and specifically suspicious of an executive who "pretended" to see them as equals. They thought Felix was patronizing them, trying to win their confidence in order to determine whether they were loyal to the company. Felix digested this advice and modified his leadership accordingly. He organized agendas and told the members what he needed from them; he asked specific questions about each department in the company and assigned the members to dig out specific data; he set and enforced deadlines. After a few meetings under this revised leadership, the workers began to respond to Felix's style and to produce good ideas. The final report, although a little late, was thorough and sound.

As these two cases illustrate, a leader's job is to figure out what needs to be done to realize the potential within a specific group of people working on a particular task. To find out what is needed, a leader must be flexible enough to alter behavior to fit the requirements identified through analysis.

An adaptive approach to leading takes it for granted that leaders, members, tasks, and situations are all flexible and dynamic. The leaders' job is to identify and respond to the particular contingencies that characterize the situation by choosing behaviors appropriate to these people in these circumstances. No abstract rules will substitute for analysis and adaptation. The adaptive approach further assumes that individuals, including leaders, exercise substantial control over their effectiveness through the choices they make. We do not believe that leaders are born, nor do we think that leaders are defined by external circumstances. Rather, we conclude that effective leadership results from careful analysis of task, members, and situations. Analysis and behavioral flexibility are not magic, nor are they innate qualities; they are the results of thought, experience, practice, and commitment to the challenge of leadership.

GAINING AND HOLDING LEADERSHIP

The adaptive view of leading emphasizes the idea of process—of changes over time in the nature and requirements for leadership in a given situation. The process character of leading is especially evident as we examine the distinction between gaining and retaining the role of leader.

Gaining leadership and maintaining it are separate activities that call for distinct abilities and actions. Hollander, a prominent leadership theorist, identifies two primary issues relevant to earning leadership: conformity and motivation. To be successful, an aspirant for leadership must demonstrate loyalty to a group's norms, values, and goals in order to demonstrate strong membership character.[20] Second, a contender for a position of leadership must display motivation to lead. The person needs to be visible through high and vigorous participation. As Hollander notes, "attaining a leader role involves drive"; would-be leaders need to show "a willingness to put themselves forward, to take stands, and to be exposed at the center of things."[21] Conformity to group norms and demonstrated motivation provide the basis for a leadership bid.

Once leadership has been earned, however, different qualifications assume prominence. At the top of the list is competence. To retain influence, a person must produce results by providing direction and structure for members and by being instrumental in helping the group achieve successful outcomes. Responsibility is a second criterion for retention of leadership. Leaders are regarded as more responsible than others for their actions and for the ultimate effectiveness of the group. Third, a leader who wants to continue leading must fulfill member expectations. Those who fail to satisfy members lose legitimacy and thus their influence over others.[22] This requirement underscores the importance of clear understandings between leader and members about what each expects of the other.

Once a person has secured the role of leader, he or she gains considerable freedom to deviate from group norms and to innovate—even to alter established norms of interaction and task work. This freedom is earned by previous demonstrations of membership character. By initially conforming to the group's norms, a leader establishes a base of trust with members and wins the right to engage in some innovative moves within the unit.[23] This latitude enables a leader to set and enforce norms that assist a group in meeting its objectives. In this sense, a leader does have more authority and influence than members. Yet the source of these rights is members' confidence, which a leader must earn and continually re-earn through demonstrations of competence and commitment to group goals.

Leadership emergence and maintenance are distinct processes. The former requires a person to win members' confidence and loyalty by demonstrating conformity and motivation; the latter requires a leader to retain members' confidence by demonstrating competence, accepting accountability, and satisfying expectations. Furthermore, there will be ongoing changes in what is required of a leader over the course of a group's life. A leader must stay constantly alert through analysis and must be ready to adapt to the ever-changing nature of the situation.

PREPARATION FOR LEADING

We've just noted that leaders are regarded as more responsible than others for what a group accomplishes or fails to accomplish. Because leaders have special responsibilities for group outcomes, they need to prepare carefully in four major respects:

1. Organizing the agenda
2. Analyzing the group and individual members
3. Controlling the physical situation
4. Planning personal style

The Agenda

To be effective, a leader must have a full grasp of the issues a group will discuss, and must organize them in ways that facilitate group progress. This does not mean that a leader has to know each issue in great detail, but it does mean a leader should understand the overall context of the problem and how various parts of it are related. Leaders who have solid overviews of the task can provide effective guidance.

Competent leaders often prepare two outlines: one that is private, and one that is distributed to members. The private outline identifies key issues and the leader's questions or concerns about each. Specific questions or comments may be noted, and potential resources may be penciled in. The second outline, known as the *public agenda,* is for members and should be distributed in advance. The purpose of the public agenda is to inform members what will be covered at a particular meeting so that they can prepare for productive, informed discussion. Leaders who distribute public agendas in advance of meetings close the prime escape hatch: "I didn't know we were going work on that tonight, so I'm not prepared to report." The public agenda need not be lengthy; its purpose is to inform everyone of the topics that will be covered. Here, for example, is a public agenda for an initial group meeting:

AGENDA FOR THE OPENING MEETING

1. Why was this group set up?
2. What are we charged to produce or do and for whom?
3. How were the members of this group selected? Do we have special talents, experiences, etc., pertinent to the task?
4. How do we want to run this group? What do you expect from me as leader? What kind of schedule is reasonable for meeting dates and times?

**Please come prepared to discuss *all* these items at the opening meeting at 4 P.M. on Monday, November 12, in 107 Klutz Hall.

Members who receive an agenda like this will realize the leader is organized and are likely to come prepared for productive discussion.

The Group and Its Members

We've repeatedly cautioned that leaders must understand the members as well as the overall group. Let's look more closely at some of the basic understandings a leader needs to acquire in order to adapt to members. First, a leader will want to know why members volunteered or were appointed to the group. When members are volunteers, a leader may assume they are interested; but they may not be fully informed, and they are likely to be biased. People who volunteer to work on tasks usually have some preconceived idea about the right solution. When working with appointed members, a leader should figure out what issues are at stake and how each member's involvement can be secured. Also, the leader may need to provide greater background information on the issues to people who are appointed and thus may have limited knowledge of the problem.

Astute leaders attempt to discern the personal qualities of individual members. Careful observation of members during early meetings should help a leader recognize particular talents and problems (remember Professor Seville's strategy?). The leader can then use these insights to help each member become as comfortable and effective as possible. Individuals with obvious communication skills may be the group's primary interviewers; articulate members may be asked to represent the group to outsiders; those with a flair for details may be assigned to work on data collection and analysis, and so forth. The goal is to find ways to realize each member's potential for constructive contribution to the group goal. Through observation, a leader can also spot behavior tendencies in members and find ways to manage them. The leader may want to calm those who tend to dominate discussion and encourage those who tend to withdraw; members who are involved and conscientious may be delegated additional responsibilities while the leader rides herd on those who are inclined to procrastinate.

Many experienced leaders report they find it useful to spend a few minutes after each meeting reviewing what happened. They want to determine whether there were any incidents or issues that call for attention before the next meeting. For example, it is wise not to let hostilities fester. If two members engaged in a heated argument, it may be important for the leader to do some informal checking on whether there is any residual animosity. Dropping in on each of the two or

A leader tries to understand the talents, problems, and personalities of individual group members. (© Druskis, 1979, Taurus)

going out for coffee with each may allow the leader to smooth any ruffled feathers and preserve good relations in the group. If the group rejected someone's idea, the leader may need to support that person in other areas or work with that person to revise the idea before the group meets again. If a normally productive member seemed ill at ease or uninvolved, the leader may want to call that person aside to find out whether there are problems external to the group that are affecting the member's participation. A member experiencing job strain or personal crisis may be unable to contribute much to the group at the moment, but a leader who gives support and understanding preserves the possibility of future contributions from that individual.

A problem-solving group is composed of individuals with special personalities, skills, deficiencies, and self-images. Each member has personal hopes and dreams and values that need to be honored and furthered when possible. The leader's primary responsibility to members is to help each one find ways of being an effective, valued member of the unit. Leaders who invest the time and thought required to understand individual members and to enable each one to achieve reap the reward of seeing a collection of diverse individuals welded into a smoothly functioning unit.

The Physical Situation

While the physical situation in which a group meets is less important than task and interpersonal issues, it should not be ignored. The leader should attempt to make the physical context conducive to effective problem-solving. Furniture should be considered. As we noted in Chapter 3, the optimum arrangement for group discussion is decentralized, so leaders should seek rooms that have tables and chairs which can be moved. Basic comforts should be provided: pads and pencils, ash trays (assuming the group has reached some agreement on smokers' and nonsmokers' rights), water and cups or better refreshments if the group has a budget. The meeting room should allow members to stand up and stretch, and bathrooms should be nearby. Ideally, a conference setting should have blackboards, tripods, and projectors. Most leaders prefer settings that are not centers of traffic; passersby distract members from the task, as does the noise of people talking in the halls outside a meeting room. Of course, there may be good reasons for veering from these suggestions. For instance, a leader may decide informality is appropriate for an initial meeting in which the group needs to get acquainted. Less businesslike physical features would then be sought. A final meeting, following a successful report, might be held in a home or restaurant to celebrate a victory. Whatever the focus of deliberation, a leader should consider how physical features can be arranged to enhance group goals.

Personal Style

Leaders need to be aware of their personal skills and weaknesses as well as their potential for impact on others. Only by understanding personal potential and limitations can an individual leader make informed choices regarding how to lead. Leaders need to be especially sensitive to the basis of their position. If a person has been appointed by someone outside a group and the group had its own candidate for leader, there are obstacles to be overcome, including earning loyalty and learning the norms of the group.[24] Appointed leaders generally have to overcome the stigma of appearing to be agents of the organization, rather than independent thinkers interested in working with members on common goals. If members' actions suggest they regard a leader as an "organizational person," it may be advisable for the leader to confront the problem directly. The leader may explain the constraints imposed by organizational higher-ups and then identify the latitude of freedom remaining to the group and the ways in which the members' values and input can have impact. If the members formally or informally selected the leader, he or she should understand the qualities admired by members and strive to continue providing them in order to meet members' expectations.

Of primary importance is understanding what members want in terms of leadership. Some members will desire tight authority, while others will appreciate greater independence. Some groups expect a leader to fulfill a strong procedural role, while other groups seek task or climate roles from their leaders. Conversations with members are a rich source of clues regarding expectations of a leader. Ultimately, leaders must try to find a viable meshing of their preferences for leadership style with members' requirements. Without sacrificing personal integrity or values, a leader should be able to accommodate the critical needs of a group and to persuade the group to accommodate him or her on other issues.

STRATEGIES FOR LEADING

Leadership succeeds or fails on accomplishments. Effectiveness in achieving group goals grows out of a leader's action choices, which influence five dimensions of problem-solving: members' perceptions of the task, members' perceptions of each other and themselves, members' perceptions of the group as whole, members' judgments on substantive issues, and the pace of deliberations. True to the systems perspective, these five kinds of persuasive action interact. These five dimensions of persuasion comprise a concise yet comprehensive description of the actual behaviors that make up leadership.

Influencing Members' Perceptions of the Leader

Consciously or unconsciously, leaders influence how members perceive them. The most effective leaders do this at a conscious level in order to control how they appear and thus how they influence others. Leaders who act informally and socialize with members promote perceptions of themselves as relaxed, unassuming, and part of the team. This can be helpful in putting members at ease and in minimizing status differences between leaders and members. It may also be appropriate when an appointed leader first takes charge and wants to show members he or she is not stiff and does not intend to run the whole show. The leader should be careful, however, not to act so informally that it is not possible to tighten up later if the need emerges.

A leader tends to be seen as task-oriented and efficient when he or she relies on formal procedures and directive comments. This kind of presentation may be appropriate when time pressures are keen or when a group seems undisciplined. The leader who confines comments to the task and who curbs members from digressive talk generally instills businesslike attitudes in members. The tradeoff may be resentment if members really do not want to work on the task and feel they are being forced. Thus, a leader should balance the potential loss of goodwill against the need for group progress.

Leaders may use very different styles over the course of a group's life. There are times when directiveness is the order of the day; at other times, gentle, democratic guidance fits the bill; and at still other points, the leader may need to do nothing but observe competent members doing their work. Through communication, leaders tell members who they are. If you are a leader, contemplate the self-image you present to members and the methods by which you achieve it. If you are a member, ask yourself how your leader seems to come across and why. These questions should lead to some intriguing insights.

Influencing Members' Perception of Each Other and Themselves

Group work is a cooperative enterprise in which each member affects the whole unit. Further, all members are affected by the overall climate of the group, which may encourage or discourage participation. For these reasons, leaders need to think carefully about how they want to influence members' views of themselves and each other.

A leader who recognizes members heightens their commitment to group goals and their motivation to contribute. Whatever members do for the group deserves acknowledgment, and exceptional contributions merit special praise. Leaders can set an example for mutual supportiveness by being generous with good words that call to everyone's attention the work of individuals. Recognition that is discriminating and distributed among members tends to strengthen a group's sense of pride and to enhance members' respect for themselves and each other. Of course, leaders should avoid so much praise that it ceases to mean anything. Likewise, leaders should be cautious of lavishing extensive praise on one or two members, since this might create divisiveness within the group.

The leader can further enhance respect among members by demonstrating interest in what each says. There is no better way to undermine individuals than to yawn or doodle when they are addressing the group. A leader who is inattentive or who appears bored tells other members that they need not respect what is being said either. Thus, leaders need to choose actions that demonstrate respect and therefore persuade members to think highly of themselves, each other, and their work as a group.

Leaders' actions influence how members perceive themselves and what they regard as appropriate orientations to group work. Through references to each member's participation, achievements, and skills, a leader contributes to role development in the group. By appointing people to record, present position papers, or report on research, a leader enhances their visibility. Punctuality and attendance are encouraged by leadership actions that censor violations. If members start dragging in late or skipping meetings, the leader should indicate disapproval quickly before members conclude it is acceptable to miss meetings. Norms form quickly, so a leader must act with dispatch. Leaders may ask the group to draft a letter to someone who is absent more than once or may remind a tardy member that the meeting began some time ago and lateness is an insult to everyone who bothered to come on time. By putting individuals on the spot, the leader can enforce discipline without resorting to heavy penalties. Also, the leader demonstrates to other members that lateness and absenteeism are not condoned. Remember, the leader is a prime setter of group norms.

Influencing Members' Perceptions of the Group as a Whole

The ways in which members see their group decidedly affects how they participate and what they achieve. Effective leaders work to help members see group goals as important and as the focal point of deliberation. The leader should make every effort to keep members from thinking participation is a means of gaining personal points, an attitude that fosters competitiveness within the unit. The leader should act in ways that promote a team orientation. It is particularly important that leaders avoid singling out particular members for special privilege or harassment.

Persuading members to see the group as talented and able is a primary concern for leaders. This need not result in Knute Rockne pep talks, but a leader should highlight group progress and remind members of any past successes. Emphasizing particular members' talents may also bolster group confidence so long as the leader is careful not to play favorites.

Leaders can encourage creativity and productivity by persuading members to conceive of the group as relatively free of external controls. Administrative committees sometimes see themselves as under the thumb of outside authorities, and this can diminish enthusiasm for the group's work. Astute leaders minimize references to outside authorities as much as possible. Further, it is often advisable for leaders to point out ways in which external agents are dependent on the group and to remind members of times when such agents have been receptive to the suggestions of similar groups. Members are generally willing to tolerate some restrictions from outsiders as long as the leader defines the range of influence members genuinely have.

Involving members in matters of task and procedure tends to stimulate commitment. Leaders who ask questions and respond seriously to members' suggestions encourage members to take active responsibility for the group's progress. The leader who wants to heighten members' involvement will look for areas in which members can legitimately participate in running the group. Naturally, there may be some aspects of discussion that a leader reserves judgment on, but there are usually other areas in which members can legitimately and constructively participate.

Influencing Substantive Judgments of the Group

Because leaders have the greatest responsibility for a group's results, they need to devote special effort to helping the group move in sound directions and draw appropriate conclusions. Sometimes members become attached to idealistic plans that have slim chances of working, or they resist coming to a recommendation that violates preconceived biases. At such points, a leader's responsibility is to persuade the group to reexamine decisions, to guard against prejudices, and to be realistic about what can be achieved.

Generally leaders should try to avoid acting as advocates, because they have strong influence over members. Sometimes, however, advocacy is necessary. When it is, the leader should distinguish between personal views and those associated with the positions of leader. For example, "The executive committee will never accept the plan we're discussing. They've turned down every committee proposal that restricts executive privileges. If we want to have any impact on corporate policy, we'll need to find the next best plan." This comment reflects the role of a leader. By contrast, a personal stance is reflected by the statement, "I don't believe in that, and I want an alternative."

Leaders influence how members perceive issues by the design of agendas. Particular items may be given emphasis on an agenda distributed in advance, thereby putting members on notice that these issues are central. Conversely, issues included as final items tend to be perceived as relatively unimportant. Leaders may also influence judgments by the ordering of agenda items. By putting several simple matters first, the leader helps the group approach more difficult issues in a mood of success.

Leaders may represent positions by assuming roles. Sometimes direct advocacy is threatening to people, so leaders need to find more indirect ways of presenting positions. One leader, a chair of a committee charged to evaluate registration procedures at a large university, wanted to persuade the committee members to consider students' rights and preferences in generating policy. The members seemed interested only in faculty and staff convenience and resisted discussion of students' concerns. To encourage attention to the needs of students, the chair said this: "Throughout today's meeting I'm going to act as if I were a student representative. I'm going to question you and argue with you from this role. This will help us avoid the charge that faculty groups ignore student views." With this statement to justify his action, the chair was able to focus attention on students without incurring hostility from other members. They saw the chair as playing a role, not as a leader expressing a personal opinion. A leader can introduce a variety of controversial or unpopular issues into discussion by similar strategies.

Influencing the Pace of Discussion

Some meetings seem to drag on forever without accomplishing much of value. On the other hand, most of us have been in discussions that moved so quickly we felt railroaded into a decision. An effective leader tries to avoid both extremes by encouraging members to work at an efficient pace, neither so fast that they make hasty judgments, nor so slow that everyone becomes bored.

One way to influence the pace of discussion is to enumerate the items of business that must be dealt with within a defined amount of time. When there is a great deal of work to be done in a single meeting, the leader not only has to persuade members that it can be done, but also has to generate a mood of efficiency. One way to open a meeting of this type is to specify what must be accomplished and then suggest the amounts of time to be allocated to each issue. This kind of schedule helps members gauge their progress as they move through the agenda and helps the group stay generally on target.

Leaders sometimes expedite work by presuming closure on particular issues. Consider, for example, a leader who needed to complete and submit a written report covering the initial work of the committee. She called a meeting and told members they would be responsible for completing the report during the session and asked the writers of the report to distribute copies to all members in attendance. These actions informed the writers that the leader approved the substance of the report and that the focus of the meeting was to edit it for style. While members might have preferred to discuss the issues a little longer, the leader knew the report was solid, and she exercised her authority.

To slow the pace of discussion, leaders may inject questions and encourage elaboration of ideas. Sometimes leaders need to calm an enthusiastic group in order to prevent premature settling on issues. The leader may say, "Hang on, Bill, I'm not clear on the details of what you just proposed," or "Just for the sake of the record, let's pin down some of these general points," or "I think this may not be the only possible solution, although it seems to be the only one we've generated. Can any of you help me identify some options?" Communication of this type sets a tone for questioning and probing. If members are not being critical and careful in their own thinking, the leader must persuade them to be so.

Leaders are persuasive agents who influence their groups in the five dimensions we've just considered. Each action a leader takes, each comment made can affect the climate of the group, the investment of individual members, and the quality of the outcomes that result.

SUMMARY

Previous approaches to leadership are limited by their static and deterministic assumptions and by their neglect of the communicative dynamics at the core of leading. By contrast, the adaptive view of leadership maintains that both leaders and members are dynamic and therefore constantly engaged in efforts to adapt to each other in order to maintain goodwill and produce solid work.

Leadership cannot proceed by general rules, nor by abstract formulas for effectiveness. Instead, it is based on informed, sensitive analysis of members, situations, and tasks, and appropriate adaptations to each. Effective leaders are people who know how to think productively about group work and group dynamics and who know how to vary their own self-presentations in ways consistent with what a given group needs. A skilled and committed leader can make the difference between enjoyable and successful group work and failure.

REFERENCES

1. E. P. Hollander, *Leadership Dynamics* (New York: Free Press, 1978), pp. 13–16.
2. C. U. Larson, "The Verbal Response of Groups to the Absence or Presence of Leaders," *Speech Monographs,* 38 (August 1971), pp. 177–181.
3. Hollander, *Leadership Dynamics,* p. 3.
4. Ibid., pp. 64–65.
5. Erich Fromm, *Escape from Freedom* (New York: Holt, Rinehart and Winston, 1941).
6. F. Thrasher, *The Gang: A Study of 1313 Gangs in Chicago* (Chicago: University of Chicago Press, 1927).
7. Charles Bird, *Social Psychology* (New York: Appleton-Century-Crofts, 1940).
8. R. M. Stogdill, "Personal Factors Associated with Leadership," *Journal of Psychology,* 25 (1948), pp. 35–71.
9. K. Lewin, R. Lippitt, and R. K. White, "Patterns of Aggressive Behavior in Experimentally Created 'Social Climates,'" *Journal of Social Psychology,* 10 (1939), pp. 271–299.
10. L. B. Rosenfeld and G. Fowler, "Personality, Sex and Leadership Style," *Communication Monographs,* 43 (1976), pp. 320–324.
11. J. K. Hemphill, "The Leader and His Group," *Education Research Bulletin,* 28 (1949), pp. 225–229 and 245–246.
12. L. T. Howells and S. W. Becker, "Seating Arrangement and Leadership Emergence," *Journal of Abnormal and Social Psychology,* 64 (1962), pp. 148–150.
13. R. F. Bales, *Interaction Process Analysis: A Method for the Study of Small Groups* (Reading, MA: Addison-Wesley, 1950).
14. K. Benne and P. Sheats, "Functional Roles of Group Members," *Journal of Social Issues,* 4 (Spring 1948), pp. 41–49.
15. D. C. Barnlund and F. S. Haiman, *The Dynamics of Discussion* (Boston: Houghton-Mifflin, 1960).
16. F. Fiedler, *A Theory of Leadership Effectiveness* (New York: McGraw-Hill, 1967).
17. J. T. Wood, "Leading in Purposive Discussions: A Study of Adaptive Behavior," *Communication Monographs,* 44 (June 1977), pp. 152–165.
18. W. E. Jurma, "Effects of Leader Structuring Style and Task Orientation Characteristics on Group Members," *Communication Monographs,* 46 (November 1979), pp. 282–295.
19. J. T. Wood, "Leading as a Process of Persuasion and Adaptation." In J. W. Pfeiffer and J. E. Jones (eds), *1976 Group Facilitators' Annual Handbook* (La Jolla, CA: University Associates, 1976), pp. 132–135.
20. Hollander, *Leadership Dynamics,* p. 41.
21. Ibid., p. 54.
22. Ibid., pp. 127–128.
23. Ibid., pp. 40–42.
24. Ibid.

RECOMMENDED READINGS

Fiedler, Fred. "The Trouble with Leadership Training Is That It Doesn't Work." *Psychology Today* (February 1973), pp. 24–30 and 92. This is an interesting article, written for general readers. Fiedler describes a variety of leadership training programs, reports on their results (or lack thereof), and offers his explanation of why leadership training is a pointless venture.

Hollander, Edwin P. *Leadership Dynamics.* New York: Free Press, 1978. This is an excellent and highly readable desk manual for practicing leaders. Hollander, who was a primary source for this chapter, elaborates his transactive approach, which conceives of leadership as an exchange between followers and a leader and which explains the responsibilities of both.

chapter 7

Making Informed Choices About the Management of Conflict

"Conflict in a social system which is handled destructively can lead to the destruction of the system; the absence of conflict in a social system can lead to stagnation."[1] This quotation suggests the themes of this chapter. Conflict is essential to productive group problem-solving. To realize its potential value, however, conflict must be managed effectively. Most groups that deal with matters of consequence discover that there are two kinds of conflict. The first, argument about personalities or extraneous matters, tends to divide a group and renders it ineffective. The second kind of argument, which centers on ideas relevant to the group, helps members achieve informed positions on the issues. This chapter is about conflict and how to manage it. We'll show how you can deal with disagreements in ways that are productive for the group and how you can recognize and correct disruptive modes of conflict if they occur.

Conflict is a neutral term. It is neither good nor bad in itself, but it can be handled well or poorly and it can be applied toward worthwhile or petty ends. If a group is to be effective, members should have the independence of mind necessary to think and act for themselves and honor their own principles. This means that you examine information yourself, reflect privately on what the data say to *you,* and express your understanding of the data, as well as your attitude about them, as clearly and cogently as possible. In addition, independent and cooperative thinking means that you remain open to what your colleagues have to say, objectively consider points of view different from your own, and work to find ways of combining your ideas with those of others. All this is done for the goal of building the most careful, thorough group report possible.

We've now set forth an ideal for expressing and managing disagreements. However, this ideal is not always realized. Often people try to avoid conflict or suppress it. The result of such tactics is frustration for members and ineffective solutions by the group. Let's consider an example of how conflict can be muffled.

Four faculty members are meeting to consider an appeal for change of grade from a college sophomore, Vala Dictory. Justin Case and Al Ternative are full professors; Teresa (Terry) Micin is an associate professor; Sterling Silver is a newly hired assistant professor. Their deliberations follow.

CASE: I think this case is pretty clear-cut. She wants to raise her grade average and needs an A instead of the B she has. There's nothing new here. I think we can dismiss this quickly.

TERNATIVE: Dictory is just another one of those students who thinks the world owes her a living. She thinks she can get her grade raised just by asking for it. The gall!

SILVER: Perhaps we're being a bit rash. After all, Dictory did show that her papers were borderline A/B. She says her attendance and participation were excellent, so perhaps that should give her a benefit of doubt.

CASE: We have no way to measure the quality of her class participation! As for attendance, so what? Students are *supposed* to attend classes. I see no grounds for a grade change.

MICIN: I have to agree. Every student wants an A naturally. We just can't grant them on that basis.

SILVER: But I read one of her papers before we met today. She got a B on it, but I would have given it an A. It was quite good.

TERNATIVE: Come now, Silver. I might give a C or D to some essay you would grade as a B, but so what? We cannot override the judgment of a fellow faculty member.

SILVER: But if the grades awarded to individual assignments were unfair in the first place, then the final grade in the course might be cumulatively unfair. Isn't that the function of an appeals board, to decide whether grades were fairly awarded?

CASE: You're missing the point. Appeals committees exist because students feel they should have some resort, and the dean does not intend to deal with this kind of issue. Our function is certainly not to reverse our colleagues' judgments.

TERNATIVE: Yes, every student believes she or he deserves the best grade possible. That doesn't mean we agree. Silver, you're rather new here, so you probably do not know our grading standards. We've been through many appeals, and there is nothing noteworthy about this one.

SILVER: I'm just not convinced that Vala Dictory doesn't have a good basis for appeal. I see merit in her claims.

MICIN: Sterling, there's always some merit in every claim, but there simply isn't enough here to justify a grade change. If you stay here as part of this faculty, I think you'll come to understand the importance of honoring standards.

SILVER: Well, perhaps. . . .

CASE: Good, then we're all in agreement, and we can get back to our offices, I presume.

Regardless of which point of view you respect in the foregoing discussion, most people would agree that there was flagrant suppression of conflict in the committee. The three senior faculty members refused to deal with the new person's objections. Eventually Sterling Silver succumbed to the pressure to conform to the majority viewpoint. He did not do it because he was convinced by good evidence or reasons. Instead, he did it in response to pressure. It is hard to know where reason ends and intimidation begins, but it is clear that a new faculty member with no job security does not have sufficient power to oppose senior faculty colleagues. As for Vala Dictory's case, it may well have been unfairly judged. This committee, however, will never know, since the members did not openly, seriously discuss the issues.

When others oppose you, it is easy to give up a stand. It is tempting to justify desertion of your position when pressured to be agreeable or to "go along." As we noted in Chapter 3, conformity pressures are well-established problems in group work. It is important that all members guard against exerting or giving in to unfair kinds of pressure such as Silver encountered. Serving as a devil's advocate or supporting a minority viewpoint are useful methods of combatting conformity pressures in group deliberations. The film *Twelve Angry Men* dramatized jurors' deliberations about a murder trial. It showed that people can be reasonable about differences of opinion and if others discuss them substantively, they represent a genuine contribution to the group. On the other hand, if expressing dissent generates anger, people may back off, drop their objections, and stop thinking. Only a person who holds a minority position very strongly can withstand group pressure to agree for the sake of agreement.

Conformity pressures, however, are not the most troublesome responses to conflict. Worse yet is the nondeliberate avoidance of conflict, the unrecognized suppression of differences of opinion. This tends to happen when members feel an urgency to reach agreement, when they face a crisis and want the comfort of unanimity, or when they have become so cohesive that there is a tacit norm against disagreement. When members suppress conflict and critical thought without conscious intent, *groupthink* has occurred.

In the remainder of this chapter we will look at groupthink and its counterpart, constructive conflict. We will suggest how to manage conflict so that it contributes to the group's progress and how to recognize symptoms of constructive and destructive forms of conflict so that you can control the climate in your group. These emphases underscore the major theme of this book: *Members control the quality of their work through the choices they make.* Conflict, like all other aspects of discussion, can be handled skillfully or poorly, depending on how members *choose* to behave.

GROUPTHINK

Irving Janis, a noted sociologist, has analyzed the reasons behind ineffective decision-making by national policy-makers.[2] According to Janis, badly formulated policies are often the result of groupthink. Groupthink is a drive for consensus at the cost of realistic analysis and critical thought. Janis believes that groupthink marks a deterioration of mental processes and occurs because individual members suppress their personal ideas and their normal reflective attitudes in order to reach agreement and preserve friendly, cohesive relations in a group.

Groupthink has two important characteristics. First, the suppression of ideas and critical attitudes is generally not deliberate. Nobody comes right out and says, "Let's have no disagreements." Instead, members fail to recognize issues that need to be explored, questions that ought to be raised, positions that should be challenged. They unconsciously turn off their critical orientations. Second, groupthink cannot be explained in terms of individual psychology. It is a group phenomenon that occurs as a result of system forces that arise out of the interaction among members. An overall norm emphasizing agreement tends to become so entrenched a part of the group's *modus operandi* that members' critical faculties are paralyzed. They become unable to see points where disagreement would be appropriate. As you might predict, the result tends to be sloppy decision-making.

To understand better the nature and consequences of groupthink, let's review several actual examples of it. In 1961, the United States was embarrassed by its disastrous mismanagement of the Bay of Pigs invasion of Cuba. The decision to attack Cuba came from a prestigious group of advisors who served President John Kennedy. The decision to attack was rash, and the planning of the attack was entirely inadequate because the advisors suppressed questions that should have been raised and alternatives that should have been considered.

Similar problems characterized the White House group surrounding President Nixon at the time of the Watergate break-in. In 1974 members of the Committee to Re-Elect the President decided that Cubans had been contributing to the Democratic party. To secure evidence of this, they authorized a burglary of the Democratic headquarters and later collaborated in frantic but ill-considered plans to cover up their involvement. These decisions led to the downfall of Nixon's administration.

In 1941 a military advisory group failed to heed sound intelligence reports about an imminent invasion from the Japanese. Consequently, American bases were unprotected, and the result was Pearl Harbor. In the late 1960s, President Johnson's advisory group encouraged him to escalate the Vietnam war despite increasing evidence that American efforts were not having the desired outcomes and despite growing questions about the rightness of our mission in Vietnam. The United States lost further credibility as the war escalated, yet the advisors refused to reconsider their decision.

Here are four cases involving groups with members of substantial intelligence, talent, and experience in handling national and international problems. In each instance, a decision was reached without adequate effort to identify and consider seriously different points of view. The transcripts of these committees' discussions clearly demonstrate that some members knuckled under to group opinion, others rationalized going along, and still others simply could not see beyond the "party line." If highly trained and intelligent advisors can succumb to groupthink, then all the more so can members of everyday problem-solving groups.

Please realize we are not saying conformity is necessarily bad. Sometimes people change their positions because they have been persuaded by legitimate means (reasons, evidence) that their ideas were flawed or that someone else's views were better. This is reasoned consent, and it is valuable in group discussion. However, when people give up ideas just to avoid rocking the boat or when they cease to think critically, the result is injury to the entire group and its goals.

Since groupthink undermines problem-solving and since it is very difficult to detect once it has really taken over, it is important for all discussants to recognize the early symptoms.

SYMPTOMS OF GROUPTHINK

The single best indicator of groupthink is the presence of *concurrence-seeking norms* in a group. Every group has norms about how agreement is reached. When a group seems to value agreement above all and is willing to accept it on any terms, it is a sign of groupthink. The best evidence of this state of affairs is that when an idea is first voiced by one person, other members are likely to nod assent or to offer verbal reinforcement. Members do not ask questions or challenge evidence, nor do they argue, typically because members have unconsciously turned off their critical thinking capacities in the interest of achieving harmony. Members retain a sense of security, because each person feels that "if we agree, the idea must be right." An uninformed consensus is fostered.

When there is an uninformed consensus, we-feeling overpowers respect for the rights of individuals. Anyone who disagrees is regarded as an opponent of the group, a barrier to progress, an undesirable. Usually the group just ignores them until they leave of their own accord. If "undesirables" keep on disagreeing, they are nudged out of the group. If they resist, they are often thrown out.

When President Kennedy's advisors deliberated on policy toward Cuba, there was an atmosphere that defined Cuba as an enemy and a threat to American interests. There was a presumption favoring attack. Those who initially dissented were ridiculed or ignored. Arthur Schlesinger, who disagreed with the majority attitude, was slowly screened out of the group; he was not even invited to the final meeting at which members voted on the invasion plan. Another example of concurrence-seeking norms is provided in Jeb Magruder's account of Watergate. Magruder reported that none of the members of the Committee to Re-Elect the President was comfortable with the idea of breaking into the Democratic head-quarters, yet they all went along with the plan because conflict would have destroyed the cohesion and the security within the committee. When groupthink operates, members tend to agree on ideas and on methods of operation. Anyone who tries to dissent will be reprimanded, criticized, or ostracized from the group. A recent laboratory investigation of groupthink supported this point. Courtright found that the absence of disagreement was the single most pronounced symptom of a groupthink mentality in discussion.[3]

A second major symptom of groupthink is members' belief that *their group is invulnerable.* This illusion of invulnerability is cherished because members can feel secure when they can convince themselves their group can do no wrong. Typically, members think their group has unlimited power and is incapable of error. As you might predict, this attitude can lead to rash decision-making and inadequate analysis of ideas. When group members cease to be skeptical of what they're doing, when they do not check for contradictory ideas, and when they refuse to consider the possibilities of problems inherent in their plans, they are bound to make mistakes. Most frightening of all is the probability that no one will notice the mistakes because members have an overriding interest in maintaining consensus, no matter how uninformed it may be.

One of the most dramatic examples of the illusion of invulnerability occurred in Admiral Kimmel's advisory group in late 1941. Kimmel was repeatedly warned that Japanese aircraft carriers could not be sighted by radar, and it was likely they were headed for Hawaii. Despite clear evidence and multiple warnings, nobody in Kimmel's group would consider the possibility that the Japanese could actually attack Pearl Harbor. The members believed their group was invulnerable until the attack took place.

The illusion of invulnerability also permeated the Committee to Re-Elect the President. After the burglars had been arrested at the Watergate Hotel, Magruder reported that no one in the group could believe they had been caught, because "our people are professionals." Magruder also comments that during the planning of the burglary, committee members believed what they were doing was ethically right because they felt they were incapable of immoral actions (if this strikes you as circular thinking, we agree!). The advisors were blinded by the irrational belief that "our group cannot be wrong and cannot fail." When groupthink operates, members of a group believe they are beyond error or reproach; they cannot see any evidence that contradicts this illusion.

Rationalization is a third symptom of groupthink. It is the process that tends to minimize evidence which threatens a group's basic assumptions and plans. Members rationalize away any contradictory information in order to sustain the group's prized sense of unanimity and rightness. This allows members to label contrary evidence as false, to discount warnings as unfounded, to wave off all disagreement as contentiousness, and to impugn the motives of those who object.

Admiral Kimmel's group was so effective at rationalization that the members persuaded themselves it was impossible for the Japanese to attack an American base in Hawaii. They held this belief right up to the moment the bombs fell on Pearl Harbor. The men involved in the Watergate coverup continued to declare they were acting in the interest of national security right up to the fall of the administration. In the grade appeal discussion we presented earlier, the senior faculty members rationalized their superficial consideration of the case by convincing themselves that Vala Dictory was an irresponsible student looking for an easy grade. Student groups sometimes rationalize away criticisms of their work by claiming instructors "have it in for us." Rationalization is comforting in the short run, but it prevents a group from reconsidering its assumptions and operations while it is still possible to revamp effectively. (We might recall the French

Academy of Science rationalizing away Pasteur's argument that bacteria caused an epidemic. What silly fool could believe in creatures so tiny they could not be seen? With that attitude, who would raise a public objection?)

Once a group has affirmed its strengths and quality, it is difficult for disagreement to occur from within. Dissent threatens group morale. Consensus is easy under these circumstances, but of course it is not well grounded. When consensus is forced or when it is not based on thorough analysis and reasoning, it is not laudable. Constructive disagreement is vital to legitimate consensus.

A fourth symptom of groupthink is *developing and promoting negative stereotypes of outsiders.* Anyone not in the group may be branded as "the enemy" or as inferior to the select few who hold membership. Members enmeshed in groupthink strengthen themselves by defining outsiders as competitors. Members pull even more tightly together to combat the enemy. In other cases, members stereotype anyone outside the group as impotent, incompetent, or otherwise ineffective; thus, members may fail to perceive real threats when they do exist. Admiral Kimmel's committee stereotyped Japan as a "midget nation" that wouldn't dare attack the United States. Consequently, members never believed the intelligence reports of the oncoming invasion. President Kennedy's advisors regarded Castro as a joke and believed he was incapable of leading a successful attack on America. Those who disagreed were branded "Communist sympathizers." The Committee to Re-Elect the President considered the Democrats immoral and subversive, labels that justified any actions against them. The faculty group in the grade appeal deliberations stereotyped students as looking for easy outs and thinking the world owes them a living; thus they justified lack of attention to a particular student's case. President Johnson's advisors held doggedly to their view of the Vietcong as inept fighters, despite the relentless loss of American lives. By developing and promoting stereotypes, a group builds cohesion, creates a basis for harsh, frequently unethical treatment of outsiders, and fosters careless, unsound reasoning.

We have now considered the four primary symptoms of groupthink: concurrence-seeking norms, illusion of invulnerability, rationalizations for decisions and beliefs, and negative stereotypes of outsiders. No group is immune to groupthink, so it is important that members be able to recognize early warning signs of the phenomenon. Any time you find yourself agreeing with collective positions too quickly, suspect groupthink. Any time you find yourself discounting opinions of outsiders that differ from those of the group, be wary. Any time you sense overconfidence about the group's powers, back up and reconsider your position.

The assumption that groups should act cooperatively is important, but it can be carried too far. Striving for consensus can be a legitimate goal, but it is not always the only way nor the best way to make decisions. Furthermore, consensus is valuable *only when it represents a genuine agreement based on thorough analysis of a range of viewpoints.* In the book *Change,* Watzlawick, Weakland, and Fisch advocate that every group try to find one or two "left field" ideas as a method of breaking out of conventional assumptions.[4] Sometimes far-fetched solutions are precisely what is needed, either for the process of discussion or for its ideal outcomes. A group cannot discover optimum solutions if it makes premature commitments to assumptions about what comprises a right answer. Left-field ideas help members stay open to possibilities and minimize the chance that they will prematurely freeze their thinking.

CORRECTIVES TO GROUPTHINK

Because groupthink can incapacitate problem-solving groups, it is important to know how to avoid or correct it. At the outset we emphasize that it is far easier (and possible) to deal with groupthink through preventive action or very early intervention than through delayed efforts to reverse it. Once groupthink is established and becomes the norm, there is usually little that can be done. So our emphasis is on how you can build a group climate that does not allow the development of groupthink and, if necessary, how you can respond to early symptoms in time to correct them.

Minimizing the problems of status differences among members is useful preventive medicine. As we noted in Chapter 2, high-status members have the potential to influence other members. This can happen, however, only if members allow high-status persons to dominate opinion. Someone must set a tone for questioning ideas, including those contributed by powerful members. Any member can do this, and all should. Further, high-status individuals should watch their own behavior and responses others make to it. If a powerful person sees that other members uncritically accept any ideas she or he offers, then that person may need to be self-critical. Tentativeness in presenting ideas encourages questioning and criticism. It is entirely appropriate to say that you're not sure of an idea you volunteer; this leaves the door open for other ideas. High-status members can also be quite effective in lending support to ideas offered by those whose status is not so high.

President Kennedy apparently appreciated the advice we just offered. During the Cuban missile crisis, he maintained a nonpartisan stance in deliberations in order to avoid influencing others. He was determined not to allow groupthink to operate again, as it had during the Bay of Pigs fiasco. One of Kennedy's techniques was to avoid attending meetings and to ask for a report of the content. He realized he was too charismatic, too influential to participate without biasing the discussion. Because he was not present, deliberations were marked by varied ideas and healthy debate over them.

Because the leader has the highest status, the role of devil's advocate is sometimes valuable. If the leader reserves the right (and acts on it) to criticize anyone's ideas and to represent minority points of view if they are not represented in the group, members will get the idea that it is important to examine opposing points of view. Devil's advocacy can be gently played, and it is contagious.

There is another element to this also. When the leader sets the norm for generalized disagreement and criticism, dissent becomes far less passionate. The opposite of groupthink is not anarchy; it is a mood of tolerance for dissent. Irreconcilable conflict is rare in this kind of group. The most dangerous conflict comes when one or more people dares to thwart the "group will." If "group will" is not allowed to develop until agreement satisfactory to all is reached, conflict will be easy to manage and constructive to the group.

A second way to work against groupthink is to seek information that challenges emerging consensus in a group. Remember that a primary symptom of groupthink is members' unwillingness to regard contradictory information as credible. A group can protect itself against this attitude by agreeing at the outset that it will actively seek information and opinions that differ from those of members. In so doing, members assure themselves that any agreements they can sustain after considering the most cogent challengers are likely to be well grounded and successful in the long run. The group may then take legitimate pride in how thoroughly ideas have been investigated and how rigorously they have been scrutinized. Members may play devil's advocate themselves at this point, or they may invite outsiders to meetings in order to hear possible objections raised by people skilled in offering them. Either way, the group avoids the trap of being selectively inattentive to important information.

A third valuable corrective is to develop a norm that legitimizes disagreement in discussion. Genuine argument and vigorous analysis of ideas are imperative to competent decision-making. Group members are obligated to suggest ideas, to review them critically, and to subject them to every known challenge. Whatever positions survive these methods are likely to be well reasoned and publicly defensible. The norm allowing disagreement needs to be established early in a group's history if it is to be viable at times of tension. Members should engage in questioning from the outset. It is important to demonstrate that questioning and challenging are methods for furthering group goals, not individual egos. Members should attempt to make their queries tentative and issue-centered. Admitting doubt about your own positions and ideas is also valuable in creating an overall climate that defines disagreement as legitimate.

Groupthink is a dangerous phenomenon. Every group is potentially subject to it, so all of us need to understand what it is, how it arises, and how to prevent and correct it. We have identified four primary symptoms and three corrective methods. These provide you with an informed basis for doing your part to prevent the groupthink mentality from hindering your group's efforts to solve problems effectively and ethically.

THE ROLE OF CONFLICT IN DISCUSSION

We have repeatedly noted the value of conflict in serious discussion. Only through consideration of differing ideas can complex problems be understood, much less solved satisfactorily. We find it necessary to emphasize the values of conflict because most people, including experienced committee members, seek to avoid, muffle, or gloss over any disagreements in deliberation. In an effort to understand the prevalent negative attitudes toward conflict, we looked the word up in Webster's dictionary and found this definition: "disagreement . . . war, battle, collision, emotional tension, . . . the opposition of persons. . . . "[5] Is this definition representative of general views held by people in our society? To find out, we asked students in some of our courses to define the term. Here's a sampling of the responses we received:

> "Conflict is when members of a group are closed-minded."
>
> "It happens when one person really believes in an idea and pushes it on others."
>
> "It's basically hostility among people."
>
> "Conflict means somebody wins and somebody else loses."
>
> "Conflict destroys closeness and breaks up relationships."
>
> "Conflict occurs when people don't know how to be cooperative."

Both the dictionary and our students define conflict as a negative force that results from lack of interpersonal skills and that leads to undesirable consequences. Research and experience, however, demonstrate that when conflict is *appropriately managed,* it is highly constructive. In fact, members of groups with consistently impressive track records regard conflict as essential to their effectiveness. Three distinct values of conflict merit our attention:

1. Conflict allows a group to entertain diverse ideas. This in turn helps members gain a broad understanding of the multiple facets of a problem.
2. Conflict encourages the expression of divergent points of view and thereby provides a group with the potential for a greater number of alternatives from which to select a final solution.
3. The excitement generated by healthy conflict stimulates interaction and involvement among members.[6]

The first objective of problem-solving discussion is to reach an understanding of the problems the group intends to solve. At this stage it is necessary to examine carefully background information and all manner of issues that potentially have bearing on the specific task facing the group. In this process of exploring and defining the problem, members should voice differing perspectives, and they should offer alternative interpretations of the task.

One member may see something that others haven't noticed; another person may think the problem has political or social implications not recognized by others. These views must be laid on the table so that the group as a whole can arrive at a definition of its task based on wide-ranging considerations.

A second value of conflict is its potential to increase the number of solutions a group considers. By the time a group gets to the solution stage, members may be so weary they are ready to grab at the first solution that appears. If fatigue is compounded by consensus-seeking norms, then the group may agree quickly on a superficially examined idea. Furthermore, if members have not legitimized disagreements, it is unlikely that more than one or two solutions will surface. Why? Because once one member has volunteered a solution, others will hesitate to criticize it or challenge it by presenting an optional solution. The result is incapacitation for the group.

Peter Drucker, a widely respected management consultant, maintains that one of the most important functions of disagreement is to provide alternative solutions, since these are necessary if a group is to achieve something that is not hasty and superficial.[7] Without considering alternatives, a group cannot have real confidence in its solution, although groupthink could delude a group into believing its solution was handed down on a stone tablet. Furthermore, without alternatives a group has no backup solutions if the preferred one is not accepted by the charging authority. Well-reasoned recommendations tend to result from lively deliberations about a number of alternative ideas.

A third value of conflict pertains directly to the climate of a group and indirectly to the outcomes of discussion. Constructive conflict focused on issues heightens members' interest and sharpens their participation skills. When differences are welcomed and considered earnestly, each member may feel free to volunteer ideas and to respond thoughtfully and honestly to those of colleagues. This kind of deliberation can be genuinely interesting. Creativity in discussion seems to thrive on constructive conflict, on the welcoming of differing viewpoints as legitimate, and on the willingness to respond with care and thoroughness to each viewpoint. Without some disagreement, discussion can become lethargic and—frankly—boring.

These values of conflict are substantial. Yet all of them are contingent on proper management of conflict. When members do not handle conflict well, the benefits will not occur, and in fact some negative outcomes may result. So members must not only realize the importance of conflict, but also understand how to manage it to achieve its potential values.

TYPES OF CONFLICT

Conflict exists on a continuum ranging from purely disruptive to purely constructive. While most instances of conflict fall somewhere between these two extremes, we will confine our analysis to the pure forms. This should allow you to recognize the essential character of ideal conflict management and its counterpart.

Disruptive conflict occurs when members do not know how to handle their differences effectively. Typically, disruptive conflict is characterized by a sense of competition in which members feel they are pitted against one another, and only one person or one faction can emerge victorious. They fail to realize that collective interests are at stake, and that all members will win with the best solution. Members tend to become ego-involved with their ideas, so that any criticism or disagreement is perceived as personal attack, and winning becomes more important than achieving common goals.

In disruptive conflict situations, members are likely to feel apprehensive and threatened. Consequently, they become defensive and may act aggressively or may withdraw resentfully. They may try to hurt one another's feelings in order to win.[8] Under such conditions, it is nearly impossible for members to consider ideas intelligently. If disruptive conflict is allowed to continue for long, the group may factionalize. Team spirit will go out the window, and along with it any possibility of compromise.

A characteristic of disruptive conflict is face-to-face confrontation between contenders. Combatants act as if they are trying to compel their adversary to change his or her mind. The rhetorical view suggests, however, that argument must be directed toward decision-makers, either neutrals or authorities. Defusing disruptive conflict sometimes requires nothing more than generating mutual respect between advocates and urging them to address their remarks to the rest of the group. If mutual respect can be extended throughout the group, members will build a reconciliation usually by taking some ideas from each. This is the substance of negotiation and compromise.

Constructive conflict, on the other hand, develops when members understand they are using disagreement in order to reach an ultimate agreement on the best way to achieve common objectives. The disagreements are managed within the perspective of collective interests, so a win-lose attitude is improbable. In constructive conflict situations, members tend to support each other's presentations of ideas, even if they disagree with the content of those ideas. Equally important, members tend to invite others to critique, question, or modify ideas they present. Discussion stays focused on issues, not personalities, and the channels of communication remain open.

Constructive management of conflict benefits everyone concerned. Members broaden their perspectives on the problem; they generate enough solutions to compare relative merits and identify backup positions; and they become increasingly cohesive because they have engaged in vigorous conflict without dividing the group. Members learn to trust and respect one another when they discover it is possible to talk intelligently and productively about differences of opinion.

Conflict can be a positive group force when it is properly managed. (© Bermack, 1978, Jeroboam)

CONFLICT IN THE SYSTEMS PERSPECTIVE

To analyze the values and forms of conflict thoroughly, it was necessary for us to focus exclusively on conflict. However, as you probably realize, conflict cannot be understood accurately in a conceptual vacuum. The systemic principles introduced in Chapter 2 have a bearing on our discussion in this chapter. Conflict must be viewed within the context of the entire group system, because it influences and is influenced by all other parts of that system. To integrate and summarize our discussion of conflict, we focus on two system-related issues: interaction between conflict and climate, and the influence of communication on how conflict is managed.

Conflict and Climate: Reciprocal Influence

Group climate and conflict interact dynamically. Each affects the other. Climate is the interpersonal tone of a group. It provides a context that affects how conflict is regarded and how it is handled. The ideal climate for discussion is cooperative, open, and rhetorically sensitive, because these qualities encourage productive, invigorating conflict that furthers group goals. In turn, constructively managed conflict assists in creating and maintaining an ideal climate because it builds trust, respect, and cooperation among members.

Neither conflict nor climate always occurs in its ideal form. A climate may be excessively cohesive, insistent on conformity, and overly deferential. Groupthink typically grows out of this sort of atmosphere and supports its continuance. On the other hand, climates that are competitive, closed, and divisive also tend to result in disruptive conflict that compromises both group goals and individuals' integrity. Conflict that is disruptive feeds back into climate to reinforce the negative, combative tone. Tubbs underscores the distinction between constructive and disruptive conflict when he notes that "The point of balance is very delicate between conflict that is managed so that it produces growth and conflict that is managed so that it produces disruption and incapacitation."[9] Because both conflict and climate are so strongly related to the effectiveness of problem-solving, members need to ensure the quality of each. Central to this objective is appreciating the ways in which communication can contribute to climates that promote constructive conflict and to conflict that fosters effective climates. That is our final consideration in this chapter.

Communicating to Build Constructive Climates

As we've noted, the ideal climate for serious problem-solving deliberations features cooperativeness, openness, and rhetorical sensitivity. These qualities are critical because they encourage free expression of ideas, efforts to understand and fairly consider differing viewpoints, and an awareness of shared goals that transcended individual positions on particular issues. Members should work on climate from the outset of group meetings so that they can establish a tone which will enhance the group's ability to manage conflict when serious disagreements begin.

A healthy climate does not arise of its own accord. Instead, it results from a series of communicative choices members make from the onset of deliberations. These choices encourage or discourage development of a vibrant, engaging tone for interaction. Let's look more closely at three major qualities of communication that promote a healthy climate for deliberations and conflict management.

Cooperativeness A cooperative spirit is the foundation of effective problem-solving.[10] Members must work together to achieve the common goal of solving the problem that initially brought them together. They should regard each other as allies, collaborators, members of one team with a singular goal.[11]

A cooperative orientation is facilitated by communication that emphasizes the notion of team. Terms such as "we," "our," "us," "our committee," "team effort," and "mutual concerns" underscore the collective nature of problem-solving and discourage feelings of competition. Equally germane to a cooperative orientation is supportive communication. Acknowledge the contributions others make; take a moment to compliment a person who makes a particularly insightful comment; voice support for a well-reasoned idea; indicate your interest in what others have to say. Even when you don't agree with another's ideas, it's possible to be supportive of their motives and their honest efforts. You may ask for clarification, elaboration, or further support for an idea. It is also appropriate to state honestly that you disagree and invite the other person to think with you to figure out the basis of your disagreement and to find a mutually agreeable position.

To promote cooperative, team orientations, it is generally advisable to minimize authorship of ideas. It matters little that Ellen suggested X and Jacob proposed Y. Comparisons couched in terms of "Ellen's position versus Jacob's position" are likely to create polarization in the group and may invoke competitiveness between Ellen and Jacob. What does matter is that the group has the advantage of two ideas, both of which everyone should want to consider and evaluate. It is the X/Y issue that is important to the group. Should it be X, or Y or X_Y or ^XY or XY? This approach honors the value of disagreement while preserving a cooperative climate.

Openness Effective climates are marked by *openness,* which is the perceived freedom to express and explore ideas without fear of ridicule, intimidation, or attack. People need to feel it's okay to make mistakes along the way to solutions.[12] Like cooperativeness, openness is created and sustained through members' communicative choices throughout discussion. To encourage an open climate, members should strive for active, balanced participation by all.[13] You want to demonstrate that you trust other members and can be trusted by them. Responses to ideas are critical. You should be careful not to make derogatory judgments. Nobody should be penalized for an honest effort. After a few harsh judgments have been made, communication may cease: Who wants to jump into pirhana-infested waters? Even if you think a comment is foolish, diplomacy is in order. How you respond has an impact beyond a specific exchange—it influences the overall climate by indicating to all members how ideas may be treated.

Openness is also advanced by the manner in which ideas are presented. It is appropriate to offer your ideas in a tentative way that suggests you are open to other ideas or to criticisms and modifications of your own. We are not advising you to be timid, but we are cautioning against dogmatism and zealotry. Tentativeness may be indicated by phrases such as "Perhaps we could consider another way of going about this," or "I have a suggestion all of us might be able to refine and build on." Each of these phrasings keeps open the channels for discussion and invites teamwork on ideas.

Rhetorical Sensitivity   As you may recall from our previous discussion of rhetorical sensitivity, it is an attitude that honors the person speaking, the people listening, and the integrity of communication itself. Every communicative act consists of content and indications of the speaker's attitude toward those who are addressed.[14] Rhetorically sensitive communication not only aims for sound content, but also for a balanced recognition of speakers' and listeners' rights and responsibilities. Speakers have a right to be heard, yet they also have a responsibility to think before speaking so their ideas will be valuable to those who listen and will take into account the perspectives of others. Listeners have a right to expect a speaker to adapt to their level of knowledge and to respect their views, yet they also have a responsibility to listen fully, actively, and fairly. When members respect the rights and responsibilities entailed in communicating, they enhance the value of interaction and enrich the human relationships that exist in a group. Effective, sensitive listening and speaking are two halves of a whole, and they are equally important in creating an ideal climate for discussion and constructive conflict management.

TROUBLESHOOTING

We've described ideals for group climate, so you should have a good idea of what kind of tone you want. To establish and sustain an effective climate, you will need to monitor constantly for signs of any problems. The goal is to diagnose any trouble before it becomes sufficiently serious to interfere with the task at hand. The best, most reliable measure of climate quality is communication. Members should be familiar with verbal and nonverbal behaviors that indicate the mood of a group.

Verbal signs of a healthy climate include balanced and lively interaction, proportionately more questions and tentative comments than strong statements of advocacy, expression of differing opinions, focus on the issues of contention instead of members' personalities, and talk that emphasizes group goals and concerns. Nonverbal signs of a healthy climate include relaxed postures, frequent eye contact among members, egalitarian seating patterns, lack of fixed seating combinations (that is, a lack of cliques who always sit together), and attentive listening. These verbal and nonverbal cues generally reflect a healthy, productive climate for problem-solving.

Just as important as knowing the signs of positive group tone is the ability to recognize early symptoms of a poor group climate. An undesirable climate exists when a group is excessively cohesive or when it lacks adequate cohesion. An overly cohesive group generally cannot exercise critical, reflective thought, and groupthink is typically at work. We've already discussed groupthink and pointed out its major symptoms, so you should be able to spot it in the early stages.

A different climate problem is low cohesion, often accompanied by aggressiveness, lack of trust among members, and little or no effort to work cooperatively as a unit. Typical of this climate is communication that focuses on individual goals and ideas instead of group concerns and attacks (subtle or otherwise) on competing positions. Often such a climate includes comments that place blame, defend personal opinions, and focus on personalities rather than content. Listening is minimal in a competitive climate, since nobody cares much what others have to say. Nonverbally, a low-trust climate may be indicated by closed postures, seating cliques among members, withdrawals from discussion, scant eye contact, and tense physical positions. The tone of conversation is frequently hostile, combative, and dogmatic. These verbal and nonverbal behaviors reflect a climate that is not conducive to effective problem-solving.

If you spot any of these warning signs, you should attempt to correct the climate before a negative tone is established. To do this, you may make communicative choices that indicate cooperativeness, openness, and rhetorical sensitivity. You thus model a constructive orientation toward discussion. Others may pick up on your style and respond in kind. It may also be appropriate to call an intermission in task work and involve the entire membership in an analysis of the dynamics of the climate. This should not be anything like a sensitivity training session—there's no need for heavy disclosure or amateur pychoanalysis of members' motives for behavior. It is possible, however, to talk in a civilized way about what is going on in the group and to collectively generate some ways of correcting shared problems. The group may be able to devise some useful rules to guide deliberations. One group we observed, for instance, developed this list of communication rules in response to their recognition of competitiveness creeping into their interaction:

1. Interruptions are not allowed. The person speaking has the floor until he or she finishes.
2. The first response to an idea may *not* be negative. If we need to criticize an idea, that comes after responses which recognize the contribution and its meritorious aspects.
3. We will not have sideline conversations between members while someone is talking.
4. When two or more members seem locked in disagreement, they will be asked to meet together to work out a mutually acceptable position.

The group found these rules useful in helping break some undesirable habits that were beginning to interfere with effectiveness in problem-solving. After several meetings in which the rules were rigidly enforced, members found they no longer needed to police their communication. They had developed different and more productive communication norms and consequently had promoted a much healthier climate for working.

SUMMARY

Conflict is vital to effective problem-solving. Without it, a group cannot have maximally broad perspective on a problem, cannot examine a variety of possible solutions, and will not have the kind of vigorous, exciting climate that promotes critical, productive problem-solving. To achieve these substantial values, members must understand how to manage conflict constructively.

Effective management of conflict involves knowing how to diagnose a group's climate as healthy, negative due to excessive cohesion (groupthink), or negative due to inadequate cohesion. Members who understand the communicative behaviors associated with each of these climates can be effective in troubleshooting for the group. All participants in discussion should aim to communicate in ways that are cooperative, open, and rhetorically sensitive. Efforts in these directions encourage a group climate that invites constructive conflict over issues. Members who build this kind of climate should be able to count on having differences of opinion and on being able to manage them in productive, effective ways.

REFERENCES

1. Stewart Tubbs, *A Systems Approach to Small Group Interaction* (Reading, MA: Addison-Wesley, 1978), p. 257.
2. Irving L. Janis, *Victims of Groupthink* (Boston: Houghton-Mifflin, 1972).
3. John A. Courtright, "A Laboratory Investigation of Groupthink," *Communication Monographs,* 45 (August 1978), pp. 228–246.
4. Paul Watzlawick, John Weakland, and Richard Fisch, *Change* (New York: Norton, 1974).
5. *Websters Seventh New Collegiate Dictionary* (Springfield, MA: C. & C. Merriam Company, 1967).
6. Julia T. Wood, "Constructive Conflict in Discussion: Learning to Manage Disagreements Effectively." In J. William Pfeiffer and John E. Jones (eds.), *1977 Group Facilitators' Annual Handbook* (La Jolla, CA: University Associates, 1977).
7. Peter Drucker, *Management* (New York: Harper & Row, 1974).
8. Jack Gibb, "Defensive Communication." In Robert Cathcart and Larry A. Samovar (eds.), *Small Group Communication: A Reader* (Dubuque, IA: William C. Brown, 1974); Mae A. Bell, "The Effects of Substantive and Affective Verbal Conflict on the Quality of Decisions of Small Problem-Solving Groups," *Central States Speech Journal,* 30 (Spring 1979), pp. 75–32.
9. Tubbs, *A Systems Approach,* p. 257.
10. Morton Deutsch, "Toward an Understanding of Conflict," *International Journal of Group Tensions* (1971), pp. 42–55.
11. Robert Blake and Jane Mouton, "The Fifth Achievement," *Journal of Applied Behavioral Science,* 6 (1970), pp. 413–426.

12. Gibb, "Defensive Communication."

13. Nancy L. Harper and Lawrence Askling, "Group Communication and Quality of Task Solution in a Media Production Organization," *Communication Monographs,* 47 (June 1980), pp. 77–100.

14. B. Aubrey Fisher and Wayne A. Beach, "Content and Relationship Dimensions of Communicative Behavior: An Exploratory Study," *Western Journal of Speech Communication,* 43 (Summer 1979), pp. 201–211.

RECOMMENDED READINGS

Deutsch, Morton. *The Resolution of Conflict: Constructive and Destructive Processes.* New Haven, CT: Yale University Press, 1973. Deutsch is a recognized authority on the effective management of conflict. This book is quite readable and offers sound advice.

Janis, Irving L., and Leon Mann. *Decision-Making: A Psychological Analysis of Conflict, Choice, and Commitment.* New York: Free Press, 1977. This book builds on Janis's landmark study of groupthink. The thrust of this work is improving decision-making by providing techniques to reduce the probability of groupthink and other interferences with sound deliberation. The book is somewhat advanced, but worth the effort required to read it.

chapter *8*

Standard Agenda Phase One: Understanding the Charge

GOALS

To understand where we stand.
Why are we here?
What authority do we have?
What do we have to turn out?
Who gets it?
What do they do with it?

OUTCOMES

Questions about the charge adressed to appropriate persons.
A written specification of the final task.
A record of our understanding of the task.

MEMBER TASKS

1. To raise questions about the nature of the group task.
2. To raise questions about personal responsibility to the group.
3. To raise questions to be addressed to higher authorities.
4. To raise questions about schedule or agenda.

LEADER OBLIGATIONS

1. To raise necessary questions pertinent to understanding the group task.
2. To transmit and interpret information from higher authorities.
3. To act as liaison between the group and higher authorities.
4. To ensure that agreements and understandings of the group are written into the record.

We have included an outline like the one above at the beginning of each of the chapters about steps in the standard agenda. Each outline will identify goals, outcomes, member tasks, and leader obligations for a particular phase of discussion. Refer to the outline as you read the text. It may be useful to make copies to keep before you when you actually participate in discussion. They will enable you to help the group be sure that it has not omitted an important discussion issue or ignored important considerations or responsibilities.

GOALS OF PHASE ONE

In Chapter 1 we referred to the old Chinese proverb, "If you don't know where you're going, any road will take you there." The primary goal in this first phase of the standard agenda is to find out where the group is going. Once the group understands what it is supposed to accomplish, it can examine the options for accomplishing it.

The beginning steps of discussion are often underemphasized by novice groups eager to get to the exciting issues that lie ahead. Chairpersons have often been heard to say, "I think you all know why we're here, so I won't waste time going into that." Unfortunately, however, people do not always know why they are there, and it is important that they do. If members do not know what is expected of them or understand the limits placed on their decision-making power, they may find their jobs in jeopardy. Unfocused members sometimes go beyond their authority, do sloppy work, solve problems that do not exist, or fail to solve the assigned problem.

It should be obvious that discussion groups are part of larger organizations. Other components of the organization are dependent on the work done by problem-solving groups. Nonetheless, organizational communication consultants report that participant confusion about the nature of the group task is the most frequent problem they encounter. Leaders assume far too often that members know what to do and how to do it. Many participants are asked to serve in a group without being properly oriented. They are eager to get to work (or to get it over with). Yet if they are not properly briefed, they can get involved in counterproductive activities.

Furthermore, members do not want to appear "ignorant." In the corporate world, advancement may often be based on their performance in groups. They may assume everyone else in the group understands what is going on and think that if they ask for direction, they will appear incompetent. The stakes are often very high for participants in the group process. Groups make decisions that have major effects on human lives. Furthermore, group participation is an important criterion on which advancement of personnel is based.

In groups outside the corporate world, there may be even more at stake. Community groups, for example, usually seek solutions to major problems: waste disposal, zoning, improvement of the economy. These are not trivial problems, and inept decisions can often have a drastic effect. It is important to get a good start. But failure to discuss where the group is going and why wastes countless hours of human energy and is one of the major reasons for failure in problem-solving.

EXAMINING THE CHARGE IN CLASSROOM GROUPS

Understanding the Assignment

If you are a member of a classroom discussion group, it makes good sense to get a specific definition of the assignment. What output does the instructor want? Does your group have to define its own problem? Within what limitations? Are there any checkpoints you can use to make sure you stay on the track? What instructions do you have, and does everyone understand them? How will you be evaluated? What part of your grade depends on individual performance, and what part on group output? Is this assignment purely academic, or are there ways in which your decisions can have actual influence? These questions are exactly like those asked about real-world issues.

Becoming Familiar with Colleagues

It is important to get to know the people you are working with. We do not mean the kind of "knowing" you might be after if you met them at a cocktail party. Their family status and social interests are not important. What you want to know is the stake each of your colleagues has in the discussion.

Is your group comprised of people who share a common interest? If your group came together because you live in the same area or have the same free time available, does this have anything at all to do with the kind of problem you select?

Good participation in a classroom discussion group entails a number of responsibilities. (© Siteman, 1980, EKM-Nepenthe)

Are your interests supposed to have something to do with the problem the group is working on? Once you agree on a problem area, do you all have the same perspective on it? Why did the people in the group choose this problem?

If you are in a group outside of class, under what authority does the group meet? How did you get there? Are you a volunteer? Are the other people volunteers? Do you all have the same motives for volunteering? If you were appointed, who appointed you, and what does that person expect the group to do? Is the group a regular organization, or part of one? If it has met before and solved other problems, what were they? Do you and your colleagues solve the same kinds of problems, or do they get different kinds of problems to solve?

What talents and points of view do your colleagues have? Who represents a special interest? Who has technical skills or knowledge the group might need? Who is best suited to keeping records? Who should handle arrangements for meetings? What appears to be their initial styles of talk?

Legitimacy of Topics

Some additional considerations apply to groups in discussion classes. Sometimes classroom groups choose topics that are beyond the scope of the participants, like "What Should Be America's policy in Central America?" or "How Can We Eliminate Racial Prejudice?" Groups that deal with such problems must understand that they are engaged in an academic exercise in an area in which they have no authority. No one except the instructor will ever see their output. Groups that address such broad topics often seek only to impress the instructor. It is more effective to choose topics for discussion that have some meaning to the participants. Even if a discussion is conducted in a classroom, there is no reason that it cannot deal with a topic important to the students or that the results cannot be sent to authorities who may have the power to do something about the problem.

If your group was formed because the members were interested in a particular problem, then you can proceed to consider the goals you would like to achieve. On the other hand, if your classroom group has been told to find a problem, then that search must become your first priority. The first source of suggestions ought to be the group itself. What problems can members suggest? Are there particular issues of importance to them? What activities and interests do members have? Do these activities and interests suggest any problems of collective interest? The group may want to examine newspapers and periodicals for possible ideas. Are there current campus, local, national, or international problems worthy of deliberation? What possibilities are suggested by examining letters to the editor? What current controversies are being talked about on listener-participation radio or television talk shows? What possibilities are suggested by the content of everyday conversations?

Considering these suggestions and others that your instructor might offer should provide your group with a list of possible problems. The larger the list, the greater the likelihood that your group can select a problem that interests all members. Be careful, though, that your group does not spend so much time trying to find a problem that it has no time left to spend solving it.

Ascertaining Your Authority

Almost as important as specifying the problem is determining the authority of the group. The classroom group has little power; no one has to cooperate with it. A blue-ribbon government commission can command support from all parts of the community, but a group in Mr. Schmidlapp's discussion class can request help only from the people around it and use general public resources. The classroom group has no budget, and anything that gets done has to be done by the people in the group. A classroom group is a classic example of a group with responsibility but no initial authority. However, groups without authority have been known to move mountains. Neighborhood improvement groups, social action groups, disgruntled employee groups, and protest groups have all been known to start with no authority, no resources, and little power, yet they sometimes change the entire community or organization. By inquiring into what must be done to reach an authority, members of the group will understand their persuasive responsibility.

Most groups have some authority. They may have the power to summon people to give information, or they may have access to files and records. They may even have funds for travel or for secretarial support. Most important of all, they will know who is to receive their final report and what the final report is to contain. That information can help the group define its task and parcel out work to the various members.

Whether your group has much authority or none, the members must understand at the outset what they are up against. This is why it is so important not to slough off the task of understanding the charge to the group. Time must be taken to talk about it and to make sure members understand it, for it provides the impetus to goal-setting.

Knowing When You Are Done

Another important matter to understand is how the group will know when its work is over. What will happen when the group has finished its task? What will the final report look like? What address will be on the envelope that contains it? What will happen to it when it gets to its destination? Raising these questions at the outset will help the group establish realistic goals.

Some groups may be able to get a clearer vision of their final product than others. A group of concerned citizens trying to reduce accidents on a busy highway could set as its goal elimination of accidents; yet such a goal could take the group forever, and chances are that the members do not have that much time. Instead, the group needs to visualize intermediate steps as goals: asking the state highway commission for a traffic light, getting it installed, pressuring the city council for a traffic census, petitioning the police for extra patrols at peak traffic hours. When the ultimate goal is distant, the group must set lesser goals first. On the other hand, a group designated to screen candidates for a position is clearly through with the task when it transmits the paper nominating the required number of candidates to the hiring officer.

For most groups, the final product is some kind of action, which may include a presentation and/or a written report. Reports and presentations can vary in length and complexity, but they usually include a preamble detailing the nature of the problem. The solution will be presented, and sometimes discussion of solutions that were rejected. Some reports may include argument directed either to the decision-maker so to some identified constituency; others may include a plan for administration along with the solution. During the charge period, the contents of any future final presentation or report must be specified so everyone can see the whole task. It is important that a group know when it is done. Finishing authorizes you to have a party or some other appropriate celebration —unless, of course, you are in one of those groups whose reward for completion of a task is another task.

Looking at Leadership

Make sure you know who the authorities are in the group. Did you have a say in selecting the leader? If not, who selected the leader? What authority does the leader have? What style does the leader use? What power does the leader have over your grade, career, or life? Can you get rid of the leader if you find him or her to be ineffective?

GENERAL OUTCOMES OF PHASE ONE

Your classroom activities are legitimate rehearsal for group participation in industry, government, and community. No matter where your group is located, nothing should be done until everyone involved understands the nature of the task. The actual discussion about your charge must center on what your group needs to know about its end product and its rights, privileges, duties, and obligations. With these things clear, the group is on its way to achieving the desired end. At the end of this phase of discussion, the members should understand the following points.

How the Group Articulates with the Larger Organization

In class, this means the instructional system. You must know the importance of the assignment, the method of grading, the learning goals. What must you convince the instructor of in order to earn an A?

In a business, government agency, or community, you must know whether the group has legal standing, who receives the report, and above all, the scope of authority of the group. Who must be convinced in order to make your solutions operative?

What Brought the Group Together

What is the occasion for the meeting? Is this a standing group that meets regularly? If so, what has been its history? What kinds of problems does it work on? What happens to its output? What has been its record?

If it is an ad hoc group brought together for a specific purpose, who decided what the purpose is? What is the outlook for the future? How urgent is the matter under consideration?

Who the Members Are

How did you get picked for the group? If it is a volunteer group, what do the volunteers represent? What skills, attitudes, knowledge, and personal interests are represented in the group?

The Rules of the Game

What are the rules of order? What resources are available? (Consider meeting space, furnishings of the facilities, expenses, secretarial and clerical help, deadlines, formats for solutions, etc.) You will also want to know what legal, practical, and ethical limitations are placed on you at the outset.

Defining the Output

Does the group turn out a written or oral report? How long should it be? Who is it directed to? Who will be responsible for preparing it (if written) or delivering it (if oral)? What happens after that?

There is often no formal written report of this stage of discussion, but the group's conclusions ought to be entered into a group record. There may be times during subsequent discussion when the group will want to refer to its original understandings.

For some groups, especially those established by a higher authority, the precise charge may be put in writing. A written record of a group's charge offers several benefits. It serves, first, as a sort of contractual understanding between the group and the higher authority. It also initially binds the members of the group together through a common understanding of what they are to do. Clarification of the charge reduces the possibility that the group will work on a problem outside its province or one that has been assigned to someone else.

Any administrator who presents a charge to a group usually expects that a particular piece of work will be done. If that precise purpose is not clear, the group should seek clarification. Questions concerning what the group is expected to turn out, who gets it, and what is to be done with it may serve to clarify an otherwise ambiguous charge.

Whenever possible, a group's record should include not only the charge, but some kind of description of where the group fits in a larger scheme. If the group is a voluntary association, the members should agree on their own conception of the direction of their efforts. Are they going to try to persuade the local school principal, traffic administrator, or city council, or are they simply going to seek publicity for their ideas in the local paper? Are they going to make a presentation to a large and influential organization or agency to try to get action on their behalf? Such decisions should be made early, when formulating the charge. A group may adjust its goals as facts are obtained or as the situation changes, but it is pointless to flounder at the outset without an objective.

Whenever a group is part of a larger organization, it should have a copy of the organization chart on file. This chart should identify the chain of command, the people in charge of various parts of the organization, and the people outside the group but involved in the solution to the problem.

Examining its charge carefully will also help the group deploy its resources. This is another important reason for recordkeeping. The group ought to be able to check back to make sure it is not moving down blind alleys. Groups are easily sidetracked into working on topics that are captivating and avoiding the hard work involved in the topic on which they are charged, unless they keep reminding themselves about their main business. During the discussion of the charge, arrangements should be made for recordkeeping, notification of membership, distribution of agendas, and other housekeeping business.

Some groups, especially those functioning within organizational settings, may be fortunate enough to have the services of a professional secretary or stenographer who will prepare and distribute minutes of meetings. Other groups, including classroom groups, will need to select a recorder or agree that the members share that responsibility. The use of a tape recorder is a valid substitute for formal recordkeeping, although sometimes groups find they have stored more than they can possibly use. Decisions should be made about what is worth saving. Some recorders dictate minutes and records more easily than writing them down. The problem with tape-recorded records, however, is difficulty in distribution. Somehow the membership of the group has to have access to stored information.

It is seldom necessary to keep records of everything that is said, though some formal groups may require such transcripts. The items listed under outcome in the outlines at the beginnings of Chapters 8 through 13 serve as general guidelines for recordkeeping. In most instances, groups will want to keep a written record of these decisions.

MEMBER TASKS IN PHASE ONE

In Chapter 1 we presented basic guidelines for discussion. Understanding these guidelines and selecting behaviors that support and demonstrate them are important member responsibilities throughout all stages of discussion, but this is especially true of this first stage. Your participation will help establish the tone and style of deliberations and will affect future interactions and relationships. Participation during this phase will be instrumental in contributing to the thoroughness, efficiency, and ultimate productivity of your group.

Your Options

By the time you reach the end of this book, you will undoubtedly be tired of being reminded that you have options, but you do. At this point, you have the option of raising necessary questions about the nature of the task. Why has the group come together? If by assignment, what is being asked for? Does the group task seem to be clear? If not, what needs to be known? If necessary, repeat what you have heard to make sure you heard it correctly. If you are participating in a classroom discussion, this is the time to understand the nature of the assignment and to clarify what is expected of your group.

Asserting Your Position in the Group

This is also the time to raise questions and make statements about your own position within the group. Are the reasons you volunteered to be a member of the group potentially useful to your group? You may want to say something about them. How about the others? Do you know who they are? Why are they participating? Try to assess what your colleagues expect from you and from each other. If you were assigned to the group, who assigned you and why? If you are working for a company, try to discover how your membership in the group relates to your total job responsibilities. Can you understand why your background and talents might be of use to this group?

Establishing Agenda and Routines

Another area you will be able to explore during the discussion of the charge is the anticipated schedule or agenda of group meetings. If the task is part of your normal employment, there should be no particular problem. In most cases, time will be made available for your group to meet. If, on the other hand, you have volunteered for the group or have been asked to participate as an assigned activity, you will want to know the demands group meetings will make on your time. How long will it take your group to produce the requested output? An emergency situation may require immediate and extended meetings. You may, on the other hand, be addressing a problem that can be explored in a leisurely fashion over a period of several months. Long-range planning groups are a good example of this kind of problem.

To be a responsible member of your group, you must accommodate to the schedule of meetings and plan your time accordingly. If you are a volunteer participant and if you anticipate demands from other sources that are more important to you than the group, in all fairness to the group you should probably terminate your membership at the outset.

Time Estimates

Furthermore, whatever the time estimate, consider it conservative. The basic law of group problem-solving is that everything takes a good deal longer than you think it will. Problems that appear simple at first become much more complex as you obtain some facts and discover the stake various individuals have in the outcome. Solutions that are easy to state are often not so easy to defend in a final report and are perhaps even more complicated when it comes to generating an administrative plan. Remember that Murphy was a committee chairman when he said, "If anything can go wrong, it will!"

Maintaining Orderly Procedure

Although consideration of a committee's charge involves a great deal of talk about issues and possible solutions, you should avoid anticipating the later phases of the discussion. We have said that the phases of discussion are not necessarily inviolable, but there is an advantage to considering complicated issues in order. If your group gets carried away and begins sharing examples and personal experiences or if someone makes a premature commitment to a solution, the rational order of the process of inquiring may be so disturbed as to render the group ineffective.

Avoiding Premature Decisions

Leader and members should take care to avoid jumping ahead too rapidly. If members choose sides on solutions at the very beginning of a discussion, they may resist reasonable consideration of the factual data your committee has yet to discover. Premature judgments may also prevent your group from considering enough alternatives to arrive at the most effective solution or plan. A discussion group is especially ineffective when it becomes a debating society, and premature commitment to choices almost guarantees that this will happen. Thus, your concern in the first phase of discussion should be that you and the other members reach a full understanding of the task.

Establishing Your Image

Although you have options (remember, we told you that you'd hear it again), your image with colleagues is often shaped during the initial group sessions. During phase one of the agenda you should concentrate on making a variety of contributions so members do not come to expect a particular kind of behavior from you. If you are interested in specialized service to the group like leadership or serving as recorder or information storage and retrieval specialist, you will have your chance during the opening phases.

Establishing Norms

It is important to concentrate on conciliation, respect for others, and conflict resolution during the opening group sessions. Patterns or norms form during the opening sessions, and they are very hard to reverse later on. If the group gets off on the wrong foot and early sessions are argumentative and filled with hostility and conflict, it may be very hard to change the climate or work things out during later stages. Agreement on procedural matters, theoretically, is easier to reach than agreement on substantive issues. That is why most international conferences start out working on procedural issues. The idea is to write a record of success by reaching agreement at the start. This sets a norm for later agreement. Your personal contribution to developing constructive norms is very welcome to the group.

LEADER OBLIGATIONS IN PHASE ONE

In the event the person who convened the meeting is not to serve as discussion leader, that person should at the outset make arrangements for leadership. We remind you again that although leaderless discussion is possible, it is important to know where responsibility lies. Someone must be responsible for keeping records, announcing time and place of meetings, and liaison with the sponsoring organization. Understanding the charge must include some agreement on the way leadership is to be exercised and on any chain of command that may be important to the process of problem-solving.

Appointed Leaders

If your group is a formal one, the leader will probably have been designated in advance and will have had a chance to prepare for the first meeting. If your group is part of a larger organization, the official convener or leader presumably has done homework and has prepared information for the first meeting. Customarily, when an executive appoints a group leader, that leader is briefed on how the problem to be solved fits in the larger scheme of things: how serious the problem is, how urgent it is to find a solution, and what resources are available to the group. Usually the appointed leader is also expected to serve as liaison between the group and the higher authority, providing periodic progress reports and seeking information and advice.

Self-Appointed Leaders

Sometimes the leader or convener of a group is self-appointed; that is, the leader is the person who pulled a group together to deal with some problem. It may be a problem in the apartment building or the community, or it may be a response to a more general problem in the society. The formation of community interest groups and groups like Mothers Against Drunken Driving are examples of leaders pulling together persons with similar concerns to form a group. In this case the leader must come fully prepared with information to satisfy the curiosity and concerns of the voluntary members and to focus them on a task.

Recently a group of people in a central Pennsylvania town banded together to form a countywide theater group. The convener of the meeting, the drama coach at the high school, came to the first meeting equipped with details on government grants. He had plans and blueprints for remodeling an old theater in the area, information about other groups in the area that might offer cooperation, and plans for fundraising drives to get the theater group off the ground. He may have been overprepared, for some of the people who came to the initial meeting felt that the convener was pushing too hard. He was able, however, to convince the group that he was eager, not pushy, and in subsequent meetings they learned to appreciate the level of his preparation.

Leadership Preparation

In any event, someone has to be prepared at the first meeting, and the leader dare not assume that it will be anyone else. (Nature hates a vacuum—in most groups where leadership is not predetermined, the person who is best prepared for initial meetings usually ends up as leader.) The leader must recognize the importance of the initial phases in influencing members' attitudes toward the problem and in stimulating their interest. The leader needs to be ready to handle any questions, ease any fears, and meet with solid information any concerns about where the group stands and what is expected. Ideally a first meeting takes care of all these matters, so the group can get right to work after its first exploratory session. Most important is not to go too far or press too hard at initial sessions. If a group overreaches itself, it is very hard to backtrack and reconstruct the foundation.

Leadership Tone

The tone of leadership tends to be set at early meetings. By encouraging members to talk and giving their questions careful attention, the leader can set a norm for participation. If questions cannot be answered immediately, the leader can set another pattern by generating a system that ensures answers to questions are provided at the next meeting, either by the leader or by members who volunteer or are designated to prepare answers. A leader should not be afraid to divide the labor. By passing questions on to others, leaders indicate that they welcome cooperation in leadership, thus encouraging other members to engage in leadership acts. The spirit of goodwill necessary to move the group ahead requires sharing the work. Goodwill does not necessarily mean that members socialize and be good friends; rather, it means that all should be knowledgeable, willing, and responsive to the efforts of others.

Wrapping It Up

The leader's final obligation in any first session is to make certain that all agreements are recorded and that there is a plan for the remainder of the meetings. The leader may take the initiative in appointing or having elected a recorder-secretary, or may assume the role personally until some appropriate arrangement can be made. Once again, the pattern of keeping careful records that are made available to all should be set at the first meeting. These records will be very important in the future. This is one of the most important reasons for avoiding leaderless groups. Members may assume leadership roles at any time during substantive discussion, but no group should take it for granted that volunteers will spontaneously assume responsibility for the logistics and liaison required of most problem-solving groups.

AN UNSPOKEN CONTRACT FOR SERIOUS GROUP
PROBLEM-SOLVING

To conclude this chapter, we want to review what we have said about group discussion in general. This review takes the form of a statement of the obligations assumed by each individual group member. The unspoken contract might sound something like this:[1]

> I am not here to waste my time, to make idle chatter, or to solve my personal and emotional problems. I am not here to make friends or do combat with enemies. I am here for a purpose, and I suspect that the others here have a purpose as well. I do not expect them to agree with me or to support me in all things I do, but I expect them, like me, to be reasonably dedicated to the accomplishment of the group task that brought us here in the first place.
>
> I know I cannot handle this problem alone. If I could have I would have, because I know that working with a group takes time and effort, and like all other human beings, I would prefer to do the best job I can in the easiest possible way. We all have the same potential strengths and weaknesses, but together we can pool our strengths and overcome our weaknesses.
>
> I have the obligation to speak up, to make my point of view known. If I just sit here, I will waste my time and the time of others. I must present my ideas clearly so that others can understand them well enough to criticize them sensibly, and I must listen to the ideas of others in a critical but not hostile way. It is my job to analyze what is said and to report the results of my analysis.
>
> I understand that group problem-solving is not a haphazard enterprise. I am prepared to curb my enthusiasm and impatience and to follow the steps that will raise our chances of reaching a logical, effective, and well-reasoned solution.
>
> I have the obligation to defend my points of view when necessary. I have no right to be truculent, to polarize the group, or to attack other members. Furthermore, I am not compelled to curb my own personal moral commitments or understandings. Still, I cannot be dogmatic; I cannot demand my way and concede nothing to others. Although I know that agreements are generally imperfect, I must do my share in forging agreements. When I am wrong I must concede it, and I must understand that my ideas may deserve modification just as much as the ideas of other members. Still, controversy is often useful, and I must respect it and learn from it even though it may take a great deal of time. If we become irrevocably divided, I will recognize that division itself may be an "answer" for us.
>
> I know that sometimes groups fail. They fail because individuals get impatient, unreasonable, distracted, or bored. I must take care to avoid these particular "deadly discussion sins." If we do fail, I have the obligation to try to discover what went wrong, but I also know that nothing is gained from accusation and recrimination. We shall simply learn from failure and do better the next time. By the same token, if we succeed I must fight against feelings of overconfidence. Each new group, each new problem, is its own challenge. There is nothing in history or science that will predict the outcome.

And that is the pleasure I take in the process, for I know that I can contribute, and to do so makes me feel more of a human being.

With these understandings in view as the personal outcomes of successful first sessions, we may move on to consider definition and specification of the problem. We are on our way through the standard agenda for group problem-solving.

REFERENCE

1. Adapted from Carroll C. Arnold, *Criticism of Oral Rhetoric* (Columbus, OH: Charles E. Merrill, 1974), pp. 42–43. (Arnold's "Unspoken Contract for Serious Oral Communication" inspired the adaptation to group problem-solving.)

RECOMMENDED READINGS

Goffman, Erving. *The Presentation of Self in Everyday Life.* Garden City, NY: Doubleday, 1959. This entire work is a classic on the rituals of human behavior and misbehavior. Of particular interest is Goffman's discussion of the presentation of self in small-group situations.

Phillips, Gerald M., and Eugene C. Erickson. *Interpersonal Dynamics in the Small Group.* New York: Random House, 1970. Although this entire book is relevant to students of discussion, of special note are Chapter 2, which discusses entry into the group, and Chapter 4, which considers the interpersonal communication transactions in small-group settings.

chapter 9

Standard Agenda Phase Two: Understanding and Phrasing the Question

GOALS

To agree on what the problem is.

To phrase a question specifying the problem that allows the maximum range of possible answers.

To agree on the type of question (fact, value, policy).

To agree on a focus (symptoms or causes).

OUTCOME

A precisely worded question to guide the group to the most appropriate solution.

MEMBER TASKS

1. To raise questions about the nature of the problem.
2. To register preliminary attitudes about the nature and severity of the problem.
3. To offer information about the history and causes of the problem.
4. To point out what information is needed to begin the study of the problem and to assist in obtaining it.
5. To make proposals about the wording of the question.

LEADER OBLIGATIONS

1. To ascertain that all members understand the problem.
2. To guide members to tasks they can perform that will equip them to participate in future phases of discussion.
3. To make sure the group understands the cause-symptom issue and how it has been resolved.
4. To make sure members understand differences among questions of fact, value, and policy, and agree which type of questions they will pursue.

5. To make sure that group understandings are reflected in the wording of the question.
6. To make sure the question is appropriately written into the record.

"Clearly, what we need is new equipment," Smith declared to the group. "We'll never meet increased production schedules without it." "I disagree," responded Jones, "new equipment won't solve anything as long as we keep the same personnel in that unit. It's time that we cleaned house and showed them we mean business." "Nonsense," said Johnson, "both of you are talking stupidly. There must be some way to generate a campaign to work on the causes of this problem!" Foster, the old vice-president, interrupted: "I think we'd better go back to the beginning and try to find out what our problem is." Too many discussions begin like this one, and too seldom is there a member like Foster who knows the group needs to back up to initial issues.

Moving too quickly can seriously hamper a group. Becoming solution-centered before the group has become problem-centered is a real hazard. Although disagreements about solutions can be productive in later phases of discussion, they are seldom useful until the group has agreed on the precise nature of the problem and has formulated a question to guide its deliberations. The primary goal of phase two is to accomplish both these tasks, and this chapter will describe how to do it. By taking the time to understand a problem and to generate a question that encourages good inquiry, your group can increase the likelihood that your work will be efficient, productive, and consequently satisfying.

When members propose solutions prematurely, they prejudice the case. They predispose themselves to think only along certain lines. Once the group becomes solution-oriented, it is very hard to do the thorough job of foundation-building an effective group needs. In phase two the idea is to get focus, to lay the ground rules for the content of the discussion. Phase one set the form of the discussion. It specified who was to do what, when work was to be done, where the group was to meet, what the amenities were to be, how long meetings would last, and how the group would know when it was done. Phase two seeks a definition of the topic. It lays out the limits of talk, ruling on ideas that relate to the topic of the charge and specifying the criteria by which digressions can be identified.

GOALS AND OUTCOMES OF PHASE TWO

Once a group understands its charge, the next phase is to word its problem in the form of a question so that:

1. All members of the group understand it in the same way. Unless members agree on what they are talking about, they will talk past each other.
2. The question defines whether the group is to find facts, evaluate a situation, solve a problem, make a decision, or lay down a policy. These types of questions are nested. A group that seeks to evaluate a situation must first find facts. Groups that seek to solve problems must evaluate condi-

tions; so must decision-making groups. Groups that seek to lay down policy must have a general overview of the situation, including facts, evaluations, problems and solutions, and decisions previously made and their effects.

3. The question guides the group to discussion of symptoms, causes, or both. Sometimes groups face emergency situations where the best they can do is put "bandaids" on recent wounds; this is a symptomatic focus (a citizens' group considering ways and means of cleaning up after a flood, for example). Sometimes groups face serious situations by investigating how they came about; this is a causal focus (the citizens' commission designed to develop ways and means of permanent flood control, for example). Most of the time groups must deal with both symptoms and causes of problems.

Even though a committee's charge may specifically ask for a written report detailing a solution to a problem, the charge rarely contains an exact *definition* of the problem itself. The board of directors may understand there is something wrong with workers' morale; they do not know the details. It is rare that those who identify the problem know the details. Legislatures have special committees to investigate the details of problems before legislation is proposed. Investigating committees not only seek facts that describe the problem, they also solicit opinions from experts, as well as people who have a stake in the outcome. Thus, a charge provides instruction about the region of the problem, but not its details. The reason a problem must be carefully phrased is to focus the energies of all members of the group in roughly the same direction.

To begin phrasing the problem, group members will need to test themselves on their understanding of the background of the problem, the setting in which it occurs, the reasons it is seen as a problem, and so forth. To guide you, we provide the following set of standard questions that can help the group at this stage. In this phase of discussion, the group must concentrate on preparing a careful history of the problem, as well as on understanding why the matter has become an issue now. The following outline identifies the questions that must be asked before a problem can be suitably phrased.

I. How did this issue come up? (Who decided there was a problem at all? Is it the result of routine evaluation? Is there some kind of emergency? Check the charge for information about the source of the problem.)
   A. Is everybody similarly aware of it? Is it a problem for the "brass," or do the troops see it as a problem? (When workers in the auto industry were receiving top wages, they did not see the same economic situation that the boards of directors saw.)
   B. Did it arise at the complaint of an injured party or parties? Who complained? Who got hurt? How seriously? Does that injury have anything to do with the common good? (A lawsuit from an aggrieved customer may be an isolated case. On the other hand, it may be a sign of declining product quality.)
   C. Did it arise out of another issue? Sometimes solving one problem leads to another. It's easy enough to lay off workers to cut company costs, but

if everyone lays off workers, who will have enough money to buy the products? Remember, in the systems approach, issues and solutions are interrelated.

    D. Is someone trying to anticipate trouble before it arises? What evidence do they have there is or will be a problem? Are we making a mountain out of a molehill? Is there some solid evidence to support projection of an upcoming problem?

    E. Are other groups dealing with this problem? Maybe this is a generalized problem. Maybe we can't deal with it alone. Maybe we'll have to work with others to solve it.

II. Has this issue come up before?

    A. Is it a recurrent problem? Has it happened before? What did we do about it then? How did that work? (This echoes an old vaudeville joke: "Doctor, I got a pain here." "Did you ever have it before?" "Yes." "Then you got it again.")

    B. What other bodies have dealt with it? Has the government dealt with it? With what effect? Have private citizen groups dealt with it? How about other companies? We can learn from the experience of others.

    C. How similar were they to us? No point looking to some other type of operation for help if there is no analogy possible.

III. How did other bodies deal with it?

    A. Did they bury it? One of the easy ways to deal with problems is ignore them. A distinguished college administrator once said, "I never deal with problems. Only 5 percent of problems ever become crises. I only deal with crisis. I don't work as hard that way." Sometimes things just work themselves out.

    B. Did they partly solve it? Groups often quit before they complete their job. They are satisfied with partial solutions. How many parts of solutions can you find?

        1. What did they solve?

        2. What did they miss?

        3. What was the residual effect?

        4. Did any previous solutions bring undesirable side effects?

        5. Has anything been done about those unexpected events?

IV. Is there anything we can learn from what has been done before?

    A. In what way are conditions similar?

    B. In what way are conditions different now?

    C. In what way are the groups similar?

    D. In what way is personnel similar?

Your group may use any or all of these questions, as it sees fit. The answers will help you get a preliminary picture of the problem, which will, in turn, help you to phrase that problem. Remember, though, as your group works through these questions, that the focus of your inquiry ought to be on gathering background information. Be careful that your group does not leap ahead to premature discussion about solutions. The search for background information will enable you to understand the problem in a preliminary way; you will then be ready to convert the problem to a usable question. This conversion to a question is necessary in order for the group to focus on discussion of the facts in the case. Phases two and three are very closely related. The questions asked to phrase the question provide information to discuss once the question is phrased. The background information gathered in phase two leads to identification of necessary information to seek in phase three.

PHRASING THE QUESTION

The main concern in phrasing a discussion question is quality. The question must be posed so that it does not polarize the group, so it does not beg the question, and so it allows for the widest range of inquiry and potential answers. It must specify who is to act (the subject of the question) about what (the object of the investigation). Questions that start "What are we to do?" imply that it is the discussion group that takes action. Questions that start "What is the Griffle Company to do?" do not specify who is to act. The appropriate subject of the question is usually the agency that made the charge. "What should the president (board of directors) of the company do?"

The idea of phase two is to keep group members focused on the problem until they understand it well enough to direct their work. Proper wording of the question can stimulate inquiry rather than debate, and it is inquiry in which you want your group to engage. The question "What can be done to meet future energy needs?" is open to a variety of answers. The question itself, however, is unspecific. It does not say who is to do something. If it were worded "What can we do to meet future energy needs?" it would at least focus on a particular group. If the group had some status in the field of energy, the answer could have some real clout. However, if the group is a voluntary association of neighbors, the "we" wording might make them feel the effort was futile. They might prefer "What proposals do we want our congressional representative to support in the field of energy?" This wording would focus attention on the group and on the direction of the solutions, but it would limit the group's considerations to proposals that had already been made. The group might prefer to generate its own energy policy and report it to a friendly legislator. In this case the question might be, "What advice do we wish to give our representative about our position on energy?"

This discussion presumes that the members of the group have some common understanding of what is meant by the word "energy." To clarify that term, it might be necessary to specify the problem by asking, "What advice do we wish

Questions that are answerable and related to the problem facing the group can produce productive discussion. (Eckert, EKM-Nepenthe)

to give our congressman regarding our position on nuclear reactors in our region?" Wording the question this way would assume more status for the voluntary group, and since the members are local residents, are able to vote in congressional elections, and are dealing with local matters, their representative might be very much interested in what they have to say.

We may conclude that just because there is a perplexity, there is not automatically a properly phrased question. "Should we encourage the development of nuclear energy?" looks like a question, but it does not make clear who is to do what about what. We do not know what "encourage" looks like, we have no definition for "nuclear energy," and we do not know where we are to encourage anything. It may well be that nuclear energy is to be encouraged in Basutoland because there is no hydroelectric power, but discouraged in Pennsylvania because it would interfere with the coal industry.

Furthermore, the question is worded in such a way that it would tend to polarize people. The logical answer to a "should we" question is answered either "yes" or "no," and this is precisely what we wish to avoid in wording a question for discussion. If we wanted to go all out and choose sides for a debate or for minor combat, we could word the question, "Do we want nuclear power or fossil fuels?" It would be like choosing up sides for a game. Furthermore, the use of the word "want" would nullify the effect of this question, because there is no way of knowing the target of desire. Does it mean "to heat our houses," "to run our factories," "as the major emphasis of national energy policy"? As a rule, groups should avoid questions that can be answered simply "yes" or "no" or with a single word (solution). For example:

> POOR: Should we do something about housing for the elderly?
> POOR: Should we provide apartments or group homes for the elderly?
> GOOD: What advice should the Forest Slough Senior Citizen's Council offer Congressman Phil E. Buster about House Bill 766 on housing for the elderly?

This third question not only permits the group to advise on whether to vote for or against the bill, but also permits it to suggest modifications. It also says who is doing what, so that the group does not exceed its authority. The group knows because of the way the question is worded that it is advisory, and it will not delude itself about its power. Furthermore, by realizing it is advisory, the group may also realize it must persuade the congressman in order to get him to heed its advice. It is very important to keep a realistic notion of who is to do what so as not to become excessively fanciful in proposing solutions.

Another example:

> POOR: What should the company do to beat out the opposition in grommet sales in 1985?
> GOOD: What should be our 1985 sales program for grommets?

Presumably, the group knows the name of its company. To focus on "beating out" another company may be unrealistic, and anyway the word "opposition" does not refer to anything in particular. "Sales program" has specific meaning.

We might assume that the members of the group had some standing in the company. The same procedure would be followed if the question were: "How can production of grommets be increased?" (This begs the question. Maybe what is needed is fewer grommets of better quality or better shipping.), or "How can the production schedule be reduced so that $51,000 can be saved in the next six months?" (You see, the answer to that last question could be, "Let's stop producing grommets, since the Pushkin Company has us beat anyway.") It's premature to settle on saving $51,000 as the solution before a thorough investigation has been conducted.

Still another example:

POOR: Should we meet the students' demands to change graduation requirements?

GOOD: What graduation requirements pertinent to academic majors should the university senate recommend to the trustees?

The first wording is clearly a debate topic. It allows only two options and does not define the word "we." The second wording allows for the possibility that no change at all is necessary and specifies the agency that is to make the changes. The group can work with the prerogatives and powers of that agency in mind. The question also clarifies the meaning of requirements as those within majors. Furthermore, the question makes it clear that the senate can only recommend and the trustees have the power to decide.

To make sure that your question is clear, you need to remove all ambiguous terms and avoid words that have no obvious referents. A good procedure for producing clear questions is:

1. Be sure the members of your group understand the question. You might ask people outside the group to read your question and see whether they understand who is to act about what.
2. Your question should state as specifically as possible the body that is to act, the form of the action, and the problem situation.
3. Make sure there are no yes-no components to the question, expressed or implied. Options should range from nothing to everything.

UNANSWERED AND UNANSWERABLE QUESTIONS

In his book *Levels of Knowing and Existence,* Harry Weinberg suggests a method for attaining precision in phrasing questions.[1] Weinberg makes a distinction between unanswered and unanswerable questions. An *unanswered* question is one for which we do not presently have an answer but for which we can generate a method for finding one: "What, if any, mechanical malfunctions contributed to school bus accidents in 1985?" Safety experts and accident reports for 1985 could be consulted concerning bus accidents. Although you might not be able to make determinations for all cases, you could reasonably rely on technical reports to bring you close to an accurate, general answer. This would be an unanswered, but an answerable, question.

Questions like "What is the role of morality in the home in shaping the degree of commitment students make to academic life?" might make for an interesting philosophical discussion, but there are too many words that cannot be pinned to real events and occurrences. Moreover, the causal relations can never be fully known. Even if a group of experts made up questionnaires that purported to measure morality in the home, student commitment, and the various aspects of academic life, there would be considerable argument about "reliability," "validity," "design procedures," and so forth. It would not even be clear where to look for data. The question is *unanswerable.*

It would be somewhat more useful to ask, "What relationship, if any, can be documented between parental encouragement of study and students dropping out of school?" This wording provides at least some specific questions that can be asked of particular kinds of people. On the other hand, the answers to the questions might still be insufficient for generating a policy to deal with school dropouts.

This leads to another conclusion about questions. Just because questions can be answered does not mean that they are necessarily worth asking. Someone might believe it is interesting to discover the relationship between anxiety in baseball fans on rainy days on which games were canceled. No one might care to do anything about it. Questions are useful to discussion groups only when they are related to some issue of importance to the group or the organization the group represents.

Make sure that your question (1) relates to your problem as presented in the charge, (2) can be answered, (3) is worth answering, and (4) is presently unanswered. Following these guidelines helps you develop a strong foundation for your work.

AMBIGUOUS LANGUAGE

We must warn again that vague and confusing language can creep in and make even the best question unanswerable. "What should be done about increased tuition costs?" fails to specify who is asking and for what reason. "How can tuition costs be brought down?" begs the question, for it assumes that present costs are too high. "What can be done by the financial aid division to provide increased financial assistance to students who are handicapped by the recent increase in tuition?" is somewhat better, but it does not clarify whether the focus should be on providing more money for people presently receiving money or on providing some money for more people. The word "handicapped" may also be confusing, for its connotations may weaken the economic thrust of the initial problem. A question like "What should be the policy of the financial aid division in the light of the recent increase in tuition?" focuses on an agency, specifies that the problem is a symptom of a particular change, and allows the widest leeway for solutions, including the possibility that the group may choose to sustain the present policy.

There is often a temptation to show partiality in phrasing a question. The tuition problem could also have been phrased as "How can the university be prevented from ripping off its students?" This question not only assumes tuition is too high, but clearly fixes guilt. No group can genuinely inquire with that kind of question. On the other hand, equally biased questions like "How can the faculty be made to assume its responsibility for the teaching of writing?" are often readily accepted if the biases they contain are consistent with those in the community. The head of the English department at a large university recently offered just such a question to the university senate. The question was almost accepted, despite the fact that it assumed the problem of responsibility had already been settled, which it had not.

Another kind of bias can be found in phrasing like "How can we stop the potentially disastrous increase in the number of nuclear power plants?" Bias, or at least an assumption that a policy has already been accepted and should be reversed, is reflected in the word "stop"; "disastrous" presupposes that a final evaluation has been accepted by all. However, the purpose of the discussion might well be to deal with the potential hazards of nuclear power plants. An unbiased phrasing might be, "What should be the policy of the Federal Power Commission toward controlling potential hazards from nuclear power plants?" The group could deal with the projection of possible hazards. It would have the leeway to conclude that what was presumed to be a hazard is not hazardous at all, or that the hazard is worth the risk, or that the hazard is minimal, moderate, severe, or critical. It could then propose policy to the commission. In this case the group would be required to examine data, evaluate them, and then proceed to a solution based on prior analysis. This kind of phrasing also allows a group to go to a final solution or stop anywhere along the line if it finds that further discussion is not fruitful. This is generally the most effective way to word a discussion question.

The idea of referring to the proper agency is important. In the first place, when there is a formal charge to a group, the power of the agent presenting the charge must be recognized in posing the group's problem. Thus, if the group is planning a sales campaign for the Grabbitt and Hyde Company, the wording of the problem question must reflect who is going to make what specific decisions and on whose behalf. One wording might be, "What should be the nature of the fall sales campaign by the sales department of Grabbitt and Hyde?" This kind of specificity will help to keep everyone's mind on the real scope of the problem and on who must execute whatever plan is finally produced.

If the group's assignment is very broad, an effective wording might specify the interested parties to be thought about and addressed: "What should be the roles of interested parties (sales, marketing, advertising, public relations, production, and so forth) in implementing the fall sales campaign for Grabbitt and Hyde?" This question allows the group to plan the fall sales campaign and to specify the activities of each of the units that might be involved in some way.

However, inclusiveness has its dangers. Universal problem-solving must be avoided, even when the group is voluntary. Phrasings like "How can we improve the neighborhood?" or "How can we eliminate traffic fatalities in Forest Slough?" set a group up for an almost lifelong task of problem-solving with no specifications about when to stop or to whom to report. Voluntary groups must take real care to specify their targets early in discussion (unless, of course, the discussion is merely an excuse to get the neighbors together once a week). A focused discussion on improving the neighborhood might deal with "What statement do we wish to make to the Forest Slough Zoning Commission at its November meeting?" Such a question requires a complete output; it fixes the target for the output, and it fixes the problem on zoning, which, of course, has something to do with the quality of the neighborhood and yet it is sufficiently open-ended that the group can deal with its choices among the several issues relevant to community zoning. A question on accidents might be worded, "How can the police be optimally deployed to deter accidents in Forest Slough?" This wording also implies a target: the police department. It is sufficiently open-ended that the group could, if the facts warrant, concede that the police are already optimally deployed.

Notice that for voluntary groups we are suggesting that the specification phase of discussion should reinforce the charge. The reason for this suggestion is that voluntary groups often word their questions to charge themselves and to specify the work they are going to do. However, groups assigned to a task do not usually have this freedom to formulate their own charges.

The goal of phase two of discussion is to phrase a question that enables the group to get on with its business efficiently and with clear purpose. Sometimes after fact-finding it is necessary to revise the question to accommodate new information. A carefully worded question will guide your group to effective fact-finding, and each revision will bring you closer to the core of your problem.

To review what we have said so far about discussion questions:

1. The question must be clear in meaning.
2. The question should provide for the widest possible variety of answers.
3. The question should pinpoint who is to act.
4. The question should identify whether the group will focus on symptoms, causes, or both.
5. The question should reflect the limitations placed on the group.
6. The question should avoid explicit and implicit bias and question-begging.
7. The question should be in harmony with the charge. In voluntary groups, the question should specify the charge.

The most effective question is one that indicates some person or agency is to take some action about some set of conditions with some intended effect. For example: "What can be done by our managers to increase our production by 3 percent within the next quarter at expenditures not to exceed $100,000?"

TYPES OF QUESTIONS

The question, once agreed on, informs the group about the type of problem with which it is dealing. Questions may be of fact, value, or policy.

Fact Questions

The simplest possible question is the question of fact, a question that asks about the distinctive nature, scope, and limitations of observable phenomena. A question of fact is asked to determine to what degree something does or does not exist or what its nature is. "What mental health problems are experienced by students at our university?" and "How was the budget expended in 1984?" are questions of fact. Somewhat more subtle are questions like "What patterns of choice, if any, are reflected in students' selection of elective courses?" and "What proportion of students fail to finish college, and what reasons do they give?" Responses to these questions would produce relatively factual, general conclusions. These conclusions might also serve as bases on which an administrator could invite another group to decide whether a problem exists and, if it does, to assess its gravity and possibly propose solutions.

When a group is confronted with a job of fact-finding, a question of procedure is implicitly raised: "How can this group most effectively organize itself to do the job at hand?" Group members and leaders must recognize that much of their fact-finding work may be done outside the group: in libraries, in interviews, in discussion with various authorities. Group meetings are used to examine each bit of factual information: to assess its credibility, to decide to what degree it is related to the problem and the extent to which it might be biased, and to ask about what still needs to be discovered.

Since virtually every group gets involved in some fact-finding, our next chapter will detail the most common methods for examining and assessing facts. Fact-finding is time-consuming and sometimes boring. It is the phase of inquiry in which groups may slip into groupthink by filtering what comes into the group. Therefore, groups should give special attention to getting relevant information, as well as to checking and rechecking the reliability of sources.

Groups function well in interpreting results. Indeed, it is here that groups tend to do better work than individuals. If you find yourself in a group that is devoted exclusively to fact-finding, it is important that you acquire some basic skills in understanding data. You will need these skills to be a contributing member of any such group. You may need to learn about statistical and experimental methods and ways of observing and interviewing. Finally, of course, you need a general ability to reason analytically. If you expect to function in business and industry, you might prepare yourself for fact-finding by taking some college courses in methods and techniques of analysis.

Value Questions

Group members must also deal with questions of value. Such questions deal with the issues of "desirability," "value," or "worth," and are often expressed by statements that embrace or reject a particular attitude. Value questions are raised to help a group decide whether a given set of facts adds up to a problem.

For example, "What is the responsibility of the university in recruiting students from minority groups?" is a value question, for it asks about the desirability and morality of a general course of action. (The group would have to gather facts about the proportions of minority students in the school and then evaluate them to see if there appears to be some problem.) If the group decides that the university does have some specified responsibility, a different kind of question, a policy question, can be raised: "How can the university recruit students from minority groups?" Discussion of the policy question should be preceded by a fact-finding discussion on the question, "What is the state of recruitment of students from minority groups?"

Value questions are also raised by groups that do not seek to do any particular business, but exist to provide their members with opportunities to share opinions, ideas, and interpretations. Groups that discuss "great books" or "great ideas" may deal with questions like "Is Saul Bellow worthy of the Nobel Prize?" "How useful is Aristotelian reasoning in today's politics?" or "How much economic planning is good for the country?" Such questions evoke much good discussion and heated exchanges, and they often sharpen people's insights or ideas. Value deliberations are typically part of policy-making. However, they do not normally produce the kinds of formal decisions that lead to the solution of problems. Our focus is upon purposive, problem-solving group discussion.

Value-based questions can also arise at the point in discussion when fact-finding is complete and the group must decide whether it needs to go on at all. Thus, "Is this situation serious enough to warrant action?" "What priorities should we assign to the various situations we have discovered in our fact-finding?" "Where should we devote the bulk of our human effort and resources?" are questions that are implicit in all policy-making discussions. In any case, it is useful to stop after fact-finding to make sure that everyone agrees on the gravity of the situation; if the problem is not serious enough to warrant concern, the group is free to stop.

Policy Questions

The type of question that most frequently engages problem-solving groups is the policy question. Questions of policy ask about possible actions by some individual, group, agency, or organization. The action can be a decision about some event, it can be the design of a program to remedy some problem, it can be the creation of a set of policy guidelines for an ongoing operation, and it can be a combination of all those things. The kind of group with which this book is primarily concerned is the group that attempts to do something about something. What such groups do may be reach a decision, make a recommendation, or implement a policy.

Essentially, these groups deal with the validity, feasibility, and desirability of courses of action applied to the events or situations that brought the group together in the first place. For example, "What should the Forest Slough City Council declare to be its policy on rezoning area B?" is a policy question. Other policy questions (taken from the weekly agenda of council committees in one town) include: "What can be done to handle the expense of leave time for the police?" "What should be the structure of the administration agency handling the new water legislation?" "How should the Streets and Highways Committee proceed in gathering bids on the extension of Crawdad Avenue?" "To what extent does the council wish to work with the local university in developing a summer intern program?" and "What should be the local policy on the hiring of homosexuals in the police department?" The council of this town will take action on each of these policy questions—sometimes the action of deciding to ignore the question.

Most of these questions involved gathering facts. The problem of rezoning required a complete survey of the local area and surrounding areas by a group of people hired to do the job. The Public Safety Committee sent out several letters to towns of similar size to inquire how these communities handled leave time for police. A subcommittee of the Administrative Committee worked with the town solicitor and a consultant from a management firm to create an administrative plan to handle the new water legislation. The purchasing agent and his two assistants checked the files to find the bidding procedure used in previous road projects similar to the one in question. A joint committee of council members and university professors met on the question of the summer intern program. They invited a federal projects specialist to meet with them to discuss alternatives in federal funding. Finally, two council members and representatives of homosexual organizations met informally to discuss whether there was reason to believe that discrimination existed on the police force.

Although most of the problems just cited led to some action by the council or one of its committees, virtually all of them necessitated fact-finding and value discussion as well. In the following paragraphs we assume that you are going to deal with questions of policy, but we must also recognize that most of those questions will involve you in fact-finding and, very likely, in considering questions of value as you evaluate goals, programs, and situations.

MEMBER TASKS IN PHASE TWO

This phase of discussion is important because if you fail to understand what is going on here, you may very well become confused and slow down the group in later phases of discussion. Most of this phase is devoted to testing yourself to see whether your understanding of the question is the same as that of your colleagues. If you seem to be seeing things differently from the others, you have the obligation to speak up. Common understandings are essential at this point.

If every member tries to keep every other member clear and informed while the question is being worded, some major troubles can be avoided. A careless examination of the history of the question, for example, might lead your group to misunderstand causes and come up with a solution that does not solve the problem or that addresses only part of it. Furthermore, unless the question is worded in such a way that all understand it, you may also find yourself engaged in debate at later stages of the discussion.

Failure of members to participate during this phase of discussion can be directly responsible for the kind of problems we examined in Chapter 1: the feeling that discussion is a waste of time, that individuals were suppressed, that the group was not always focused, and the sense that individuals sometimes acquiesced to others. Note that each of these difficulties could come about because individuals shirked their responsibilities in the stage of formulating the problem question. Member participation is important, and particular types of participation are crucial at this point.

You will need to raise questions about the problem, its nature, and its severity. How long have you or others been aware of the problem? What does it mean to you and to the others in your group? How do you think it affects others, including people outside your group? Is there a need to reconstruct the history of the problem, and to do this publicly, together? Can you identify its onset? What factors seemed to have contributed to the problem? How did it grow? Do you know of any attempts to deal with it? How did earlier groups deal with it? Is any other group trying to deal with it now? What is happening with these groups? Did any earlier solutions solve part of the problem or contribute to its severity?

As you listen to others report and comment on the problem, think of what information is missing and where it could be obtained. By pointing to missing information, you may help the group word its problem so that sensible, comprehensive fact-finding can be carried on.

Make sure that the wording is concise and multivalued and that it reflects necessary limitations. Does the question specify who is to do what? Does the question specify the agency under which the group operates, if this is important? Will your final solution explain who is to do what to whom, or what at what cost and with what intended effect? If you are in a classroom group, you may want to ask your instructor to comment on your question.

LEADER OBLIGATIONS IN PHASE TWO

We remind leaders of their regular duties: (1) to control traffic, (2) to summarize, (3) to introduce new material, (4) to referee conflicts, and (5) to maintain the record and to move the group ahead.

Given the goals, output, and members' obligations for this phase of discussion, obligations of leaders should be clear. Leaders must be particularly careful about keeping their groups centered on problems and not on solutions. They can maintain such a focus by making certain that all group members understand the problem in the same way. Obviously, leaders need to be in command of background information. Those who were appointed in advance should have had a briefing and understand some of the resources available to the group. Leaders who have emerged from the group may not have time to prepare special background information; and they will need to make sure that this information is identified and secured before phase two closes. The leader must restrain the group from jumping ahead until the necessary information is available. The leader will need to help the group coordinate all information-gathering efforts and must also see that tasks are parceled out and completed.

When an adequate understanding of the problem has developed and the leader is sure that everyone understands, it is time to formalize agreement on the question. Whoever is leading the group should be skilled in phrasing problem questions in order to improve upon the members' efforts. The leader may even need to become a "consultant," showing the members how to form a good question and perhaps making some suggestions for the wording of the question if none comes from the group.

When the group reaches agreement on the precise phrasing of its question, the leader should remind the recorder to register the question in the record so that the group can move on to the next phase of the standard agenda. The recorder may wish to make copies of the problem question, with any necessary definitions and agreements about its meaning and scope. Distributing these copies to the members will provide them with a constant reminder of the focus of their deliberations.

Now that the first two phases have been completed, we can turn to the complicated matters of gathering and evaluating information. The next chapter provides guidelines that will enable you to decide what data you need and to evaluate the importance and accuracy of the information you gather.

REFERENCE

1. Harry Weinberg, *Levels of Knowing and Existence* (New York: Harper Brothers, 1959).

RECOMMENDED READINGS

Gulley, Halbert E. *Discussion, Conference and Group Process.* New York: Holt, Rinehart and Winston, 1968. This is an excellent general reference despite rather heavy writing style. Particularly useful is Chapter 4's discussion of preparing for deliberations in the small group. Your authors are of the opinion that the 1968 edition is superior to the newer one.

Wagner, Russell H., and Carroll C. Arnold. *Handbook of Group Discussion,* 2nd ed. Boston: Houghton-Mifflin, 1965. Chapter 3 of this book provides several suggestions for choosing subjects for discussion and offers advice about their phrasing.

Zelko, Harold. *Successful Conference and Discussion Techniques.* New York: McGraw-Hill, 1957. This is another excellent basic work that provides useful pointers on how to prepare effectively for discussion.

chapter 10

Standard Agenda Phase Three: Fact-Finding

GOALS

To obtain information about the nature of the problem, its causes, and history.

To obtain information about similar problems at other places at other times.

To reach a decision on whether symptomatic or causal treatment is appropriate.

Revise discussion question, if necessary.

OUTCOMES

A library of factual information, authoritative statements, and evaluations.

Conclusions about the causes of the problem.

Formal reconsideration of discussion question and, if appropriate, modification in light of discovered facts.

MEMBER TASKS

1. Do necessary research. Find facts, statements of authoritative opinions, and other relevant information.
2. Participate in evaluating reliability and validity of all facts presented.
3. Participate in identifying causes of the problem.
4. Participate in decision about whether symptomatic or causal treatment is necessary.
5. Participate in reconsideration of and rewording the question, if necessary.

LEADER OBLIGATIONS

1. Direct and expedite gathering, evaluating, classifying, and storing information and opinion.
2. Direct and expedite decision about nature of treatment.
3. See to it that the discussion question is evaluated and reworded if necessary.

Without adequate information, group discussions are bull sessions, at best. However, it takes considerable effort to find the kind of information needed to conduct an effective discussion. Many groups evade this step of the standard agenda simply because it is so difficult; others become fatally bogged down in a morass of facts. In this chapter we will show you how to avoid both problems.

Fact-finding cannot be a haphazard process. It is possible to be overwhelmed with facts. For example, the library of a major university once set up a statistics committee, charged with gathering numerical data on the university's operations. The result was something like an un-indexed edition of the *Statistical Abstract of the United States.* The facts were there, but it was impossible to find anything anyone really needed. Successful fact-finding must be a careful process of finding information needed to answer important questions. Each member must participate in figuring out what information is needed, finding it, and evaluating it.

BASIC FACT-FINDING QUESTIONS

To guide your fact-finding efforts, we provide the following set of questions that should be raised about any problems. Consistent use of this set of questions in any discussion spares you the indignities of fact overload, wandering around libraries wondering what to do, or sitting and staring into space wondering what all the fuss was about.

1. *What are the evidences and symptoms of the problems?* Who reported there was something wrong? On what evidence was the report based? What is happening now that was not happening previously? What is not happening that has been happening? Who is complaining about what? Consider the three towns on the bank of House Bayou: Travesty, Mudsink, and Forest Slough. A new factory opened in Travesty. Most of the workers live in Mudsink. In order to get to work they have to go through Forest Slough. Downtown Forest Slough merchants are complaining that traffic is so heavy people are not able to stop and shop. Factory management is complaining about congestion that keeps workers from getting to their jobs on time. Workers are complaining about the tension of getting to and from work. All in all, it is not a pleasant situation.

2. *What is the effect of these symptoms?* Who is being affected? How serious is it? Does it matter? In what way? In our example, virtually everyone is displeased. The citizens of Forest Slough resent their town being used as a traffic funnel. Workers are upset about travel problems. This affects the quality of their work. Factory managers wonder why they opened the plant in the first place.

3. *Has this ever happened before, and how was it handled?* How has the problem been dealt with before in the present locality and in other places? There never have been traffic problems like this in the area. The tri-towns were sleepy little places where people moved slowly. But downstream, in Vapid City, it was necessary to build a traffic bypass to channel cars from Wombatville to Wafflesburg. The state paid part of the cost.

4. *What caused the condition?* What motivated people involved to change what they were doing? Why did the company locate in Travesty? (Could the tax rebate program enacted by the Travesty town council have

anything to do with it?) Why did most of the workers come from Mudsink? (Could the fact that Mudsink is the most populous of the three towns and the Mudsink Mush factory recently went bankrupt have anything to do with it?) Causes may be easy to find; often they are hard to remedy. The group will have to make a decision here about whether to concentrate on the traffic problem (symptomatic focus) or work on the whole economic condition of the region (causal focus).

5. *What have other interested and expert parties had to say about this issue?* First you must define who qualifies as an expert, and on what. Do you need traffic experts, personnel experts, legislators, regional planners, or all of these?

6. *What might happen if the problem is not dealt with?* It is important to estimate possible consequences. The economic consequences take little imagination to calculate. The factory can pull out. But if the factory stays, the downtown area of Forest Slough can be ruined.

7. *In the light of new information, what is our problem now?* The original broad question may have been "What can the town council of Forest Slough do about changed traffic conditions in the downtown area?" Do they warrant changing? Should a regional planning issue be raised? Should the mutual dependency of the tri-towns be studied? Before moving on, the question should be properly revised so the group can work on some manageable problem.

Fact-finding is done to inform the group's activity. Your search for information may reveal there is no problem, or that nothing can be done about what is going on. You may find immediate action is necessary, or you may opt for a long-range program. More likely, you will discover the problem you set out to consider is not the real problem at all, and you must modify your question and refocus your search for information. Fact-finding continues until your question is refined and you have enough information to handle your new question. You should not be overcritical, however; don't wait for *all* the information, for you will never get it.

To demonstrate how universal the preceding questions are, try to apply them to some simple problems in your own college community. Take problems like the cost of textbooks, availability of academic advisors, the losing soccer team, rising tuition costs, the quality of food in the dormitory dining halls, student health care. Phrase a discussion question (see Chapter 9), and then try to figure out what kind of information you would have to seek in order to answer it.

CRITERIA FOR EVALUATING INFORMATION

Information comes in various forms. You may have statements of fact, generalizations, definitions, authoritative statements, and reasoned conclusions. Each must be evaluated against the criteria of credibility and competence, replicability or confirmability, currency, relevance, and sufficiency.

Credibility refers to the reasons for believing the information. A statement is credible if it comes from a believable source, if it can be confirmed, or if it is consistent with other information. Any statement that appears unusual or out-landish must be checked. For example, if you are investigating sales losses in various regions and you get a report that one salesman has increased business by 75 percent, it is good sense to check again for the possibility that inaccurate information was transmitted or unusual circumstances accounted for the unusual fact. Credibility can also be tested by examining biases and prejudices that might exist in information.

Statements that a particular substance is harmless (when all other informa-tion shows it is harmful) may be the result of influence by people with a financial interest in selling the substance. Information that appears biased is not always inaccurate, but whenever bias is suspected, accuracy should be checked.

If you are getting information from an eyewitness, for example, you must check to see why the person was observing and what the person could see. Sometimes eyewitnesses are so startled by what they see that they miss important details. In other cases, eye witnesses are biased and see only what they wish to see. It is important to confirm eyewitness testimony. Lawyers who try criminal cases will tell you that eyewitness testimony is often not reliable and frequently can be refuted through examination of circumstantial evidence. A witness may see a car swerve left when tire tracks show the car swerved right. In such cases, the circumstantial evidence is more trustworthy.

Competence refers to the ability of the reporting source to understand what he or she sees. Untrained personnel can observe technical operations first-hand without having the vaguest notion of what they are seeing. Competent sources are able to understand the details of the event, situation, or process on which they are reporting. For example, a recent newspaper story reported that detectives

Interviewing can often produce accurate and extensive information. (Leinwand, Monkmeyer)

present at a hostage situation were "unarmed." The reporter simply did not know that plainclothes detectives keep their weapons concealed. This is a trivial example, but it illustrates that information is not reliable if it does not come from someone who understands the details of what is being observed.

It is important to ask what the source knows. Inquire about training, sophistication with what was being observed, and general knowledge of the situation. A machinist and an engineer will give very different accounts of the state of the equipment. Neither is necessarily wrong, because each has been trained to look at different aspects of the operation. In general terms, accountants are more likely to understand financial details and overlook important aspects of production. Production engineers will spend little time thinking about money. That is why a great many different kinds of people are needed in discussion groups.

A great deal of information is gained from experimental research. Many problems can be clarified through formal investigation. If the question is about what machine produced the most defects, formal observation of production accompanied by statistical tests will produce reliable information. Ideally, every discussion group should have a member sophisticated in research design and able to understand technical reports of experiments. If such a member is not available, an expert may be consulted. Experimental data are often so complicated they can mislead those not trained in interpretation. Furthermore, all experiments must be replicable; that is, other people should be able to set up the experiment and obtain similar results. Conflict in experimental findings is the same as conflict in eyewitness testimony. Until there is some way to confirm the results or gain a consistent story, the information must be taken with a grain of salt.

Currency means information must not be out of date. In a recent argument over school financing, an expert witness reported on how a particular state provided funding to local districts so that all districts got a minimum level of resources regardless of their own ability to tax. The problem was, the expert was describing a situation from 20 years ago. The state in question changed its practices a decade ago, and no longer provides such extensive financial aid. It is easy to find the information you would like to find if you do not pay attention to its date. All information should be checked for date, and questions must be raised about whether there is even more current information.

Relevance is a frequently misused word. It is a transitive verb—that is, something cannot just be "relevant," it must be relevant "to" something. Fact-finding groups often find themselves overdosed with high-quality information that has nothing to do with the topic they are investigating. By referring back to the list of questions at the beginning of this chapter, you can discover whether an item of information is relevant to your problem-solving. If it helps answer those questions, it is relevant to your group. If it does not, file it for possible later use.

Sufficiency means adequacy—whether you have enough information to meet your needs in discussion. When information is sufficient, you know enough to draw conclusions about the problem. The process of fact-finding never ends; there is always something new to be learned. On the other hand, to meet the charge you need to move on to the next phase of discussion as quickly as possible. The following questions should help you make the decision about whether or not you have sufficient information.

1. Do you know the evidences and symptoms of the problem? Can you make a statement about what is going on that should not be or what is not happening that should be?
2. Do you know who is being hurt and how? Can you estimate the possible consequences if the situation continues? Have you gotten information from representative people who are being injured or who might be affected by solutions to the problem?
3. Do you have background on the problem? Do you know when it started and how it progressed? Have you gotten information directly from people involved in it? Have you examined other attempts to deal with it to find out how well they worked and what more needs to be done?
4. Have you gotten information about similar cases? Are you able to argue that the cases are similar?
5. Have you gotten information from authorities representing various points of view? Have you identified the best experts and found out what they think?
6. Are you able to set priorities? Do you know how urgent it is to find a solution to the problem?

Once you have enough information to answer these questions, you can decide whether to modify the original question. Understanding the facts in the case frequently enables groups to rephrase their questions more specifically. Furthermore, you should be able to decide whether you must deal with symptoms of the problem, modify causes, or deal with both. It is also possible that information gathering may lead a group to conclude that there is no problem.

EXAMINING PARTICULAR TYPES OF INFORMATION

Information comes in various forms. Each requires careful examination before it can be accepted as credible. Much of what you discover will come as statements from authorities made either in person or in published materials. Authorities can make statements of fact or express opinions. They make claims for their authority. For example,

> Said one umpire, "I call them as I see them."
> Said the next, "I call them as they are."
> Said the third umpire, "They are *nothing* til I call them!"

Your use of authorities must follow the principle of *caveat emptor*—let the buyer beware. You have the right to believe what you wish, and the obligation to defend it. That means authoritative opinion must be checked two ways; by checking the authority himself or herself, and by checking the statements made. Use the following cautions as your guide to credibility:

1. What form does the authoritative statement come in? Authorities sometimes write books. So do people who are not authorities. One way to estimate the reliability of an authority is to check the form of the statement. A casual statement made in social conversation should not be taken seriously. A statement made in an interview should be checked. The authority should have a second look at it so errors can be corrected. It should also be checked against other statements about the same topic. If it is inconsistent with other statements, the reason for the discrepancy should be checked. A discrepant statement may mean the authority is biased. It may also mean an important new discovery or idea. Double-checking discrepant statements allows you to find out which is the case.

Also, check the source of publication. Sometimes publishing houses print books by famous people who know little or nothing about a topic. Sometimes a person's name is used on a book written by a ghost. Some people pay to have their books published. A qualified authority is usually published by a reputable house without obvious bias and at the publisher's expense. When a person pays to have a book published, it should not be taken seriously.

2. Find out what the authority really knows. Some years ago, a Nobel Prize winner in physics began issuing statements about genetics. The statements were provocative and drew a great deal of attention. The physicist claimed geneticists were biased against him. On the other hand, experts in genetics claimed the physicist did not know enough to interpret information accurately. There were few corroborating opinions, virtually no corroborating evidence. This was an example of an authority in one area making statements in another. Be sure your authorities are legitimate experts on the topic they discuss.

Check for biases. Be suspicious if an authority expresses ideas to the advantage of those who control his or her salary and advancement.

Finally, be sure to check specific factual statements. If there are footnotes or references, be sure to check to see if information is quoted accurately from other sources. Consistent misquotes or inaccurate representation of information by your authority sheds doubt on his or her opinions.

3. Make sure your authority assumed the burden of proof. If your authority's ideas are inconsistent with other information, be sure to examine the evidence on which the statements are based. When there is an inconsistency, those who express the minority opinion have the obligation to show why their ideas differ from those of established authorities. This was the problem faced by Louis Pasteur when he attempted to show the French Academy how bacteria caused disease. Pasteur had to perform several delicate experiments before his colleagues would accept his ideas.

4. If you are using authoritative or factual statements drawn from abstracts or reports, you will need to check the reputability and bias of the publishing source. Government data are usually reliable, but they are often presented in overwhelming quantities. You will need to sort them carefully and make sure you get precisely what you are after. Corporations generally do not misrepresent information in their reports, but they may omit negative data or emphasize material that sheds the best light on the situation.

5. Reports of experimental findings or generalizations must be checked

against similar investigations. Where possible, the material should be retested. We have already advised how important it is to have contact with someone skilled in evaluating experimental designs and findings. Generalizations drawn from experimental studies, surveys, questionnaires, and systematic observations should legitimately represent the data. Do not accept generalizations without checking the data on which they are based.

6. When examples are offered, be sure they fit the generalization they are designed to illustrate. Examples are not proofs in themselves. They are offered to illustrate or clarify complicated generalizations. To be effective, they must include the main elements included in the generalization. If, for instance, you use an example to illustrate the situation of the typical mortgage holder, you must select a case that contains *all* the elements of typicality. This is often hard to do, for generalizations are averages, and it is virtually impossible to find an "average" family. Some authorities will construct an example to illustrate the average. Be alert to the use of hypothetical examples and regard them as explanations, not demonstrations.

THE USE OF LANGUAGE

A major problem you will encounter in fact-finding is slippage in the meaning of words. It is very hard to remain consistent in the use of language. For one thing, interesting writing or speaking demands the use of synonyms, which connote shades of difference in meaning. To avoid semantic arguments, you must be aware of how various types of definitions are used.

Dictionary definitions record the historical meaning of a word. Dictionaries are records of how words have been used. For example, the common word "ecology" has these definitions in a current dictionary:

> ECOLOGY. . . . 1. The branch of biology dealing with the many relations between organisms and their environment; bionomics. 2. the branch of sociology concerned with the spacing of people and of institutions and their resulting interdependency. 3. a political movement organized to protect or conserve air, bodies of water or particular units of plant or animal life from threats from encroaching industrialism. . . .

Suppose you encountered this phrase in a report: "We are concerned with the ecology of the community." Does this refer to the organisms that live in the community, relationships between community institutions, or political activity on behalf of the environment? To clarify the sentence, the author would need to use an operational definition.

Operational definitions are technical specifications of what a word means in a particular document. "By 'ecology' we refer to the relationship between the company and community institutions with which it comes in contact—for example, police, schools, business organizations, and financial units of government." Operational definitions are often used in scientific reports. They specify the conditions of meaning in a particular experiment or study. You must be alert to these types of definition, for they specify which of many possible dictionary definitions are referred to when a word is used. Furthermore, you must be alert to definitional slippage—that is, changes in meaning for the same word throughout a document.

Other types of definitions are used to make writing more interesting or to specify meaning even further. *Categorization* is used to explain the elements or components of a large definitional unit. For example, "We will consider ecology to be relationships between company and pollution enforcement agencies, company and citizen action groups, company and its customer production requirements." That definition offers three subheads for the word "ecology" and also provides some guidance about the sections of the report to follow.

Some documents will contain *metaphorical* definitions, like "Ecology is a community's family portrait." Such a definition adds no particular meaning, but it highlights aspects of meaning in order to make information more dramatic or more readable.

AN EXAMPLE OF COLLECTIVE REASONING

During this phase of discussion, group members work together to gather and evaluate information. By paying attention to the basic questions we provided at the beginning of this chapter, the group can guide itself through fact-finding so that its problem is crystal clear. The more lucid the problem, the more likely the group can find a suitable solution.

Consider the case of the Planning Commission of the Borough of Forest Slough. It has been asked by the borough council to come up with a proposal to handle the "downtown traffic problem" that has drawn a number of citizen complaints. The Planning Commission is an advisory body. It cannot pass legislation, but it can prepare legislation for consideration. It can also decide whether legislation is needed to solve a problem, or whether some other means can be used. Here is how it dealt with the questions.

What Are the Evidences and Symptoms of the Problems?

Here is a summary of the facts and important opinions they gathered.

1. A survey taken by the Chamber of Commerce last year showed that 45 percent of people living in Mudsink and working in Travesty reported being made late going to or coming from work at least once during the last three months. Residents of the west side of Forest Slough who work downtown or on the east side complain about being late both morning and evening.
2. The Chamber of Commerce reported it had received at least one complaint from every merchant in the downtown area about shipments and deliveries being delayed during the last year. Four of the larger stores presented detailed reports on how their business had been impeded because of delayed deliveries.
3. The chief of police reported he was unable to assign enough personnel to manage traffic during peak periods and still be able to cope with other responsibilities. The chief also reported ambulances, fire, and emergency vehicles had to be routed around the downtown area during peak periods. He reported that he, the fire chief, and the supervisor of the emergency room

at the local hospital feared the consequences should there be an emergency downtown during a peak traffic period.
4. An analysis of business flow in the downtown area showed a drop in revenue of approximately 2 percent because of inability of customers to reach the stores or to find parking places within reasonable proximity.

What Caused the Conditions?

The commission came up with the following statement of causes.

1. There is no regional traffic flow problem. Suburbanites traveling to and from work are forced to pass through downtown. Factories on the outskirts of town all have the same working hours.
2. The blocking of Della Street to make a downtown mall last year cut one major traffic route through the downtown area. The parking and traffic pattern designed to cope with this change appeared inadequate to handle the results.
3. Failure to complete the Luke Quarm Freeway has forced commuters to use the most congested routes.
4. Campaigns to use public transportation for access to and through downtown have failed, since public transportation also moves slowly, and some industries lie outside the area serviced by public transportation.

What Is the Effect of These Symptoms?

Formal complaints, petitions, and legal actions have been received from three neighborhoods adjacent to the downtown area. Minor traffic accidents in the downtown area have risen 18% in the last year. Two major merchants have already moved to peripheral shopping malls, and several report they are making plans to move.

Has This Ever Happened Before, and How Was It Handled?

There have been a number of recent events affecting traffic.

1. When Polly Ticko was mayor, she blocked all traffic legislation because of lack of funds to make necessary improvements.
2. The opening of the Della Street Mall in response to merchant pressure was not compensated by improved traffic patterns.
3. No one anticipated the rapid growth of two of the peripheral industries resulting in increased traffic pressure.
4. Traffic had never really been a problem in Forest Slough. There was no legislation other than speed limits and parking zones.
5. The Si Burnetic one-way street plan had been shelved during the election campaign.
6. Other communities in the region have instituted overall traffic plans. Elephant's Breath instituted a one-way street system to facilitate traffic to peripheral industries. (Elephant's Breath lies on the other side of the industrial zone east of Forest Slough.) Effluencetown applied for and received state

and federal bypass money and used it to route traffic to the industrial zone. Other towns in the region are suffering from similar traffic problems.

What Might Happen If the Problem Is Not Dealt With?

There are rumors about stores planning to close or move from the downtown area. One manufacturer has threatened not to expand his plant because of the problems with the traffic flow.

What Have Other Interested and Expert Parties Had to Say About This Issue?

1. The Taxpayer's Association has issued a statement objecting to any new taxation for traffic improvement.
2. E. C. Duzzit, city engineer, presented a formal report to the council from a consultant hired to evaluate traffic flow. The report was extensive and concluded nothing would improve without significant modification of streets and roadways at considerable cost.

In the Light of New Information, What Is Our Problem Now?

The commission redefined its problem as follows: "How can traffic flow be facilitated in downtown Forest Slough during peak periods with no major expenditure of funds?" The words "facilitated" and "major expenditure of funds" were further specified. "Facilitated" was operationally defined as "return to the traffic rate prior to the opening of the downtown mall." "Major expenditure of funds" meant "no bonding or tax increase."

Note the variety of sources Planning Commission members used to obtain information. Data on traffic problems are virtually endless. The commission could have gotten bogged down in study. However, most of the members were up to date on current writing and thinking by experts on traffic flow. Their imperative was to get information on the local scene. They relied on testimony from interested parties, recognizing that though interested parties might disagree, the *way* they saw the issue was itself part of the problem.

Later on in the discussion process, it might be necessary to ask specific questions in order to handle the details of a solution. For the moment, however, the commission is on track, focused on *a* problem, if not *the* problem, and prepared to move to the next step of discussion.

MEMBER TASKS IN INFORMATION GATHERING

Obtaining Materials   Group members must be prepared to tap all resources in order to get information. Often the first stops are the library and information retrieval systems. Books, periodicals, reports, reference works, almanacs, tables and charts, on-line computer information, company archives, minutes and similar records, financial reports, and personal interviews can overwhelm you with information. Data searches must be preceded by questions. Only if your search for information is focused will you be able to manage the flood of information available to you. There is little hope for those who wander about in libraries hoping for some inspiration to come their way. Furthermore, with microprocessor-operated information files, the only way to get information is to ask the right questions. This means you may have to learn something about how to use computers, particularly how to translate your questions into questions the computer can recognize.

Interviewing   Members may need to do some interviewing in order to get accurate and extensive information. Interviewing is a delicate task, for it requires getting a maximum amount of information in a limited amount of time from a person who is often busy or reluctant to give information. The etiquette of interviewing is important. There are four guidelines you must keep in mind.

1. No one is obligated to answer your questions. When you seek an interview, call in advance for an appointment. Explain why you need the information, and try to show the person you are interviewing how participation might be mutually advantageous. Offer an estimate of how much time you will need for the interview. Make it a point to assure protection of confidentiality if necessary. It is also good practice to indicate you will give your interviewee a copy of a transcript of the interview so he or she can correct errors.
2. Be sure you've done background biographical research so you understand your interviewee's qualifications and authority. Confine your questions to areas in which he or she is an expert. Do not ask for opinions unless your interviewee is qualified to express them. And don't try to force the issue. Your interviewee has the right to avoid going out on a limb.
3. Use only a limited time for the interview. Do it at your subject's convenience, and be sure you have your questions prepared in advance. Ask the most important questions first. Do not ask questions to which you already know the answers. Do not bait your subject or try to refute what he or she says. Just get the information, thank your subject, and leave. Within two days following the interview, send a brief written thank-you note. This is a simple courtesy, and it keeps the door open for future contact.
4. Note answers carefully. It is always useful to use a tape recorder, but you must ask permission in advance. If you cannot record the conversation, prepare note sheets to facilitate recording the information. If you cannot take notes, make sure you write down your recollections as soon as possible after the interview.

LEADER OBLIGATIONS IN PHASE THREE

The main problem the leader has in phase three is managing impatience. Going through the steps of information gathering and evaluating can be time-consum ing, and group members are often tempted to jump ahead to consideration of solutions. Fact-finding always contains a discussion within a discussion on the question, "Where can we get the information we need, and how can we interpret it appropriately?" The leader must keep careful control during this phase to make sure the group handles the logistics of information gathering. The leader uses these questions:

What information do we need? Why do we need it?

Where can we get it?

Who will do what (division of labor)?

Now that we have a pile of information, what is worth taking seriously?

Now, what does it all add up to?

Does the information suggest it is in order to revise the question?

Someone has to keep records and files. Someone has to make copies of important information. Someone has to survey archives and libraries, and someone has to interview authorities and interested parties. A great deal of information gathering is done outside the discussion group by individuals. But no individual should have a monopoly on available information.

The leader should also enforce quality control. Groups are often confronted with dramatic and exciting information, rumors, first-hand accounts, scare stories. It is easy to get carried away with them. The leader must constantly dampen excessive excitement and subject each contribution of information to the critical tests required to ensure its reliability. To do this well may mean assuming the role of devil's advocate.

SUMMARY

The fact-finding phase of discussion is often the slowest and most tedious. It requires more time from members above and beyond meetings than any other phase. Without a satisfactory fact-finding phase, however, the rest of the group's work is pointless. It is easy enough to solve problems that do not exist. On the other hand, an accurate description of the problem built from careful fact-finding is the surest way to get an effective solution.

READING AND REFERENCE

Beardsley, Monroe. *Thinking Straight.* Englewood Cliffs, NJ: Prentice-Hall, 1979. There is no substitute for this book. It explains how to evaluate information, how to spot propaganda and deception, and how to reason intelligently. It should be required reading for all discussion group members.

chapter *11*

Standard Agenda Phase Four: Setting Criteria and Limitations

GOALS

To identify moral and legal authority, institutional, logistical, and suasory limitations on the group.

To develop standards against which to test proposed solutions.

OUTCOMES

A list of limitations on group recommendations.

A list of standards for testing solutions.

MEMBER TASKS

1. To suggest and discuss suggestions that limit the group for moral, legal, logistical, institutional, and suasory reasons.
2. To suggest and develop suggestions for standards that will help the group test solutions.
3. To participate in reviewing or reworking previous steps in the agenda if necessary to generate criteria and limitations.

LEADER RESPONSIBILITIES

1. To consult external authorities regarding limitations.
2. To make sure the group understands its limitations and enters them in the group record.
3. To decide whether the group needs to review or rework previous steps in order to manage this phase effectively.
4. To work with members to generate and enter into the record a set of criteria against which solutions can be measured.

This phase of discussion, in which the group has to examine itself, is the one most frequently bypassed. By the time groups reach the end of fact-finding, they're tempted to jump immediately to solutions. It is easy enough to believe that once the facts have been thoroughly evaluated, it is a simple process to agree on a solution. But it is at this point that the organizational setting of discussion groups takes on overwhelming importance. Groups are actually limited in their solution power by a number of considerations derived from the environment in which the group is set, as well as the basic values of the members. Failure to recognize this often makes group members resent their leader's efforts to convince them to spend time to develop criteria and limitations. Usually this impatience results from not understanding the importance of phase four. To be effective, the leader should take the time to explain the importance of this phase as the groundwork for workable solutions.

Although it may seem natural to move directly from fact-finding to solutions, skipping attention to the criteria and limitations is generally counterproductive. Now that the facts are laid out, a group needs to determine what it can and cannot do and what kinds of goals are reasonable for solutions. This is what phase four is all about.

DEFINING CRITERIA AND LIMITATIONS

Criteria are standards used to judge possible solutions. Think of them as goals: What could be achieved by an effective solution to the problem that concerns you? For example, the Forest Slough group came up with these three criteria:

1. Any viable solution must allow for speedy transit of deliveries and personnel to and from factories.
2. Any solutions should involve the the other towns logistically and financially.
3. Any solution should tangibly improve the situation of the merchants who are suffering loss of business.

Note that these statements are *not* solutions. Instead, they are standards or goals that any solution must meet to be acceptable. By contrast, a solution is an action statement. It directs someone to do something specific. Criteria, then, are more general than solutions. They are specifications for building solutions. The optimum group solution must be as desirable as possible; it must also be do-able. Criteria specify the *desirable* part of the formula. Limitations help the group decide what is *do-able*.

Limitations are restraints under which the group operates. They are limits or restrictions the group must observe when selecting solutions. Limitations recognized by the Forest Slough group include these:

1. A solution cannot exceed in cost what the community can raise through bonds and taxes.
2. A solution cannot infringe on laws regarding freedom of trade.
3. A solution must be limited to recommendation, since the group is not empowered to make policy.

Each of these statements clarifies the group's scope of authority and the boundaries within which it must operate.

There are always questions at this point in discussion. The most frequent question is, "Why bother? Surely most people understand these things without having to talk them through in detail." Our experience as teachers and consultants, however, contradicts that premise. Most people, in fact, do *not* understand criteria and limits, and often this gets groups in trouble. It has been said by social critics that two major problems characterizing the work of the officials who planned the Vietnam war were (1) they lacked any criteria for judging the outcome and (2) they failed to acknowledge important limitations, such as public resistance and moral revulsion.

Throughout this book we have emphasized the orderly process of making decisions and solving problems. Taking the time to work through phase four properly is consistent with this overall focus. Another reason for care during this phase is that thoughtful attention to criteria and limitations improves the chance that your solution will do what it is supposed to do. This is always desirable, and it is especially important when a group is charged by and responsible to some external authority. As you conclude fact-finding, all you have is a detailed profile of some problem. Now is your opportunity to discuss seriously precisely what you want to accomplish. Phase four allows you to get your bearings and put the problem back into a broad perspective that includes the context and members' values.

Finally, dealing with the issues of phase four increases the probability that members can reach agreement on solutions when the time comes. Let's consider an example of what might happen if phase four were bypassed. Assume that a faculty advisory group has been charged to select one person for a visiting lectureship. Each member of the committee has mentioned one or two favorite candidates and has offered reasonable arguments as to why a favored candidate would be the best choice. Without some criteria, each member could become an advocate who supports her or his candidate for personal reasons. There is no basis for group reasoning, deliberation, and evaluation. There is nothing that can be used as a basis for reconciliation. Under these circumstances, members are likely to become locked into their positions. If a solution is eventually generated, it may reflect power dynamics among members, rather than reasonable deliberations over the relative merits of the various candidates.

The advisory group, however, is not incapable of making a sound recommendation. Members simply need to establish criteria and limits *before* they discuss the relative virtues of the candidates. Assume the chair of the committee convinces members to focus on criteria by asking them to generate a list of ideal characteristics of a visiting lecturer. Here are some statements that might appear on the criteria list:

1. The lecturer should be nationally known as an authority in his or her area of scholarship. (This will probably eliminate personal friends and candidates below the rank of professor.)
2. The lecturer must have a record of superior teaching on both the graduate and undergraduate levels. (This criterion will require advocates to present some documentation of quality from local evaluators.)
3. The lecturer should have appeal for multiple departments and for students

in diverse majors. (We don't want someone so specialized that the majority of students and faculty cannot benefit.)

With these criteria, the group could take the file on each applicant and make an appropriate choice. Inferior candidates could be identified by objective and agreed-upon reasons. Personal issues, disciplinary loyalties, and political considerations would not be allowed to influence the decision-making because they are not in the criteria.

To further guide its work, the committee might stipulate its known limitations:

1. We have authority to recommend only scholars who will come for no more than $18,000 for the semester. (This will eliminate haggles about price and the temptation to select an excessively expensive candidate.)
2. We cannot exclude anyone because of race, color, age, or sex. (The law provides this.)
3. We do not have the authority to negotiate a contract; we are limited to recommending our choice to the dean of academic affairs. (This limitation is imposed by the institution that charges the committee.)
4. Since 80 percent of past visiting lecturers have been from humanities and fine arts, we were advised to give some preference to candidates representing more technical areas. (This is a political consideration based on understanding of the larger institution.)

Establishing criteria and limitations before discussing solutions increases the likelihood that a group will be able to arrive at a genuine and well-reasoned consensus. In a recent study, Likert and Likert confirmed that listing criteria before considering solutions is effective in depersonalizing issues, decreasing divisions among members, and enhancing the probability of a final solution acceptable to all.[1]

OUTCOMES OF PHASE FOUR

At the conclusion of this phase, you should have two documents before you: a list of criteria for judging possible solutions and a set of limitations within which members understand they must operate. It's a good idea to duplicate both documents so that each member has a copy. Now let's take a more detailed look at *how* you generate each of these lists.

Establishing Criteria

To devise criteria you should review your research with care, make sure you have clear understandings of superiors' expectations, and consider your own values in relation to the issues at stake.

Research as a Source of Criteria and Limitations   Remember how the criteria for the Forest Slough traffic group just flowed out of their fact-finding? The same

Careful consideration of the implications for a solution are important at this stage. (© Gupton, Southern Light)

is likely to hold true for your group. The facts in the case suggested the criteria and limitations. The problem-solving group discovered they could not count on federal funds to help them. They discovered some merchants were abusing the issue and making threats for personal advantage. They also recognized the need the community had for industry and the need to keep industry satisfied. Forest Slough could have acted without recognizing the needs of the other two counties, but the group recognized that local chauvinism could not be an issue. Most of these ideas might have been skipped had the group not taken the time to reconsider its earlier work.

Review your research to discover major problems or deficiencies. These will suggest goals (criteria) for your solutions. You also want to be alert to causes and symptoms identified in your research. Let's consider the example of a citizens' committee charged by a local council to recommend ways of increasing voting. In reviewing its facts, the committee identifies the following symptoms and causes of chronically low voting.

SYMPTOMS

1. Wards A, C, and K voted less than 20 percent in the past two elections.
2. Only 35 percent of eligible voters under twenty-five are registered to vote.
3. Blue-collar workers vote in significantly lower proportions than white-collar workers (33 versus 62 percent).
4. Blue-collar workers tend to vote before going to work or not at all, while white-collar workers tend to vote after work.
5. The polling hours have been 8 A.M. to 8 P.M.

CAUSES

1. Ethnic voters are suspicious of city government, and they are located primarily in Wards A, C, and K.
2. There is no evidence to suggest that the schools have made strong efforts to notify students of recent changes in the voting age; there is some evidence to suggest that in some cases schools have entirely neglected to notify students.
3. Blue-collar workers tend to begin their workday at 7 A.M., while white-collar workers tend to begin at 8 or 9 A.M.

These symptoms and causes identified from a review of research suggest a number of important criteria for solutions:

1. The get-out-the-vote program should include efforts to persuade ethnic voters that they have the potential to influence city government.
2. The get-out-the-vote program should involve participation by the schools and other agencies that reach people under twenty-five years of age.
3. A registration drive should be an integral part of the program, and it should be well publicized.
4. Poll hours should be altered to accommodate the working schedules of blue-collar workers.

The third criterion is especially important, because it highlights the need for action prior to election time. These four criteria represent a good starting foundation for building a comprehensive, effective program to increase voting.

In addition to identifying deficiencies, your search for criteria should involve reviews of previous attempts to solve the problem. Your fact-finding probably unearthed a number of situations analogous to your and a number of attempted solutions. If you can figure out why a previous solution did not work, you can avoid repeating the error. You may also gain insight into ways to take parts of previous solutions that are viable while discarding ineffective aspects of them. Sift through your data carefully. They are a primary source of criteria.

Group Goals and the Charge as Sources of Criteria and Limitations   Now is the time to reexamine your goals and your charge. If you are directly responsible to some other group or individual, then your recommendations must be acceptable to that person or group. If you are an independent unit, then your solution must be one you are capable of implementing yourselves. If your charge includes specifications of deadlines or budget, these limitations must be observed in your solutions.

Moral Limitations and Criteria That Arise out of Values and Policies   Most problems worthy of serious discussion involve complicated moral issues. Personal commitments held by individual members as well as those embraced by the group as a whole suggest both criteria and limitations to be applied in your consideration of solutions. Issues such as freedom of speech, equality of opportunity, fair notice, and freedom of information frequently crop up in problem-solving ventures. You'll need to recognize these as moral questions and decide where your group stands on them. Obviously, members should have been expressing values throughout the discussion process, but during phase four these should be explained clearly and deliberated seriously.

We have pointed out three major sources of criteria: (1) the facts uncovered in phase three, (2) the charge to the group and its attendant goals, and (3) individual and group values. While these may provide some insight into limitations, they are not the primary sources. We turn now to a specific examination of limitations and the major bases for them.

Establishing Limitations

Criteria define what you want to achieve with your solution. Limitations, on the other hand, remind you of what you cannot do. All groups are limited in various ways, and all problems must be solved within certain constraints. Not understanding restrictions under which you operate is a recipe for failure.

Legal Restrictions   No solution that violates laws is acceptable. Governmental agencies, colleges and universities, labor unions, and businesses employ legal counsel to examine committee recommendations prior to sending them to agencies responsible for implementation. The legal counselors check to make sure the proposals in no way conflict with existing laws. In some cases legal limitations interfere with criteria set by groups. For instance, the most economical solution for building a community recreation center (a criterion) may violate zoning ordinances (a limitation), so a less economical plan must be recommended.

Institutional Policies and Traditions   Any viable solution must be consistent with both the formal and the informal codes of the institutions that will be affected. Suppose your company charges a task force with negotiating a medical insurance policy. The best coverage for the least cost can be gotten from an insurer that refuses to provide coverage for 8 percent of the company's employees whose work is high-risk. Will you generate a separate policy for these special cases, exclude them from coverage, or recommend a less cost-efficient insurer that will cover all employees? Your choice may be limited by company policies that ban special treatment. In large, complex businesses, it is not unusual for a committee to propose a plan at the departmental level, only to discover that approval must be secured at the vice-presidential level. In academic institutions, policies preserving academic freedom, affirmative action, and so forth often limit the kinds of solutions that are possible for a range of problems. Thus, it is most important to discover what institutional policies and norms potentially limit your recommendations.

A few years ago, a group of students at a large university decided to develop a plan to measure teaching effectiveness. The group received funds and political backing from the student government. After several months of sophisticated research, polling, and deliberation, the group recommended that anonymous monitors attend random class meetings of each course and compile their impressions in the form of a student opinion brochure. The university protested that this procedure violated academic freedom and promoted evaluations based on less than comprehensive and fair observation, practices specifically forbidden in the statement of university policies. Months of good work were wasted and the group lost credibility simply because it failed to identify a critical limitations within which its solution must fit.

Financial Limitations   Money and love are the two commodities no one can get too much of, and small groups do very little of their work with the latter. Everything costs money. Just meeting on a regular basis, costs are incurred for gas, coffee, paper, pens, duplication of important documents and findings, and so forth. Further, groups often pay professional typists to prepare final briefs, and good typists charge substantial fees. Some committees are given budgets within which they must operate. Other groups—including most student groups—have no funds provided and must rely on members' contributions. It is legitimate and realistic to face the issue of cost, and to determine how much money is available for solutions. Leaders should take some initiative in seeking funding from charging authorities when appropriate. When a group is self-charged, members may be able to exercise some imagination in finding sources of funding or in developing strategies.

Suasory Power   A group is restricted in what it can recommend by the amount of support it has been able to generate for itself and its goals. Blue-ribbon committees have great initial credibility which gives them some suasory power. Other groups have suasory status by virtue of their standing in a community or organization. Yet many groups do not start out with any firm bases of support. In these cases, part of the groups' ongoing task is to win supporters. Goodwill and credibility can be generated through professional interviewing techniques, thank-you letters sent to resource people, and concerted efforts to demonstrate how the interests of your group are tied to those of other individuals and groups. To the extent that your solutions receive even informal backing from the powers that be, you increase the probability of success.

Problem-solving groups are confronted by a variety of limitations. Among the most common ones are those imposed by laws, institutional policies and traditions, financial restrictions, and suasory constraints. Careful attention to limitations at this juncture may spare the group great difficulty, disappointment, or embarrassment later on. In some cases, of course, it is possible to overcome limitations. You may be able to get a law repealed, gain an exception to an existing policy, or petition for an increase in budget. In general, however, it is not a good idea to count on such fortune. Be prepared to operate within the limitations that exist.

MEMBER TASKS IN PHASE FOUR

Essentially, phase four involves reviewing and drawing out the implications of what has been accomplished. It is particularly important to listen carefully and critically, to ask questions to clarify points, to assert your own perceptions of criteria and limitations, and to communicate in ways that consistently keep the focus on collective goals.

Participation is critical in this phase. One strategy frequently employed to enhance participation is to ask all members to prepare lists of criteria and limitations prior to group discussion. This method provides the group with a range of ideas, independently generated yet open to collective deliberation and analysis. The possibility of groupthink is minimized, and the goal of comprehensive analysis is maximized. When differences do arise, members should first make sure they understand the alternate points of view and then concentrate on the *reasons* behind each position. As long as all members remember that they share the goal of coming up with the best solution, differences of opinion can be managed constructively.

During this phase members should not shirk from disagreements, nor should they attempt to gloss them over. Recognizing and discussing differences is vital to effective problem-solving. Further, any genuine consensus grows out of efforts to emphasize disagreements that might subvert a solution which does not take them into account. At this stage, all members must think through what they can live with, the proverbial "bottom line." Reservations must not be kept secret, and moral concerns must be expressed. This is particularly important in community groups, where members represent constituencies in the larger environment. Their concerns will reflect those of components of the community. Understanding them and taking them into account can prevent the group from agreeing on solutions that would make the problem worse instead of solving it.

Above all, members should insist on thorough discussion of criteria and limitations. It is easy to be impatient, to be tempted to rush through these issues in order to get on with solutions. Yet this can be counterproductive in terms of the overall goals of the group. Members should encourage each other to participate fully and thoughtfully. Good questions, attentive listening and response, and enthusiasm for the topics help generate the kind of atmosphere conducive to thorough work.

LEADER TASKS IN PHASE FOUR

As always, a leader is responsible for controlling conversation, summarizing deliberations, refereeing disagreements, maintaining the record, and keeping the group focused on pertinent issues. During phase four, much of the leader's work parallels that of members. A leader should encourage full and balanced participation, should model good listening habits, and should demonstrate enthusiasm both for the topics of phase four and for constructive disagreements over issues.

Leaders need to be alert to the possibility of excessive idealism as members generate criteria. Sometimes people get carried away with what they want to achieve. The result can be a "wish" list that is simply not feasible. A leader should encourage members to generate realistic criteria. As a further curb against unwarranted idealism, a leader should inform members of limitations imposed by superiors. The leader is responsible for making sure that all members recognize the unalterable restrictions within which they must operate.

The leader may also need to direct the group to return to previous stages. If there is insufficient information on some issue, more fact-finding is in order; if generation of criteria exposes a new issue, related background material may need to be obtained. Members tend to be reluctant to backtrack and may feel demoralized by suggestions that they should. In such cases, the leader needs to supply motivation and persuade the members that the detour is essential to the group's long-range collective goals.

The leader may need to make special assignments during this phase. To clarify limitations, members may be asked to secure additional information on legal issues, economic plans, or institutional practices. When members are asked to perform special duties, the leader should make sure they are recognized for their efforts on behalf of the group.

Finally, the leader should prepare the final list of criteria and limitations or delegate this to a specific member such as the recorder. Copies of this list should be given to all members to enhance the probability of informed participation in the upcoming discussion of solutions.

SUMMARY

Phase four digs out the rocks on which the solution will be built. It is the point at which the definition of the problem is refined and the implications of facts are drawn out in order to move toward the most desirable solution that is feasible.

The foundation for a solution consists of criteria and limitations. Criteria come primarily from research, the group charge, and the goals and values held by individual members and the group as a whole. Limitations consist primarily of legal, institutional, financial, and suasory constraints imposed on the group.

Phase four involves an interesting balance between idealism and realism. Both are needed in order to carve out the best possible solution under the particular circumstances confronting the group. By attending equally to criteria and limitations, it is possible to lay the foundation for a desirable *and* practical solution.

REFERENCE

1. Rensis Likert and Jane E. Likert, "A Method for Coping with Conflict in Problem-Solving Groups," *Group and Organizational Studies,* 3 (December 1978), pp. 427–434.

RECOMMENDED READINGS

Smith, William S. *Group Problem-Solving Through Discussion.* Indianapolis: Bobbs-Merrill, 1963. This book devotes an entire chapter to the topic of how to reach a genuine consensus by managing disagreements effectively.

Wagner, Russell, and Carroll C. Arnold. *Handbook of Group Discussion.* Boston: Houghton-Mifflin, 1968. This book offers a good overview of criteria and limitations in Chapter 5.

chapter 12

Standard Agenda Phase Five: Discovering and Selecting Solutions

GOALS

To generate and examine as many alternatives as possible.

To select or construct a solution.

To prepare a plan for operationalizing the solution.

OUTCOMES

A set of proposals with reasons for rejection.

Detail of a proposal with rationale for each component (budget where required).

Operations plan, complete with method of evaluation.

MEMBER TASKS

1. Review facts, criteria, and limitations to find, evaluate, and propose solutions.
2. Participate in constructing group solution, including operations plan and rationale.

LEADER OBLIGATIONS

1. Use whatever methods necessary to increase the number of possible solutions to consider.
2. Guide group through the process of evaluation of proposals against criteria and limitations.
3. Supervise development of operations plan, budget, and evaluation procedure.

AVOIDING THE OBVIOUS

The goal in this phase of discussion is completion of the group's work. The solution to the problem—an operations plan, policy statement, or reasoned decision—must be produced, complete with arguments for its adoption, a budget where necessary, and a method of evaluating it once it is put into operation.

Unfortunately, by the time this phase of discussion is reached, the group is often fatigued. There is a tendency to jump to conclusions with the slogan, "Well, it's obvious what we ought to do is. . . ." Statements like this stop thought and subvert the group's work.

When the first idea that pops into view is subjected to careful scrutiny by testing it against the criteria the group has generated for itself, it often dissipates quickly. People wonder how they could have been so foolish. Some of the statements that indicate prematurity are these:

"Well, it looks like we should. . . ."

"We've got to stop. . . ."

"Everyone knows we ought to. . . ."

"It seems apparent that. . . ."

At this phase of discussion, nothing is obvious, and nothing should be ruled out.

Because effective discussion is an orderly, reflective enterprise, the group should review the criteria by which it will evaluate solutions before proposing the first solution. Furthermore, each member should examine his or her conscience and come up with a best solution. Some groups ask members to write position papers at this point. If each person works out an independent solution, the group is guaranteed a number of alternatives to examine.

If there are not enough alternatives, the group can generate more by *brainstorming,* a process in which members propose ideas uncritically, omitting no "wild" notions. Each idea is then subjected to examination against the criteria. The process rarely produces a solution, but it often opens up some imaginative approaches to more standard proposals.

Brainstorming, introduced during the group dynamics movement of the 1950s, has become a standard method of loosening up groups in which ideas are slow in coming. It is an attempt to encourage total freedom in making proposals. The process is fun because members are encouraged to be humorous and imaginative as they follow the rules:

Anyone can offer any solution, no matter how far-fetched.

Every proposal is written down.

No one may criticize during the proposal-making period.

The goal is to get a large quantity of ideas.

Every idea must be evaluated against criteria and limitations.

There are some drawbacks to brainstorming. Creativity and originality are not necessarily signs of a good solution. Sometimes groups get carried away with the idea of creating an outlandish solution. Furthermore, brainstorming seems to work best in training settings with group exercises. The authors have rarely seen it used in real-life committees or boards, although we have seen many such groups encourage reasonable degrees of imagination and creativity in proposals. In addition, brainstorming tends to exclude shy members who have difficulty participating in such a lively, extroverted process (see Jablin et al.). Brainstorming is probably best reserved for times when groups seem irrevocably blocked and need an assist to creativity.

It is rare when a group finds a good proposal in complete form. Usually, what happens is bits and pieces of proposals are fitted to the problem as it was defined after fact-finding. The Forest Slough Planning Commission, for example, set up the following list with possible solutions matched to components of the problem.

Problem	Possibilities
1. Merchants threaten to move to the suburbs if the traffic problem is not solved.	1. Let's not take them seriously. Let's take a formal survey to see who actually moves.
	2. Let's check with the shopping center realtors to see who they are leasing to.
	3. There are other reasons for moving besides traffic.
	4. Let them move. Let's have a plan to persuade new businesses to replace them.
	5. A downtown parking garage with local loop bus service might do it.
	6. Try a one-way street traffic plan to free up circulation.
	7. How about peripheral parking with loop buses into downtown?
2. There is no way around the downtown area for commuters coming home from work.	1. Can we get the peripheral employers to stagger hours so they don't all put pressure on at the same time?
	2. How about getting some money for a freeway bypass and mass transit?
	3. Try a car pool campaign to reduce the number of vehicles.

Each of the proposals was then tested against criteria and limitations. The proposal to persuade new businesses to replace those that moved was rejected because there was no practical assurance that it would work. The freeway bypass was rejected because the group agreed it could not spend any more money. Finding out who the shopping centers were leasing to was rejected, since the shopping centers would not provide the information. And so on.

OUTCOMES OF PHASE FIVE

At the close of phase five, a group should have a great deal of information. For one thing, there should be a set of proposals made and rejected. For each rejected proposal, the group writes an explanation of how the proposal failed to fit the group's criteria and limits. This is very important to the defense of the proposal required in phase six. Whenever a proposal is made, someone is bound to ask why something else was not considered. A well-prepared group will be able to state what was considered and offer reasons why each rejected solution was not accepted.

There also should be records of particular solutions devised by individual members. These are evidence that the entire group participated in the decision-making. They also serve to ensure that the solution meets the needs of members who may represent important interest groups. If there is a substantial minority favoring a rejected solution, a minority proposal can be included with the final report.

The group should also have an operations plan prepared for the solution it proposes. An operations plan contains the following components.

1. A general description of the proposal, usually as a heading.
   Proposal for Communitywide Car Pool Program
   The following proposal seeks to generate a central office to arrange car pooling for people regularly passing through the downtown area of Forest Slough either going to or coming from their place of work.
2. Personnel involved in the program and their duties.
   There shall be a pool supervisor in the borough hall. A secretary will be assigned part-time. The supervisor will take calls and make referrals to possible pool people in the same neighborhood. The supervisor will attempt to persuade companies to arrange in-plant pools. The secretary will keep records and handle correspondence as directed.
3. A statement of resources needed.
   The solution will require a desk, regular office supplies, a file cabinet, and phone. There should be office space designated in borough hall.
4. A statement of supervision and responsibility.
   The program will be supervised by a member of the Planning Commission designated by the Planning Commission.
5. A method of evaluation.
   The traffic survey committee reports regularly on traffic flow. The program will be considered successful if traffic is reduced 10 percent and/or if there is evidence of at least 250 pool cars at the end of 90 days.
6. A tentative budget.
   Costs include salary for pool supervisor, allotment for part-time secretary, costs of office supplies, phone. Office furniture and space will be free from the borough. Merchants will be asked to fund advertising for the program.

What to Avoid in Proposal Making

Two tendencies must be avoided in proposing solutions: unwillingness to try anything new, and groupthink. Many groups seem to freeze at proposal time. They tend to propose more of the same old solutions to problems. But any program has a point of diminishing returns. If a one-way street pattern has partially solved a traffic problem, there is no assurance that more one-way streets will solve the rest of it. If a problem required funds for a solution, there is a point where spending money will be pointless. For example, budgeting for more teachers to solve a problem in education is useless if teachers are not available. It is important in proposing solutions to evaluate some ideas that have never been explored just to see if an imaginative solution is feasible.

A second problem to avoid is groupthink. It is at the proposal stage that many groups freeze and get very concerned about "getting along." On rare occasions, some pressure group representative will offer adamant opposition to an idea, but for the most part people tend to avoid argument at the proposal stage. It is important to be skeptical of agreement that seems too easy. What passes for consensus is sometimes nothing more than fatigue or apathy. By the time the group reaches phase five, many members may be exhausted, unable to make the effort to engage in the intense thinking required to reach an effective conclusion to their work. When advocates present their point of view, opposition may collapse like a house of cards. Leaders should be particularly careful during phase five to encourage members to express disagreements. Only if members feel free to object and criticize will the group be assured its ideas will receive an effective evaluation. Leaders must also be ready to take a stand against those who advocate too intensely to prevent them from bullying other members.

Creative and original ideas do not just happen, and we have already pointed out that artificial procedures like brainstorming probably will not produce them either. On the other hand, a fair and open attitude by members will encourage people to experiment. If the leader maintains a consistent pattern of evaluation and suppresses sarcasm and ridicule, members will be encouraged to try out realistic ideas to "see if they fly."

A brief word on *creativity* is important here. Creativity is a very abstract concept. One person's creativity may be another's foolishness. An idea is evaluated as creative once it has been tested. It is probably better to avoid applying adjectives like "creative," "conservative," "bold," "imaginative," "forward-looking," "breakthrough," and so on to proposals. Each proposal should be carefully checked against criteria and limitations and considered on its merits alone. The solutions phase of discussion is where cool heads are very important.

It is easy, however, to get carried away with excitement when a new idea is discovered. The Forest Slough Planning Commission might be interested to find out that in Singapore a traffic flow problem was solved by issuing stickers to motorists permitting them to use certain streets only at certain hours. That might mean shoppers would be restricted to off-peak traffic flow hours in the downtown area, while commuters would be permitted to pass through only during the time they would normally go to and from work. There would be a few problems, of course, if Forest Slough tried it. What if workers pooled their cars and their wives wished to come downtown to shop? That would mean some cars would have to apply for two stickers. Furthermore, the cost of enforcing a sticker program might be too high. There may not be enough police available even if the costs could be met. But the idea is worth looking at, for examining it illustrates the perils of complicated plans that require bureaucratic administration and consistent enforcement in order to work.

The Advantage of Position Papers

Once the list of solutions has been reduced to a manageable few that have passed preliminary tests against criteria and limitations, they must be subjected to refined analysis. The group will want to discover whether there are major objections from involved interest groups, barriers to implementation, hidden costs, and possible new problems associated with the various ideas. An effective way to obtain refined analysis is to have group members prepare position papers in which they present arguments for and against proposals or parts of proposals.

Writing a position paper permits an individual to devote serious thought to a question without having to respond immediately to questions and criticism. Thoughtful analysis, written down, can be shared among members who can then develop their criticisms or amplifications of the ideas. By circulating the position papers anonymously, the ideas become property of the group and no member needs to be threatened personally if someone objects or criticizes.

Position papers also guarantee that sufficient attention is devoted to each proposal. By taking the time to write the papers, the group is spared the hazard of making a premature commitment to a solution that might turn out to be worthless or dangerous. Often groups will get far down the road to preparation of an operations plan only to discover hidden perils they missed because they did not consider the proposal seriously enough at the outset.

Logistically, position papers require a recess of several days to allow members to think and write. They must be duplicated and circulated, and members should be given ample time to consider them and prepare responses. A position paper should deal with at least the following issues:

What would the proposal cost? Would it meet cost-benefit standards?

Who might be injured by the proposal? What is the nature of the

A quiet time for serious thought and analysis allows group members to further refine their solution to a problem. (Alper, Stock, Boston)

injury? Is compensation possible? Is there any way to reconcile people who might be harmed because of the proposal?

Are there unanticipated political barriers to the proposal?

What are the main advantages of the idea? How important are these advantages? Does their benefit outweigh projected costs? (Costs include not only money, but time and resources as well.)

If the position paper advocates a proposal, it should demonstrate how the proposal satisfies the group goals and fits within the imposed limitations.

Short of groupthink, there is no way to avoid argument at this phase of discussion. Furthermore, argument is desirable, especially at this point. Any proposal the group adopts must be defended before the charging body anyway. Thus argument within the group is rehearsal for later argument. The final report must include a defense. The argument conducted in the group helps the group discover what must be defended. However, argument on proposals must be dispassionate. It must be about the ideas and their implications and should not involve personalities. Proposal time is not the time to form political factions and disrupt group unity. Position papers reflect a combination of individual commitment and dedication to the group goal. By reading them and dealing with them without reference to their authors, argument can be kept courteous and productive.

Devil's Advocacy

The notion of consensus is sometimes interpreted to mean unanimous agreement without conflict. But unanimous agreement without conflict often results from groupthink. When things look too easy, the leader or a member should become a devil's advocate and support an unpopular side just to see if there is merit in it. The person doing so should advertise it: "Look, I don't necessarily believe this, but what if." Devil's advocacy is a process that virtually guarantees critical questions will be directed even at the most popular proposal. Once someone begins, other group members will be encouraged to rethink their ideas and raise important questions.

How Do You Know You Are Right?

The answer is, you don't! The group never knows whether it is right until the solution has been put into operation and tested. Just because seven or eight people agree that a solution is worth trying does not mean it is the best, or even a workable solution. That is why considerable care must be given to examining the details and potential impact of the solution. Consider, for example, the problems of social security because increased longevity was not considered. Consider the impact the invention of the automobile had on the insurance industry. It is not always possible to predict the future, and often the predictions we make do not come true.

By preparing a detailed implementation plan and budget and by setting up an evaluation procedure to check how well the solution works once implemented, the group is helped to check some of the details that might easily be omitted. Working out the budget is very important. It will raise intriguing questions. Consider the Forest Slough car pool proposal. Here are some of the things that came up during examination of the budget.

> "How will people hear about the program? How will it be advertised, considering we have agreed on minimum expenditure?"
>
> "Who will it benefit? The downtown merchants, of course. Why not get them to fund advertising for it?"
>
> "OK, but who will go to them to solicit their support? And what if they don't want to fund it?"
>
> "Well, to blazes with them! If they don't like what we are doing for them, they don't. . . ."
>
> "Hold it! Maybe we ought to take the time to solicit their ideas before we get carried away."

The budgeting procedure revealed a possible flaw in the solution that requires more investigation before putting it into operation. Groups will frequently find a number of reasons to pause during development of solutions in order to test reaction and get more information about implementation.

What If There Is No Consensus?

In situations where consensus does not seem likely, you cannot postpone decisions indefinitely. Most groups have deadlines. They would not be in existence if there was not some important reason for producing a solution. In these cases, it may be necessary to use a less than ideal method to resolve the decision. Although voting has the potential to polarize the group into two factions, it is efficient. Examining attitudes by show of hands or voice vote sometimes shows a preponderance of opinion on one side or another. It is not desirable to agree on a solution when the vote is close, but if it appears that a disagreement cannot be reconciled, it may be necessary to do a little logrolling for each side to give up a little in order to come to agreement. It is not wise or efficient to wait for inspiration to guide the group to unanimous agreement. Unanimity does not just happen; it requires careful and painstaking work to accomplish.

Monitoring

This refers to stipulating some method of measuring the effectiveness of a solution once it has been implemented. Working out an evaluation plan is also important. It too may reveal weaknesses in the proposal. By asking "How do we know our idea works?" the group can be led to review goals. Saying "Traffic flow will improve" is not enough. The Forest Slough Planning Commission may have to interview merchants to see if business is increasing, count vehicles passing through the area, count the number of complaints and compare them to the numbers before enactment of their solution, and so on. Building a careful monitoring plan enables the group to check the components of the proposal in detail and anticipate problems before they occur. If the group discovers there is no way to measure effectiveness, it may want to review and revise the proposal, for it may mean there is no possibility the proposal will work. If people cannot tell things are improved, there may be no point to taking action.

MEMBER TASKS IN PHASE FIVE

Things can get very moralistic during phase five. Members can find themselves getting committed to various ideas and turning into advocates. Some members might proclaim themselves defenders of the budget, others may become spokespersons for interested pressure groups. Still others may be concerned about possible legal implications. Each component of the limitations can become grounds for argument against a given proposal. The most effective members must take care to express their ideas in a way that encourages modification.

Members have an obligation to express objections and concerns about the effect of a given solution. If a member does not speak out during this phase, it may be too late. Objections raised when the group is preparing the final report are easily brushed under the table. During the solution phase, any member has the power to stop the group from moving ahead in order to consider some new possibility of trouble.

Often some members will drop out at this phase of discussion. They may choose to remain silent and let a few members work out the details of the proposal. Members should keep a list of criteria and limitations in front of them and make sure their objections are considered and answered in *every* case. All should participate in writing position papers and reading the papers submitted by their colleagues. Each should avoid premature commitment to solutions. Each should avoid attacking another person because of his or her point of view, no matter how repugnant the point of view is. Some basic rules should be observed by every member during this phase of discussion.

1. If you make a statement, you are required to support it. If you offer information, you must document it. If you offer an opinion, you have the burden of proof.
2. If you disagree, you must base your disagreement on something more than personal feeling. You must be able to show the proposal may not meet the goals, violates the limitations, or will bring unforeseen unpleasant consequences.
3. When you object, you must focus your objections on the ideas, not on the person presenting them. However, if you are questioning the statements of some outside authority, you may question his or her credentials, objectivity, or interest in the outcome.
4. If you offer a criticism, you should be able to state the standards on which your criticism is based. If you say a proposal will cost "too much

money," you should be able to answer the question "How much is too much?" If you say a proposal is "impractical," you should be able to specify some standards for impracticality. Simply saying "It won't work" or "I don't like it" is not enough.

5. If you ask a question, you should be able to show how the answer is relevant. Sometimes members ask irrelevant questions in order to trap another member or discredit his or her ideas. Questions should be relevant to the case. Furthermore, questions must be asked. Don't sit back with confidence someone else will ask what you want to ask. You may be the only person to have a particular idea, and your idea could be very important to the group. It is terribly disruptive to a group to have to go back and answer questions that should have been asked earlier.

6. Keep contributions brief and clear. There are rare moments in discussion when a person may have to function as a technical expert, but most of the time limited contributions and taking turns are important to facilitate the give and take of constructive discussion. When one person is functioning as an expert, be sure to ask questions when you feel them warranted. No one has the right to demand to give a lecture during the discussion process.

Most of this advice applies to any phase of the discussion process, and you have heard it all before. We offer it again here because it is crucial to deal with proposals as carefully as possible.

Perhaps it is because people have the human tendency to want to win that discussion literature deals so much with personal feelings. A group discussion is actually an arena for controversy. It is possible to get a feeling of personal victory if your ideas are chosen over others. Some members will get very involved in argument and do not consider others. They ride roughshod over quiet and restrained people, cut other speakers off in the middle of their remarks, and constantly demand attention by shouting and interrupting. It is also easy to get trapped into personal argument. After all, how could anyone who disagrees with you be anything more than a fool?

It is easy to say people ought to know how to defend themselves. This, in fact, was Aristotle's original idea, that every idea ought to receive a good defense. It is difficult for most people to speak skillfully. No matter how dedicated, well informed, and concerned they may be, they are no match for a truly skillful arguer. Their self-esteem can be injured when their good ideas are beaten down simply by someone else's eloquence.

Thus, steps must be taken to ensure each member's integrity. But training people to get along sometimes suggests they must *go* along with each other. While it is necessary to be courteous in discussion, it is not necessary to give in just to avoid conflict with others. Furthermore, when groups are excessively attentive to personal feelings, groupthink may set in. A task group has a goal to accomplish. The situation is quite different in a therapy group. Therapy groups may accomplish some business, but it is not necessarily important to the therapy. Task groups may do some therapy with individual members, but that should not be their goal.

We advocate adherence to the agenda and effective leadership as a method of ensuring the rights and feelings of individual members. By working to meet the requirements of each phase of the standard agenda, members can be guided away from personal combat toward attention to the common commitment. Leaders can devise ways and means for individual members to be heard and prevent aggressive members from bullying those less proficient at extemporaneous speaking.

Everyone has the obligation to stay awake and responsive in discussion. By working to protect the rights of others, you ensure your own rights as well. Everyone must understand that they cannot get all they want. Everyone must give a little in order to get a little. These ideas, more than anything else, will protect members from being abused. Everyone in the discussion has the right to courteous consideration and the obligation to give it to others.

LEADER OBLIGATIONS IN PHASE FIVE

Leaders must be aware that phase five is potentially the most volatile phase in the discussion process. This phase represents the culmination of the group's effort. By the time it is reached, members are tired. They have been meeting for a long time. They want to be done, to get on with the next task. Some may be impatient just because they have other things to do. Some may be sensitive because certain elements of the solution are very important to them.

Furthermore, by the time phase five is reached, there may be a history of hostility between particular members. Factions may have formed. Some members may have formed friendships, others may feel socially excluded. Some members may have achieved recognition for their work. Others may feel this is their last chance to be noticed by supervisory personnel. There are a great many reasons why individual members may be testy and sensitive during this phase.

We have been reminding you continually of the leader's regular obligations: to direct traffic, to provide summaries, to try to resolve conflict. In this phase, the leader must also attend to the content of the discussion as well as the process, for it is the leader's job to see to it that the group solution meets the requirements of the charge.

This may require the leader to prod the members, to question them, to urge them to keep working, to raise issues they must resolve, to advocate for the devil, and to work to see to it that every detail of the requirements of phase five is met. The leader must prevent the hazards we have mentioned earlier in this chapter by pushing for concrete detail, raising good questions, encouraging sensible criticism, avoiding digressions, and curbing head-to-head combat. Here are some areas about which leaders must be most concerned.

1. *Stopping premature commitment.* If members agree on a solution quickly, stop them and raise enough questions to get them involved in reconsidering their conclusion. They may be right; the problem may be

easy to solve. You will not know this until you subject all alternatives to scrutiny and test.

2. *Fighting fatigue.* It is particularly important during this phase to take time for refreshment and contemplation. You may be working against the clock, but a marathon effort may be self-defeating. As leader, you may have the obligation to deliver a solution on time, but you also have an obligation to the quality of the solution. You should be prepared to ask for a little more time if you absolutely must to ensure quality participation by the members.

3. *Assigning tasks.* Information gathering is often important during this phase. You may have to ask members to make phone calls or get information necessary to work out the details of various proposals. You cannot work around a lack of information. When information is necessary, you must see to it that it is obtained, even if you have to get it yourself. You may have to find typists, library searchers, interviewers, liaison people, archives checkers, and coffee brewers. Use your group as you must to provide what is needed.

4. *Maintaining contact with the recorder.* It is important that you know what is going on. There can be considerable detail discussed in this phase. Make sure detailed information is recorded, and make sure you refer to the records so you are certain about what has been agreed on and what remains to resolve. Pay attention to detail. Every detail you cover in this phase will make the next phase easier. Furthermore, your responsibility in the final phase of discussion is very great. You can help yourself by encouraging the group to provide all the information you will need to do the best job in phase six.

5. *Wrapping up.* Your most difficult task in phase five is stating the final solution. It is important to know when to quit. We have encouraged you to pay attention to detail and be properly critical, but at some point you must stop and declare the work done. You will need to know when consensus is working, when to do some bargaining and logrolling, and when to take a vote. It is not effective to use the same method of coming to a decision all the time. Different methods are needed for different situations. It you have one dissenter holding out when the rest of the group agrees, you may want to make a careful try to please him or her and then vote and get on with business. Sometimes several people may seem irritated about small points. That is the time to struggle for a consensus on major issues and leave the trivial business to be worked out during the preparation of the final report. Try to avoid a solution so diluted with compromise that it will not work. Paying attention to an evaluation plan will raise your chance of getting a workable solution, for trivial solutions are hard to evaluate. If you cannot find anything to look at, ask about, or count, you probably do not have an effective solution anyway. Be sure to take time to commend your members for the work they have done. Inform them about what must be done to prepare the report and get those you need involved in the process. Deploy your members to take care of extra details like minority reports, data appendixes, and so on. Leaving your members with a feeling of goodwill in this phase will be to your benefit the next time you meet them either individually or as a group.

SUMMARY

Phase five is both exciting and frustrating. There is the excitement of finally completing the job and the frustration at the amount of effort and attention to detail it takes to do it well. Whatever happens during phase five will be the payoff for the work done during the previous phases. If things go well, a sound decision emerges and the group comes to a consensus. This will be a credit to your earlier work. If things do not work out so well, you may find it necessary to retrace your steps and fill in details.

The possibility of disruptive argument is greatest during phase five. Members will be tempted to debate. They may forget their task is to propose and to work collaboratively for common goals. They may want to exert their authority and decide as if they were a legislature. The leader will need to be more in control at this time than in any other phase of discussion.

REFERENCES AND READINGS

Jablin, Frederick M., David R. Seibold, and Ritch L. Sorenson. "Potential Inhibitory Effects of Group Participation on Brainstorming Performance." *Central States Speech Journal,* 28 (Summer 1977), pp. 113–121.

Jablin, Frederick M., Ritch L. Sorenson, and David R. Seibold. "Interpersonal Perception and Group Brainstorming Performance." *Communication Quarterly,* 26 (Fall 1978), pp. 36–44.

Phillips, Gerald M., and Julia T. Wood (eds.). *Emergent Issues in Human Decision Making.* Carbondale, IL: Southern Illinois University Press, 1984. This book reviews various ways of achieving solutions, offers some case histories and reports of experiments to illustrate how groups come to conclusions, and assesses the alternatives to consensus as a goal.

Watzlawick, Paul, John Weakland, and Richard Fisch. *Change.* New York: Norton, 1974. This is a good book on how to get outside the system in order to find creative solutions.

chapter *13*

Standard Agenda Phase Six: Preparing the Final Report

GOALS AND OUTCOMES

Content of Final Reports

1. A preamble that contains a statement of the charge, a review of the problem-solving process, and the routing for the report.
2. A report on the background of the problem indicating present need.
3. A detailed presentation of the solution, containing (if necessary) an implementation plan, organization chart, and budget.
4. An argued defense of the solutions, including:
   a. A demonstration of how the plan will meet the need.
   b. A demonstration of why the plan is desirable, and will bring no undesirable concomitants.
   c. Appendixes where necessary: proposals rejected with reasons for rejection; minority report if one has been prepared.

MEMBER TASKS

1. Members will work as directed by the group leader in the preparation of the final report.

LEADER OBLIGATIONS

1. To see to it that the final report is written and properly transmitted.
2. To inform the group of its disposition. Will it meet again, and when, or will it go out of business?

In the final phase of discussion, the group changes its purpose and its method of operation. Phase six requires cooperation in developing a final report according to specifications. Members must accept tasks as assigned by the leader. The leader is actually an administrator coordinating the work of several people in order to accomplish the required task.

This book is not about administrative planning. We discuss the preparation of the final report in detail only because group members are often required to participate in justifying and defending the report and because they must play a part in preparing it. When members cannot defend the solution, it casts doubt on the effectiveness of the group.

Many groups do not need to prepare formal reports. When a group has the responsibility to implement its own decisions, it can go directly to developing a plan for administration of the solution. In most cases, however, groups must submit their final report to someone else for the decision to begin implementation of the proposal. Even if your group does not require this kind of ratification, it is important to understand the elements of the final report, for they serve as criteria by which to judge the proposal you developed in the previous phase. If you cannot write an effective report on your proposal, it may indicate that your proposal is not as effective as you think.

We will be more concerned with persuasion in this chapter than in previous chapters. There is a very close relationship between discussion and persuasion. The results of your discussion will be the agenda for argument in the group that must approve it. That is why you are obligated to give your solution the best possible defense. It generally takes a good deal of effort to persuade people to adopt a solution, particularly if they are obligated to take responsibility should the plan fail.

You might assume an executive who charged a group to solve a problem would automatically accept its solution. However, organizations tend to be conservative. They resist change, and thus approval of change depends on effective argument on its behalf. A great many people in any organizations depend on things remaining precisely as they are. Changes jeopardize their authority and even their income. They can be expected to be suspicious of any proposal. Committees play a peculiar role in preparing solutions to problems. If things work, they often get credit; but if they fail, the person who administers the program is the one who takes the blame. That is why it is so difficult to get management to take risks.

It is even more important to be persuasive if you are trying to affect public policy. Legislators usually do not have the time to do the systematic work involved in preparing solutions. On the other hand, they are required to judge proposed solutions and take a public stand. The more information you can give a legislator about a proposal, the more likely the approval. People cannot approve what they do not understand. Furthermore, legislative committees are quite obscure. When there is a conflict about legislation, it is usually executive and legislative blaming each other. The patient committee work that led to the proposal in the first place is often overlooked. This spares committees from taking a great deal of blame, but it also makes the people they serve suspicious and critical. If the care and detail representative of the early stages of discussion are not reflected in the final report, the committee's work may be rejected. Remember, the legislators or administrators the committee serves were not present during the problem-solving. They cannot fill in the holes. They have only the information you give them. So your group must take great care in deciding what to present and how to present it.

CONTENTS OF THE FINAL REPORT

Preamble

The preamble usually contains a statement of the charge, a review of the problem-solving process in which group goals are emphasized, and the routing for the final report. For example:

> Report from the Forest Slough Traffic Commission
>
> We were charged by the mayor to investigate complaints about traffic congestion in the downtown area. We surveyed the complaints and discovered serious impairment in the business community and serious inconvenience on the part of workers in plants on the margins of the borough. We set as our goal to propose traffic legislation to the borough council and limited ourselves to legislation requiring neither bonding nor taxation. We present this report of proposed legislation to the borough council.

It is difficult to phrase the preamble. There is a tendency to want to say too much about what the group went through. No one is really interested in the effort the group made. In fact, it is an axiom of final report writing that *no one rewards you for the effort you made;* you are rewarded only for the effectiveness of your final product. Therefore, in presenting the final report, you must pay attention to the needs the receiver of your report has in supporting it, rather than to justifying your own hard work and goodwill.

The Forest Slough Traffic Commission (FSTC) had written a first draft of a preamble:

> With great effort, the Traffic Commission has sorted out our problem with traffic in the downtown area and presents herewith a solution to the economic deprivation that might result if the. . . .

and stopped immediately when it discovered the self-congratulatory tone. Clarity in a report should never be sacrificed to emotion. The legitimate purpose of the preamble is to introduce the issues.

It is sometimes useful in the preamble to notify the reader of the nature of the proposal to be made. The FSTC reported as follows:

> Our proposal includes a plan for one-way traffic designations on downtown streets, staggered hours in local factories, car pooling, and discovery of additional parking spaces.

The final report requires that carefully thought out detail be provided. (© Morrow, Stock, Boston)

Background

The background of the problem provides the group with an opportunity to review the case. The Forest Slough Traffic Commission worked out the following outline:

I. Traffic presented no more than ordinary inconvenience prior to initiation of the downtown mall. (Included was a review of the standard figures on traffic flow, parking spaces, violations, accidents, complaints, etc.)

II. Within one year after the opening of the mall, the situation was as follows: (The data were reviewed and compared, showing not only that there were grounds for complaint, but detailing the nature of the complaints.)

III. The standard policy for solution of traffic problems in the borough has been: (They reviewed their guidelines, including limitations on funds, liaison with police, and relationships with adjacent governmental units. They also used this point as a chance to state the limitations they placed on their solutions, such as no bonding or taxing.)

IV. The situation currently is: (A description of the problem as it stands is presented. This brings the reader up to date on the issue and prepares the ground for the next heading in the report.)

Presentation of the Plan

The proposals should be presented in complete detail. Each element of the proposal should include a statement about each of these points:

Who? (List titles of all personnel.)

Does what? (Include job descriptions that are as complete as possible.)

For what reason? (What does each job contribute to the solution?)

With what resources? (What does each job require: equipment, specialized training, machinery, supervision, etc.?)

Under whose supervision? (Show chain of command, organization chart, communication links.)

At what cost? (Budget as completely as possible. Show maximum, minimum, and most likely costs for negotiation purposes.)

To be provided by? (Where is the money to come from? No point to budgeting unless you know the cash is available.)

And evaluated as follows? (Go back to your criteria and ask how you would know a successful solution if it came to you on the proverbial platter.)

The plan should be presented in sufficient detail so that it can be budgeted and an administrator would know precisely what had to be done to get it into operation. Here is the outline of the plan presented by the FSTC.

Our proposal combines revision of the one-way traffic plan for downtown Forest Slough, with staggered hours in peripheral factories, car pool systems, and provision of additional downtown parking spaces.

I. The One-Way Traffic Proposal (effective in 90 days)
  A. Who does what?
    1. The borough engineer shall designate one-way routes around the downtown area (see attached map).
      a. Travesty Avenue should be eastbound at all times.
      b. Mudsink Avenue should be westbound at all times.
      c. House Bayou Boulevard should be eastbound from 7 to 9 A.M. and westbound from 4 to 6 P.M. to accommodate traffic to and from Grevitz Industries and the Hardy-Berne Meatball Company.
      d. Drainoff Boulevard should be westbound from 7 to 9 A.M. and eastbound from 4 to 6 P.M. to accommodate traffic to and from Planegenstya Corp. and Porto-Bar Manufacturing.
      e. There shall be no parking on Travesty and Mudsink Avenues at any time, and no parking on House Bayou and Drainoff Boulevards from 6 to 10 A.M. and from 3 to 7 P.M. on weekdays.
    2. The police commissioner should post signs accordingly and brief officers to facilitate traffic direction.
    3. The borough secretary should notify relevant companies, organizations, institutions, and the public in general about the change.
  B. Reasons for proposal
    1. One-way pattern and parking control on Travesty and Mudsink will facilitate entry and departure to downtown areas.
    2. Changes on Drainoff and House Bayou will facilitate traffic flow to and from major employers during peak traffic periods.
  C. Resources and cost
    (Included is current estimate for cost of publicity, street signs, special police training, etc.)

    D. Supervision
      1. Council president shall supervise the work and shall review the plan after 90 days by checking:
        a. Complaints on coming to and going from work.
        b. Difficulty entering and leaving downtown area.

II. The Staggered Hours Proposal
    A. Who does what?
      1. The chairman of the FSTC will contact personnel managers at the following plants (enumerated).
      2. She will solicit cooperation in the following program.
    B. The plan. In order to distribute traffic flow effectively:
      1. The following plants should start work at 7:50 A.M. and dismiss at 4:50 P.M.
      2. The following should start at 8 A.M. and dismiss at 5 P.M.
      3. And so on.
    C. The chairman of the FSTC will follow up and apply necessary persuasion for compliance and will measure effectiveness by traffic-flow data at six-month intervals.
    D. Costs will be covered by the budget of the FSTC.

III. The Car Pooling Proposal
    A. Who does what?
      1. The chairman of FSTC will solicit formation of car pools by personnel managers of the various factories.
      2. The chairman of FSTC will solicit advertising for car pools from downtown merchants who will benefit.
    B. The chairman of the FSTC will follow up and apply necessary persuasion for compliance and will measure effectiveness by traffic-flow data at six-month intervals.
    C. Costs will be covered by the budget of the FSTC.

IV. Provision of Additional Parking Spaces Proposal
    A. Who does what?
      1. The city engineer will designate parking areas for downtown shoppers as follows from 10 A.M. to 4 P.M. weekdays:
        a. St. Murphy Church.
        b. Luigi's Restaurant.
        c. Broad St. Baptist Church.
        d. Elm St. Theater.
      2. The transit commissioner will reroute downtown loop buses to cover these parking areas at 10-minute intervals. Riders can go to any downtown point free.
      3. Owners of parking lots shall be entitled to collect a 10¢ per hour fee per car to cover wear and tear and will give parkers a token.
      4. Merchants will compensate transit commission at 25¢ per person, presenting tokens to cover costs of loop bus operation.
    B. These are parking areas not used during shopping hours. They accommodate 540 cars.
    C. The chairman of the FSTC will check results.
      1. By measuring increases in customers in downtown stores.
      2. By checking whether fees cover costs of maintaining parking areas and operating loop buses.

Operations Plans

The preparation of the detailed plan portion of the report could well be the topic of another book. A number of management systems rely on group activity. One such system, PERT (program evaluation and review technique), combines group problem-solving with a mathematical formula used to check efficiency of operations and is highly effective in deploying personnel and estimating costs. Many groups will use all their personnel during the planning stages. Some may find they must supplement the group with experts of particular kinds who can offer information about technical matters involved in administrative deployment, development of organization charts, or cost estimating.

Groups must remember that solutions involve detail. A corporate group was asked to plan an honor awards event. Its report read as follows:

> The committee believes we should have an honors celebration to be held at a date to be specified in a suitable place. A committee should be appointed to decide what awards should be given and how the winners should be selected. This recommendation should go into effect two years from now.

The president of the company who charged the group was irate. He responded with the following memo:

> Your report is the worst example of buck-passing I have seen in years. You have had 30 days of meetings and you have come up with nothing! You have wasted company time and money, and believe me I will take it into account at the proper time.

He appointed a second committee and gave it two weeks, but he warned members about what he wanted and suggested they refer to a discussion training manual. This was the second report.

> The committee proposes the following:
> 1. The heads of Sales, Marketing and Merchandising, Display, Transportation, Production, Accounting, Purchasing, Personnel, and R&D should be constituted into a committee on awards.
> 2. The committee should identify employees (no more than two in each department) who have made an unusual contribution to the company. The "unusual contribution" shall be a proposal or activity which has resulted in increased sales, money saved, increased efficiency, and/or contributed to the general welfare of employees.
> 3. Awards shall be an additional week's salary to be taken in cash or vacation time at the winner's discretion.
> 4. The purchasing agent shall buy a wall plaque on which winners can be permanently honored at a cost of no more than $5,000 and a small plaque for each winner at a cost of no more than $50. The committee shall approve plaque design.
> 5. The personnel manager shall arrange an awards banquet to be held during

the week between Christmas and New Year's at a location not more than 3 miles from the office and with parking accommodation for at least 300 cars. Dinner shall be served at a cost of no more than $25 per person (without drinks) and there shall be a cash bar. All personnel will be invited and may bring a guest (spouse) at the expense of the company. The event shall be scheduled for the week of December 26, 1983.

6. The general manager shall be responsible for supervising the operation of this report and for all publicity and notifications. The general manager shall provide a speaker or toastmaster for the banquet. Award speeches shall be no longer than 5 minutes each and acceptance speeches confined to 2 minutes each.

There are details to be worked out, but the proposal is concrete and could be implemented. Considerable discretion was given to various department heads and to the general manager. They can delegate their authority if they care to. The important issue here is that the final report is the *only* opportunity the group ever has to show how well it worked. The group that presented the original inadequate report may have worked very hard, considered issues carefully, examined the facts, and participated cooperatively. They may have arrived at a consensus. The second group may have squabbled and wasted time. The receiver of the final report has *only* the report on which to base a judgment. An inadequate report is often taken as a sign of an inadequate group.

Your classroom experience will demonstrate to you how hard it is to represent your quality as a group. By the time the final report is due, group members may be fatigued. Furthermore, they may have been selected for their skill at talking, not writing. But the two cannot be separated. Whatever the form required of the final report, whether it is a written document or a presentational speech, it is the sole measure of the group's effort and the product on which they will be judged eventually as individuals as well as collectively.

The Argued Defense: Group Rhetoric

Each comment you make in the group affects your credibility. Each collective action by the group also reflects on you. As an individual member, you are required to cooperate with other members, but as a group, you are to compete for distinction in doing the task. Furthermore, there is a paradox about individual behavior in the group. Each member wants to be noticed, recognized for his or her fine work, which means each member competes for that distinction against each other member. Finally, the group must be prepared to argue in defense of its solution against whatever arguments can be raised by its consumers.

Argument is a matter of practicality and pride. If the group cannot overcome objections raised against the substance of its report, then the solution is probably not worth putting into operation. Furthermore, the act of commitment to the report involves the personal reputation and self-esteem of each individual. The struggle for individual and group recognition is not over until the solution is adopted and put into operation.

In the final phase, the group must deal with this question: *What can be done to prepare the most persuasive case possible for acceptance of our proposal?* The first step is to assess the possible obstacles to adoption. Who might speak against the proposal? Who stands to lose? Who has offered a different solution about which they might feel defensive? Each of these considerations will help you select evidence to support your argument. Take into account that the people who will pass judgment on your ideas are not entirely dispassionate: They will have their own ideas and they will not accept yours without good reason.

Examining your list of limitations may help you find arguments for the legal, moral, practical, and financial issues most frequently raised in arguing against proposals. Be sure you remain within the limits you set for yourselves.

It is even more effective to figure out what the executive or board that can give approval is looking for. Unfortunately, the world of work is not always a place where honest people who do honest work are rewarded honestly. People often owe past favors; some are influenced by people who have their own interests in mind. Decision-makers sometimes look after their own interests at the expense of the organization. To make an effective appeal, you will have to look at the personal interests of those who pass judgment. Here are some issues to consider.

> The decision-maker may have a sphere of influence. Does your proposal weaken or strengthen his or her influence?

> The decision-maker may not be prepared to take on more work. Does your operations plan provide for additional people to reduce the pressure?

> The decision-maker may be concerned about how particular individuals are affected by changes. Does you proposal displace anyone? What influence do people potentially displaced have on the decision-maker? Can you protect them?

If your target is a legislative body, your group may have to learn to lobby on behalf of the proposal. If you represent a citizen action group, you are guaranteed nothing. You will have to argue just to get your ideas considered, let alone accepted. Be prepared to bargain. Know how much you are prepared to give and where you must stand firm. When you propose legislation, there are a great many interest groups seeking consideration. No matter how skillful you were in preparing the solution, there will be others in the community whose interests are jeopardized and who will argue against you.

You may also have to use some ingenuity to lobby legislators who can initiate your idea. You may have to schedule time at public hearings or rely on the "friend of a friend" to get a hearing for your ideas. In a sense, the same process applies to industrial problem-solving, for discovering the solution is one thing, getting through the political labyrinth to adoption is another.

The persuasive theme characteristic of democratic societies becomes very important in the preparation of the final report. If the report is to be written, it requires a good writer. If it is to be delivered orally, it is important to get a skillful speaker to present it. Many fine solutions have been lost in the shuffle because they did not receive persuasive presentation in the final report.

THE STRUCTURE OF ARGUMENT IN THE FINAL REPORT

The purpose of the final report is to persuade someone to adopt the proposal. It requires that the very best job of documentation possible be done to present the proposal. We have discussed those elements already: background of the problem, nature of the problem, the details of the program, and the operations plan and budget. The core of the persuasion in the final report is the demonstration of how the components of the proposal will meet needs within the limitations and without bringing worse problems. We can examine the FSTC proposal to get an idea of how these objectives can be met in the argument that accompanies the final report.

The problem, in its simplest terms, was traffic flow: too much in the morning and evening, too inconvenient during the day. Lack of parking was part of the problem. The commission was pledged to avoid expense that would require new taxes or bonding, so such obvious proposals as a freeway bypass or parking garages would have to be rejected. Unfunded burdens on public transit would also have to be rejected. The commission tried, insofar as possible, to stay within voluntary participation and funding by the people most involved in the problem.

By presenting these limitations up front in the argument, the commission gained credibility for its solution. Even before a detailed presentation of the problem, the commission found it necessary to point out it was trying to solve an important problem involving only those directly affected and without shifting the tax burden. Thus, when it presented the details of the problem, it could present them in the context of a set of standards useful in evaluating the impact of the solution. The commission argued that its solution would be effective if there were observable reductions in the number of cars passing through downtown, or if cars passed more rapidly, or if complaints declined, or if there were more parking spaces, or if merchants reported increased sales. This was a highly effective and subtle bit of persuasion for it took note of the problem, but focused attention on the results *in operation.* That is, it assumed everyone would support the solution and moved ahead to a demonstration of how the solution would work. This enabled the commission to make a smooth transition to the core of the argument.

I. The one-way traffic proposal guarantees the following:
   A. There will always be one easy circular pattern into and out of downtown with the change in Travesty and Mudsink Avenues.
   B. The change in House Bayou Boulevard will provide a double route to and from companies east of town.
   C. The change in Drainoff Boulevard will provide a double route to and from companies west of town.
   D. The change in parking regulations will further facilitate traffic flow, but will reduce the number of parking spaces.

    E. Costs are limited to sign posting, notifying involved businesses, and reorienting police.

 II. The staggered hours proposal further reduces traffic flow:

    A. It paces traffic through designated one-way routes by staggering opening and closing hours slightly.

    B. It places a cooperative burden on employers and no pressure at all on public facilities.

III. The car pooling proposal further implements voluntary aspects of the plan:

    A. Involved employers can help solve the problem by supporting and encouraging car pooling.

    B. Car pooling will bring benefits to workers as well.

    C. Borough service and collaboration can be provided within existing budgets.

IV. The parking proposal is the result of a careful survey and private cooperation.

    A. Parking spaces will be provided in large parking lots not used during business hours.

    B. Costs will be made up by nominal charges to people who stand to benefit most from improved parking: merchants and shoppers.

    C. Burden on public transit will be limited, since there already is a downtown loop and only slight changes will be necessary.

      1. Costs of changes will be made up by private contributions.

The commission then reviewed the method of evaluation and showed how costs of evaluation would be covered. Included in the presentation is the strong suggestion that if the voluntary proposal does not work, it might be necessary to spend some real money. This provides increased persuasion to support the program since, by and large, it is relatively convenient to all, and certainly not as costly as a bypass, a parking garage, or public transit might be. By alluding to these possibilities, involved citizens are alerted to the possible content of the next act, if it is necessary. Appendixes to the report point out how convenient the three costly solutions might be, make clear how high the costs would be under present economic conditions, and forecast the increased costs if steps are delayed. This allows the possibility for the growth of sentiment favoring the more costly steps (which would suit the traffic commission). The present political climate militated against costly proposals, however, and the commission took the more convenient route to voluntary solutions.

Note how the process of discussion itself makes it possible to do an effective job of presentation and persuasion in presenting the final report. Going through the steps of the standard agenda requires the group to consider not only the details of the problem, but its relationship to the community. The charge, the definition of the problem, goal-setting, and assessment of limitations push the group to consideration of social and political realities, while the fact-finding and solution-building stages focus attention on the problem itself. Synthesis of the two into the final report completes the process in the form of a realistic solution presented in terms the public can understand.

FUNDING PROPOSALS

Groups are often required to seek funding for the solutions they propose. This is particularly true in research facilities, where the group's solution may come in the form of a study to be performed or an experiment to be conducted. Most grant proposals are generated by committees or research and development groups. The element of persuasion is crucial in seeking funding. The group must take into account the limitations imposed by the granting agency and must learn to phrase the proposal so it best suits the goals of the funding source. Furthermore, most funding agencies require carefully detailed proposals requiring painstaking formulation by the group. Here, for example, are the requirements for a funding proposal established by a state agency (which distributes over $35 million a year based on such proposals).

1. Review the problem your proposal seeks to solve or detail the conditions your proposal seeks to remedy.
2. Provide a complete descriptive overview of your program. Then provide the following details:
   What personnel will be needed? Provide a job description for each. Show how they will be coordinated and supervised. Provide organization chart.
   Where will the project be located? Show the floor plan of the operation if relevant.
   What equipment will be needed? For what purposes? How will the premises be altered to accommodate this equipment? How much space and equipment is presently available?
   Are there personnel available doing work proposed in this document? Are there personnel doing similar work? Can personnel be trained to do this work? Submit training or reassignment plan. What new personnel must be hired? Where will they be recruited? How will they be trained?
   Detail, in sequence, all operations in your plan. Submit PERT/CPM diagram, if relevant.
3. Provide complete budget for your project. Show how much of this money is available under present funding, how much will come from sources other than this agency, how much is requested in this proposal.
4. Detail an evaluation plan on which you will base decisions about success of your program. Provide a budget for same.
5. Who will benefit if this proposal is funded? In what way? Are they providing service or funds to implement this proposal?
6. What other alternatives were explored prior to preparation of this proposal? Why were they rejected?

The guidelines are useful as an agenda for groups preparing such proposals. To provide a logical flow, step 6 would be inserted before step 2. The whole would provide the agenda for a discussion following completion of an initial discussion culminating in a decision to ask for funding. The group would then shift its focus and participate in preparation of the proposal.

The final report must have some impact on those who receive it. After reading the report, the recipient must (1) be convinced that the conditions you sought to remedy were serious enough to justify the action, (2) understand the details of your proposal and precisely how it will remedy those conditions, and (3) be assured the proposal is practical, reasonable, and will bring no undesirable side outcomes. The recipient should also believe your proposal is the best of the alternatives. To review, these are the requirements for an effective presentation:

I. *Demonstrate there are flaws (impairments) in the status quo that require modification.* Show how injury would occur if the present situation were permitted to persist.

II. *There is a plan consisting of the following elements.* The plan is presented in detail (possibly following the format for grant writing provided above).

III. *A demonstration is made of how the plan will solve the problems for which it was developed.* Demonstrate there are no wasted moves, that it is fundable, that personnel are available, etc.

IV. *It must be demonstrated the plan is better than other possible alternatives and that it will bring no undesirable concomitants.* A debater is prepared to refute attacks by the opposition. Such attacks can take the following directions:
A. There is no need.
B. There is a need but the plan is unworkable.
C. There is a need, the plan is workable, but it will not solve the problem.
D. The plan is needed, workable, and it will solve the problem, but it will bring undesirable effects (too costly, violates legal or moral limitations, etc.).
E. The reasoning is ineffective. The documentation is ineffective.

The basis for argument is *presumption.* Presumption tells where the weight of the evidence lies. At the start of any argument, presumption is with the status quo. That means those who make a proposal must present convincing reasons why their proposal should be adopted. If they cannot, those with power to decide are justified in taking no action. Many groups believe their work is done if they have carefully considered an issue. The act of considering a problem in detail is very convincing, and group members generally are convinced their ideas are worthwhile. Unfortunately, the decision-maker has not shared the experience, so the group is required to assume the burden of proof and shift the presumption so the decision-maker will accept its proposal.

Every plan will have opposition. Groups that take this simple premise into account are suspicious of their own work to the extent that they will strengthen it to overcome possible objections. To do this requires the best possible presentation. We have presented here the elements of a final written report. In the following chapter, we will acquaint you with the principles of presentational speaking to equip you to do the best possible job of defending your proposal.

SUMMARY OF STANDARD AGENDA

We can now summarize the entire group problem-solving process. It involves several people who talk, share ideas, criticize, argue, amend, and improve proposals to derive the best solution to the problem they were charged to solve. In the world of business and government, discuss means *solve,* help a decision-maker meet the challenges of a very competitive world.

The process consists of six distinct phases:

1. Understanding the charge
2. Understanding and phrasing the question
3. Fact-finding
4. Setting criteria for judging solutions (including goals and limitations)
5. Discovering and selecting a solution
6. Preparing and delivering the final report

Through these phases, discussants try to answer a series of questions in logical sequence.

1. What is the required output of this group?
2. Who gets it, and how is it to be used?
3. How shall we phrase our problems?
4. How can we get the information we need?
5. Of the facts we have obtained, which are relevant, significant, and necessary?
6. Should we now rephrase our problem? Do we deal with symptoms, causes, or both? Do we, indeed, even have a problem?
7. What are our goals for a solution?
8. By what criteria shall we judge a solution?
9. What are the legal, moral, practical, and financial limitations on our power to solve and to act?
10. How would the world look if the problem were solved?
11. What are some possible solutions, and how valid are they when tested against goal accomplishment, criteria, and limitations?
12. What is our optimum solution? What are the details?
13. What shall be the nature of the final report?
14. Whose objections must we overcome in our presentation?

Members participate by devoting their minds and talk to the issues with which the group is confronted. Leaders ensure orderly procedure by staying with an established agenda. By following these guidelines, the group can enjoy the satisfaction that comes with a wise solution.

SUMMARY

A major theme in this book is that you, as a discussion participant, have a great many choices available to you. There are a number of practical and important roles you can play in a group. Furthermore, whatever your present level of skill, you can learn to be more effective by observing, thinking about, and understanding the discussion process.

We have advocated that you leave very little to chance, for group discussion is one of the best ways to display your competence to your society, employer, or other audience.

Discussion is an important part of democratic action. It is respectful of individuals and protective of common goals. You, as an individual, can become more important, more productive, and more satisfied with your own competence by learning how to share your ideas with others, to cooperate in solving problems, and to respect the interests of individuals and groups in a complex democracy.

Although the era of the rugged individualist has passed, individuality survives. It is best displayed in the process of group discussion, where each *individual* has the best opportunity to influence what groups do. In a very competitive world, we can ill afford to lose the contributions of intelligent and competent people. It is your responsibility to present yourself the best you can by learning to be an effective participant in group discussion.

It is at this point that the connection between group discussion and other phases of speech communication can best be made. You have a considerable choice of books and periodicals to read. You can get some good ideas about the contents of the final report by reading a good argumentation and debate text. In general, you will need to apply the principles of effective writing or speaking or both to the contents of your final report in order to make it most effective. In the final chapter, we will deal with the actual presentation of oral and written reports. The chapter will not make you an expert, but it will make clear some of your obligations in presentation speaking and report writing and help you identify the kinds of skills that will make you successful.

RECOMMENDED READINGS

Bradley, Bert E. *Fundamentals of Speech Communication: The Credibility of Ideas.* Dubuque, IA: Wm. C. Brown, 1979. Chapters 5 and 6 deal most directly with planning of persuasion.

Clevenger, T. *Audience Analysis.* Indianapolis: Bobbs-Merrill, 1966. This short text provides in-depth attention to the analysis of listeners as a prerequisite to effective persuasion.

Wood, J. T. *Human Communication: A Symbolic Interactionist Perspective.* New York: Holt, Rinehart and Winston, 1982. Chapter 11 focuses on issues involved in planning public presentations, and Chapter 12 continues with a focus on developing and presenting public communication.

chapter 14

Presentational Speaking and Report Writing

There is no need to labor the point about argumentation and persuasion. If your group has done its work, you will probably have all the information you need to do an effective job of presentation, provided you know the techniques. Your problem will be how to deploy what you have to meet the requirements of the audience you seek to persuade.

In this somewhat less than the best of all possible worlds, no plan is likely to be without opponents. People can be expected to oppose any plan they see reducing their material security, institutional power, or personal prestige. Furthermore, even the best of groups can make mistakes or forget details. Thus, you must expect to confront argument and opposition.

People will also raise moral issues. If you want to help people by licensing paramedics, you may insult the doctors. If you work out a program to help doctors pay for malpractice insurance, you may raise the cost of medical care or insult the lawyers. If you work out a program to produce more doctors, you may threaten the ones who are already practicing. There is no way of predicting for certain what kinds of opposition your plan will evoke. You have to be ready for anything. As they used to say on the frontier, "It's a risky job but someone's got to do it."

And you can't ignore the trivial issues. Sinus and hayfever sufferers may object to the planned picnic. Others may complain the affair is not formal enough. If you have a banquet, some might complain about the cost of dressing up, or they might not like the menu. In fact, you can always count on passionate disagreement about the menu.

Not everyone wins. Sometimes you have to hurt one group or another. It simply is not possible to provide for everyone's preferences. And the pressure groups may get you in the end. If the neighborhood group prefers recreation over traffic, or housing over business, the complaints will pour in and someone will have to deal with them. Sometimes the best programs are rejected because a pressure group had more power than anyone anticipated. You can't concede everything just to get an agreement. Sometimes you have to fight and sometimes you have to lose. The purpose of persuasion, however, is to turn disapproval into support so the new plan can be initiated. We can hope the plan works so well that support is sustained.

What it comes down to is that you have to pick your target—the board of directors, the city council, the trustees, the boss, the voters—and present your ideas as best you can. Sometimes writing is best; sometimes speaking. It is smart to be able to do both.

PLANNING AND MANAGING THE ORAL PRESENTATION

Many people fear giving an oral presentation. This chapter should provide enough straightforward information about managing an oral presentation to transform a feeling of panic into constructive energy. If you are the spokesperson for your group, required to deliver the final report orally to the person or agency that charged your group in the first place, you have the responsibility of "carrying the ball over the goal line." It requires attention to fundamentals, not brilliance.

The first thing you must understand about an oral presentation is that it cannot effectively be read from a manuscript. If a written report is necessary, you will find that it is usually long. A written report contain all the details, the facts and figures, the administrative plan. It usually has extensive appendixes and bibliographies. It is designed to be studied and pondered by those who receive it. Readers can go through a document at their own pace. They can take notes, go back to check things, even pause and write memos to the author of the report. They can get experts to interpret technical passages for them.

None of this is possible with an oral report. The listener must understand what is said as it is presented. If the listener loses a major point, he or she remains confused (and possibly resentful or angry) throughout the speech.

In spite of these limitations, oral reports can arouse action and give a solution a hearing that is not possible in a written report. The point is that written reports must be designed for readers; oral reports, for listeners. Reading a written report out loud is not an oral report. It remains nothing more than reading a written report out loud.

In spite of this, uneasy presenters frequently cling to a written manuscript in an effort to manage their insecurity. But now for the good news: In our experience working with industry, we have discovered that executives have little tolerance for written reports read out loud. Often they do not have the time to read the written report in detail. What they want from an oral report is the important stuff, the headlines. We even witnessed one manager stop a young executive who was reading a report with the comment, "If I had wanted the report read, I would have distributed copies. Put down the manuscript and get to the point!"

The point of the oral report is that it is easy to get to the point, and listeners often get the point more quickly and accurately when it is made orally than when it is made in writing. Understanding this should help you control your uneasiness about speaking in public. You don't write memos to your friends or lovers, you speak to them because that is the best way to get your business done. So it is in presenting your group report.

After you have figured out all the persuasive arguments to support your proposal, it should be easy to sum them up into a single statement expressing your purpose. We call this simple statement the *residual message*. It is what you want your listeners to remember after they have forgotten all the detail. Your group can help you work out the residual message. Perhaps you want your listener to remember:

> Failure to adopt our plan for traffic control in Forest Slough may not only mean the end of our downtown business district, it may jeopardize employment in our neighboring towns. The economic climate of our entire region depends on what we do in response to the traffic problem.

This commission has summarized its whole persuasive message in two sentences. Now it is relatively simple to document the assertions. The spokesperson must offer evidence to indicate that present conditions are ruining downtown Forest Slough, as well as show how the economic climate of the region is affected. Next, the speaker must demonstrate how the plan will prevent both catastrophes from happening. The result is a nice, neat, three-point speech.

Your best guide to writing your residual message is to complete the sentence, *"We want each member of our audience to agree that. . . ."* You ought to be able to finish the sentence with a very specific statement. If you avoid using the word "that," you are probably not clear enough. For example, "We want the audience to agree with our proposal," is nebulous. "We want the audience to agree that Forest Slough should control traffic," or "that Forest Slough should initiate one-way streets downtown," would be specific enough.

Once you have your specific sentence or sentences, you can add the words "because" or "for example," and then complete them. Residual message: We want the Town Council to agree that:

> We should use one-way streets to control traffic in downtown Forest Slough, because
>
> Present traffic load results in congestion—for example, (and provide the details).
>
> Present traffic load interferes with downtown business—for example.
>
> There is no other plan that has a chance of working because:
>
> > There is no way to reschedule industrial shifts.

> There is no way to reduce the number of people using the streets.
>
> There is not enough money available to build a bypass.

The information you include in your presentation should answer, in advance, the question any of your listeners might ask, "What is it you want me to do?" The answer is "agree with me and vote/decide my way!" Unfortunately, the issue is not always clear to the person making the presentation. The CEO of a large international food firm recently reported that a team of presenters came from the advertising agency which services the multimillion-dollar account. The board of directors listened politely while the team presented a well rehearsed "song and dance," complete with charts, visual displays, slides, and audio background music. They demonstrated media commercials and showed magazine spreads. At the conclusion of the presentation, the marketing vice-president asked, "What do you want me to do now?" There was no answer. He asked another question, "What is the problem this campaign is supposed to solve?" Again, no answer. The presenters, in stunned horror, realized they had gotten so caught up in dramatizing a solution that they had completely lost sight of the problem.

To add insult to injury, the CEO then announced: "Henceforth there will be no more meetings unless everyone involved understands the purpose. Is that clear?" It was apparently clear. The board nodded. Everyone left the room.

The best practice you can do for your oral presentation is to make sure you can answer those basic questions. What problem are you trying to solve? What evidence can you give your listeners that it is a problem? What are the major components of your plan? Why do you believe they will solve the problem? What do you want your listeners to do about it?

Keep away from detailed facts and figures. Use illustrations instead. Listeners, as a rule, will not remember the details of your presentation. The subtleties and nuances that were so important during the group problem-solving session can be embodied in the written report. The oral report should deal only with the major headings.

THE LOGISTICS OF THE ORAL REPORT

Once the group has decided on its purpose and has done the necessary documentation and outlining, it must consider the form in which the oral report should be delivered. There are always choices.

Sometimes it is most useful to designate a single spokesperson. In fact, this task is often part of the job description of the designated chairperson. Political bodies like town councils and legislatures will often hear only one person representing a group. When the oral report is to be given to an administrator, it is often more convenient just to send one person, so the administrator does not feel outnumbered and intimidated. When this is the case, the group may want to consider choosing its best speaker. Sometimes another member of the group is more skillful than the chairperson. Matters of ego sometimes impel group leaders to demand the right to speak for the group even when they are inexperienced or not too effective.

Speaking on behalf of the group is not a classroom exercise. It is a task that should be undertaken by the most skillful person or persons available. Only a person who has participated in the group meetings should be considered. The spokespersons should understand the details of the problem and its solution and be able to answer questions. She, he, or they should also be familiar with the written report.

As groups have grown in popularity, so have team presentations. Discussion class assignments often require the group to work as a team in the final presentation. The team format is useful because it can allow each member of the group to function as an expert. The role each member played during the discussion lays the groundwork for the part of the oral report each member is to present. Requests for grants and funding, for example, often feature oral presentations by individuals representing various aspects of the proposal. Each individual is able to handle his or her component virtually as a separate presentation and answer relevant questions. Research teams with complementary specialists often elect this mode of presentation.

It is important, however, to make sure everyone knows what everyone else is going to do. It is considerably easier to build a report if each group member assumes responsibility for a share of it. However, it gets very confusing to listeners if the members overlap in their presentations or if responsibility is not clearly established so just the right person can answer the right question at the right time.

There are many possible formats for collective presentations. In fact, there are so many that whole books have been written about the different ways groups can design oral reports. So that you may examine the options for group presentations, we've included some references at the end of this chapter.

Reports from groups require careful coordination of components. A major hazard in group presentations is that the speakers will lose track of the residual message. Each presenter must understand the basic outline of the presentation. It is as though each person is a human support for the group's ideas.

COLLECTIVE PLANNING

Whether the presentation is to be made by one person, several members, or the whole group, everyone must take part in planning the message. The report loses the flavor of a group effort if only one person does the planning.

Establishment of the residual message and the basic outline presents a discussion problem for the group members. They can move through the steps of the standard agenda to prepare their presentation, dealing in sequence with the following topics:

What is our residual message?

What are the most effective arguments to use on its behalf?

What sequence of ideas should we use?

Who should be responsible for what?

It is not necessary to present your group minutes. The detailed history of your group's examination of the problem and generation of the solution is not important. On the other hand, it is important that your listeners understand something of the process of the group's thinking. It is particularly important for them to understand why, if the group chose not to accept an obvious solution. On the other hand, it is important to avoid information overload. The group will need input from every member in order to make satisfactory decisions about precisely what the listeners need to know.

Listeners appreciate brevity. Your presentation should get to the point quickly. Twenty to 40 minutes is the optimum presentation time, although there may be some occasions when a longer presentation is warranted. Many situations provide even less time. That is why it is important for everyone to know the most important points to be made. It is more effective to add details to two or three important points (if you have the time) than to add points. Too many ideas can only confuse your listener.

Intricate details may be important to individual listeners. Try to provide for a question period so interested people can ask for the information they think they need. In your oral presentation, use only information of interest to everyone present.

While all presentation formats are necessarily different, the following represents a division of message presentation responsibility in a group. As you can see, the steps in the standard agenda function as heuristic questions about what should be included in the presentation.

PRESENTER ONE: Introduction of presenters and topics (Avoid extensive biographies, but be sure to indicate specialties and competencies.)

PRESENTER TWO: Definition and statement of the problem (If the question has changed from the charge, be sure to explain why.)

PRESENTER THREE: Criteria for a solution (Make sure legal and financial limitations are especially clear.)

PRESENTER FOUR: Discard solutions and why (It is important for listeners to know what was considered. Otherwise they may have to ask about it and waste considerable time.)

PRESENTERS FIVE AND SIX: Recommended solution (It is not necessary to present the operations plan, but it is important to show how the solution will remedy the problem as well as to make some statement about the practicality of the solution.)

PRESENTER ONE *(returns)*: Summary and conclusion (Solicit questions and direct them to appropriate group members for response.)

Variations can be made on this division of presentational responsibility to accommodate more or fewer presenters, though care should be taken to avoid a cast of thousands. Team presentations seem to be most effective when the number of presenters does not exceed seven, and teams of three to five seem to be most comfortable.

USING VISUALS IN PRESENTING YOUR MESSAGE

It is now common in business and industry to find almost all formal presentations using visuals—that is, some kind of printed or photographically reproduced visual support to accompany the message. The reasons for this are clear. Visuals can be designed to take the place of notes and manuscripts and help speakers recall what they want to say. In freeing speakers from notes, they serve to increase effectiveness.

The cliché about a picture being worth a thousand words is not quite true. Visuals must be integrated with talk. Visuals can facilitate understanding of a message and serve to heighten listener attention and interest, provided they are carefully associated with the oral content of the presentation. Appropriate visuals are especially important in group presentations because they provide a thread through the topic that holds the presenters together. They can prove invaluable in reinforcing the intended residual message because listeners can both hear and see the idea being stressed.

While visuals can technically include anything that can be seen or heard or both, the most popular visuals include the flip chart, the transparency or overhead projector, and photographic slides. Let's spend a moment examining each, since each serves special needs and each has a different personality.

Flip Charts

The flip chart is a large 27″ × 34″ pad of newsprint suspended on a stand to permit viewing. It is a very personal and friendly visual, and this accounts for its popularity in conference rooms and seminars when the audience numbers fewer than 20. Pages are generally prepared in advance, and like pages in a tablet can be lifted and "flipped" as appropriate. In general, large, fat-tipped felt markers are used to print or draw the visual (the same way chalk is used on a blackboard).

Some speakers like to add information or accent points by drawing on the visual as they speak, but care must be taken to avoid delivering the message to the flip chart instead of the listeners. One other advantage of flip charts is that light pencil marks in the margins can serve to remind speakers of facts or figures which they want to include at selected points in the presentation, and such notes will not be seen by the audience. This frees the speaker from notes or manuscript that may encumber the presentation. In preparing flip charts, care must be taken to avoid overcrowding. As a rule, the most effective use of flip charts is for visuals of no more than a half-dozen words, or graphs or tables with a few numbers.

For viewers to read flip charts, lettering must be at least 2 inches tall and carefully spaced. Letters should be formed with the wide part of the tip so that they are legible to more distant viewers. Black or blue should be the predominant color for lettering, since it can be easily seen.

Red makes an excellent accent color, but is tiring when used in quantity. Pastel colors should not be used because of the difficulty in being seen. Because flip chart pads use newsprint, pen marks will bleed through to the pages underneath. Similarly, printed pages in back of the surface being viewed will be visible through the paper. For this reason, printed pages must be separated by a blank page during preparation and use. Many speakers also prefer to staple the visible page and the blank page together so that when they are flipped, the next visual, rather than the blank page, becomes visible to the audience. One of the most popular uses of the flip chart in group presentations is for word visuals. Word visuals can serve as a roadmap for the presentation and help listeners follow the presentation and its main points. For example, in a group presentation the first presenter might introduce the presentation with a roadmap visual like the following:

The Problem: Joe

Criteria for a Solution: Amy

Possible Solutions: Tim

Best Solutions: Kate

Summary & Questions: Bill

Having done so, a simple transition such as, "and to present more about the nature of the problem we sought to solve, here is our second presenter, Joe." With that, the first presenter can flip to the second visual, which might look like this:

THE NATURE

OF THE

PROBLEM

Notice how the transition has been punctuated by the roadmap visual. Listeners will find it much easier to recall where they are in the presentation and what is being talked about. Often a visual like the one above remains before the audience throughout the message component. Details can be added on following flip chart pages, but each page should carry the heading identifying the phase of the presentation. If additional visuals are needed to help make points abut the nature of the problem, a second flip chart stand or another form of visual can be used. When the second presenter is finished, an appropriate transition like the following can move the message to its next component and presenter. "You now have an understanding of the problem we had to solve. Amy, our next presenter, will describe the criteria we established for an effective solution." With that, the roadmap flip chart is changed to the next visual, which might look like this, and the third presenter begins.

CRITERIA FOR

A

SOLUTION

It is entirely likely that this third component will require visuals to help describe and reinforce the criteria selected. The pattern can be followed to the end of the presentation. The main advantage of the flip charts is that they can be prepared in advance. Use of a chalkboard is risky because there is so much that can go wrong when you try to talk and write on the board at the same time. Furthermore, chalkboards are often hard for audiences to see.

Overhead Projector

Another popular form for visualization is the overhead projector which uses acetate transparencies. Its use is so common in classrooms and lecture halls it is unlikely that anyone is unfamiliar with it. Overhead projectors, like the flip chart, can be used with normal room lighting, though they require electricity. Most classrooms and conference rooms are equipped, and hotels and meeting rooms also have such equipment available upon request. The newest models of overhead projectors are so compact that they can be carried, briefcase fashion, almost anywhere, even hand-carried on airplanes. Older models are somewhat bulkier and less portable. The transparencies or clear sheets of acetate are available at most stationary supply and book stores.

The $8\frac{1}{2}'' \times 11''$ sheets of acetate may be prepared with special markers made for this purpose, since the felt-tip pens used for writing on paper will not work on acetate. The popularity of acetate memo or reminder boards found on refrigerator, office, or dormitory doors makes such pens easily available. These will produce functional transparencies. As with flip charts, black and blue should be the predominant colors. Photocopying machines can also be used to produce transparencies from typed copy.

Be careful with typed copy, because audiences find it hard to follow a point through hundreds of words on a screen. If you are using prepared transparencies, make them especially for the presentation, and think through precisely what you want. It is helpful to highlight with felt-tip pen. Draw boxes, arrows, or something to highlight the words. Make sure you work with figures at least one-half-inch high. Use of transparencies has been brought almost to an art form by skilled presenters. A little experimentation with the medium should get you familiar enough to use it easily in your presentation. Just don't forget to arrange for your equipment in advance, and be sure to bring an extension cord.

Slides

Visuals are not effectively used as "proofs" by themselves. Speakers can use facts, figures, statistics, drawings, and so on to add content to a message or presentation. For example, it is easy to recite the number of fatal traffic accidents at an intersection for the last several years, but this information will have much greater impact if it can also be seen. There are undoubtedly places in your presentation that could benefit by this kind of visual reinforcement. Use content visuals to help make them.

While roadmap visuals and content visuals account for the largest share of your visuals, there are instances when neither a word, a list, nor a fact or figure will suffice. Nothing short of a picture will do, and this accounts for the popularity of a third type of visual, the photographic slide. Words might describe the scope of flood damage, but pictures will have far greater impact. How can a listener appreciate the damage caused by arson without some pictures? Perhaps your group has been asked to select the new corporate plant site. How can you give listeners a feel for the options without some photographs? While speakers occasionally pass pictures among the audience, such a practice is often a disaster, because circulating pictures distract listeners.

Slides offer the advantage of speaker-controlled audience exposure and a large, easily seen image. Unlike the flip chart and the overhead projector, though, slides can be shown only in a darkened room. This requires that the room be equipped with room-darkening shades, that someone be available to turn the lights out on request, and that the speaker not be dependent upon notes—which, of course, can't be read in a dark room. Of the three media we have examined, slides are probably the most difficult to use. But they can be dramatic and effective when the presentation requires their use. Remember that if you choose to use slides, your presentation must be planned much further in advance. Shots must be taken and time allowed for processing and reshooting if need be. Professional photographers often take many more exposures than they anticipate needing so that they can select the best ones for presentation. Remember too that processing may take several days, and you have no guarantee your film won't be lost in processing. Nonetheless, if your presentation requires photographs and you have the necessary advance time to prepare them, slides are a very effective medium to use.

Almost all presentations can benefit from some form of visuals to map the presentation or to provide important content or support. Your group should carefully consider its visual requirements and their effective use. Thinking about visuals will help the group focus on orderly procedure in the presentation.

PRACTICING AND DELIVERING THE PRESENTATION

Whether your presentation is to be done by an individual or a group, it will require practice. There are undoubtedly cases where luck has helped an unpolished, unpracticed presentation, but as a rule, "winging it" has produced a far greater share of disasters. Audiences tend to react to presentation before content. Sloppy presentation will convince your listeners that your content is also sloppy. Nothing is so injurious to the perceived quality of your group's work than a slipshod presentation of it. Furthermore, presentations to executives and boards take a great deal of costly executive time. It is important to make as many points as clearly as you can in a short time. Your listeners will appreciate it. That means care must be taken to be sure the presentation is clear and interesting.

This is particularly important in group presentations. If you use a group presentation, *every* member of the group must be competent. One hesitant and disorganized speaker can lose an audience. Group members must be honest enough with each other to excuse those who cannot speak well from participation in the presentation.

As you practice your presentation, give some thought to delivery. While good delivery alone cannot make up for material that is poorly documented and disorganized, ineffective delivery can distract listeners and discredit even the best-planned presentations. Speakers must gain attention and hold it not with tricks and gimmicks, but with simple, straightforward, clear, documented statements based on a well-constructed outline. Be alert in your practice so you can avoid some of the major pitfalls in delivery.

The presentation of an oral report should be oriented to the listeners. (© Gupton, Southern Light)

1. Talk directly to listeners. Don't keep your eyes on your notes. Be sure you can see the expressions on your listeners' faces. By observing your listeners carefully, you will be able to adapt your presentation to respond to their questions and move quickly to regain flagging attention.
2. Avoid mannerisms like wiping your nose or face, tapping with your finger on the podium, jingling change in your pocket, or vocalized pauses ("and uh," "like I mean").
3. Make sure your grammar is correct. Sloppy grammar, poor diction, and long and complicated sentences cast doubt on your intellectual credibility.
4. Be careful using visuals. Make sure you point to visuals as little as possible. If you must point to a flipchart, use a pointer. With overheads, use a flat-sided pencil and keep it close to the transparencies in order to eliminate waves and shadows.
5. Dress appropriately.

During the dry run of your presentation, members of the group can attend to potential distractors in each other's presentations and discuss ways to minimize their impact during the actual presentation. This is also the time to plan the arrangement of seats for the group, the lectern if one is being used, and the placement of flip charts or projectors and screens. Make certain that the audience can see and that the group does not obstruct the listeners' field of vision for some members of the audience.

CONSIDERATIONS IN THE WRITTEN REPORT

Your written report can be considerably more extensive than the oral report. In fact it must be, because your written report will probably become the basic reference should your proposal be put into operation. You may not have the time to work out a complete written report during your classroom training. It is useful to read a good writing book like Thomas Pearsall and Donald Cunningham, *How to Write for the World of Work* (New York: Holt, Rinehart and Winston, 1978). There are many other similar books you can use.

Your written report can contain background information on the problem, as well as a review of the steps taken by your group to investigate it. Data you used in the solution can be placed in an appendix for reference for those especially interested. You may then make a detailed presentation of your group's work under the following headings.

The Problem

Your description of the problem should contain a careful presentation of the "impairment." Your readers should understand what was happening that should not have been, or what was not happening that should have been. It should be clear who or what was hurt or "impaired," in what way, and what its cost was to the organization. There should be some statement about the prognosis of the problem. What will happen if no action is taken?

Precedent

The second component is a discussion of similar problems in the same locality or in similar places (or types of organizations). What was done to solve the problem? With what effects? What is applicable to the present situation? Be sure to make it clear where the present situation differs from previous situations.

In your discussion of problems and precedents, you can be quite extensive in listing the facts. Explain how you decided what information was relevant, valid, and reliable (see Chapter 10). Use appendixes to list complicated information.

Redefinition

Specify exactly what situation you were working with. Explain whether you were working on symptoms, causes, or both, and why. Make sure you state and restate your problem question clearly throughout.

Proposals Examined

Explain the alternatives you examined and rejected and why. In order to do this, you will have to state your *criteria* for solutions and your *limitations* and justify them. Then show how you compared each proposal to the criteria and limitations and made the decision to accept your final solution.

Details of the Solution

The solution should be explained in detail. Be sure to state:

1. *Goals and objectives.* Objectives are signposts on the way to solving the problem. Goals are operations and actions to be taken by persons. (PERT/CPM program charts are useful here.)
2. *Statement of personnel.* Show the organization chart with the qualifications and job descriptions of each person assigned specified. Indicate the chain of command and communication flow. Be sure to specify supervision requirements.
3. *Space and logistics.* Indicate what the space requirements are for the program. Explain how movements of personnel and goods will be regulated.
4. *Records.* Indicate what information will have to be kept, how it will be stored and retrieved, and who will have access to it.
5. *Finance.* Explain in complete detail the cost of the program and indicate the source of funds. (This may be the most difficult part of your report.)
6. *Evaluation.* Be sure to explain how your program will be evaluated.

Make sure you explain how you will know it is working adequately, well, or not at all. Specify alternatives in case things do not work out.

7. *Impact.* It is useful to make an impact statement. Specify who will be affected or inconvenienced by the new program, and how you will handle their discomfort.

Writing reports is a specialized skill, worth a great deal of money in industrial and government enterprises. While your present training may not include detailed instruction and practice in report writing, keep in mind that most real-world problems require extensive formal reports. The ability to integrate oral and written reports is an important element of problem-solving.

RECOMMENDED READINGS

Brilhart, John K. *Effective Group Discussion,* 4th ed. Dubuque, IA: Wm. C. Brown, 1982. Chapter 11 describes a number of forms for public discussion.

Dietrich, John E., and Keith Brooks. *Practical Speaking for the Technical Man.* Englewood Cliffs, NJ: Prentice Hall, 1958. Despite the publication date of this book, it contains much useful advice on individual reports. Chapter 12 provides an especially useful treatment of preparing the oral technical report.

Potter, David, and Martin P. Andersen. *Discussion: A Guide to Effective Practice,* 2nd ed. Belmont, CA: Wadsworth, 1970. Chapter 8 offers a variety of public discussion methods and very practical advice on how and when to use each. You will find several chapters in this book useful in preparing oral reports about group activity.

Wilson, John F., and Carroll C. Arnold. *Public Speaking as a Liberal Art,* 4th ed. Boston: Allyn & Bacon, 1976. This is one of the most thorough and sophisticated books on individual speaking. It provides a basis for studying the theory and practice of presentational speaking.

INDEXES

NAME INDEX

SUBJECT INDEX

ISBN 0-06-045218-8

9 780060 452186

90000